MW00611084

Martin ♥

all my light, laughter & love ♥

RECKLASS
·IN THE·
KITCHEN

A year of light, laughter & love... oh, and food!

Scottie Jeanette Madden

... oh, and food ♥

Jan '20

Copyright ©2019 Scottie Jeanette Madden
Cover, interior & layout direction/design: Adam Waldman
Layout: Megan Logan
Cover and interior photography Mena Kerry Kehoe
Back Cover Portrait by M. Sharkey
Custom earthenware "Aritayaki" by Toshio Shimada/Shalom Studio
All rights reserved
ISBN-10: 0-578-53431-2
ISBN: 978-0-578-53431-2

For Mylove, always & forever

Zuzubean Press

Contact the author for questions, appearance schedule, booking, (and as always) swapping receipes at scottie@zuzubean.com

Acknowledgements

Mylove has forever been my muse, my inspiration and greatest fan of my cooking — she has been both "pillowtalk" consultant, and partner in crime for the creation of Recklass Cooking (as well as every creative endeavor for the past 3 decades). And there were scores of fantastic, wonderful people who have supported and cheered me on in the making of this book, for which I am grateful & humbled — but there are a few that I wish to thank publically, because I truly would not have finished this book without their strong, and graceful help — my original reader team: M'liss Missy Polk, Sukoshi and Mary Beth who helped me see that I was on the right track; to my foodie cuties, Donny & Vanita, Jill & John, Laura & Bobby, who's cooking and passion inspires me to make of their tongues and pallettes, guina pigs; my lifeguard, Megan who saved me from the digital quicksand, I was always a little too cocky to ever avoid: the divine angels who held me up when I wanted to crumble, Macky, Cat (& Craig) Ruthie & Jack, Mena and Aubrey and my most cherished and precious Adam and Indira who stood & stand by me unwaveringly... but this book and my completing of it would never have happened had it not been for the graceful, beautiful, inspiring golden light, laugther, love and strength of my beloved sister Kimm (and her divine hubby, Mikey). She holds me, cajoles me and gently glues the shattered pieces of my heart back together almost every day. She makes me and the world a better place with her every breath.

CONTENTS

INTRO: GET RECKLASS IN THE KITCHEN

Okay, I admit it freely… I don't just *like* fire and iron and steam and smoke and spice and sharp knives and fresh vegetables and chilies and garlic and more chilies and turning raw ingredients into magical mystery tours and more chilies…

I LOVE IT!

Maybe love isn't a strong enough word. What's the word for "nothing else *even* matters, except Mylove" (who I'm probably doing all of the above for anyway) in fact, few else even exists?

… while you figure out what that word might be — I'm cookin'.

Because juggling fire and sharp knives while balanced on the razor's edge between success and failure (try keeping everything timed perfectly for a formal multi-course Christmas Eve meal for 18) literally saved my life.

I'm not joking.

I didn't realize how deep this went until I finished my first book "Getting Back to Me" *from girl to boy to woman in just fifty years.* My editor said, "Wow, you sure work a lot of things out in the kitchen!" She was right. Since puberty, when gender dysphoria hit me full force, the kitchen and cooking and caring for others was the only thing in my life that consistently made any sense. (Later it would be Mylove's arms, but that's another chapter). Taking short "furloughs" from the dungeon in which I had imprisoned my heart by thinking of someone/something else for a few blessed moments gave me a chance to refresh my grip on reality. Immersing my entire body and soul into caring for someone else's tummy and well-being gave me a healthy channel for the trauma, despair, pain and confusion that is gender dysphoria.

So, I went all in on every meal. Even the simplest bowl of ramen in college (hey 25 cents for three packs?) got everything from me. When I couldn't afford "real" hot sauce, I made my own. A nickel for a jalapeño and a dime for the garlic, limes from the neighbor's yard across the street? It was a no-brainer. And … it worked.

Cooking (again or still) was my wingwoman when I fell in love with "Mylove" — my beloved Marcy, my spouse, muse, lover, soulmate, my everything. Since then, over thirty years ago, it's how I celebrate her, us, our love and our world.

My friend once wondered aloud (she had to be loud, to make herself heard over the din of clanging pots, slamming cupboards and the general mayhem of making Mylove, her & her hubby, dinner) *"why are you so damn reckless in the kitchen?"* This stopped me in my tracks — and I did think about it (later, of course, after I had plated another creation) and I realized, she was right. I am …

Recklass. (noun. rek-Laas) —

A wild woman who plays with fire, runs with sharp objects and is fearless in cooking from The heart!

I wear that label proudly. I will push two ingredients together that may have never met before they came into my kitchen. I will fuse together four ideas to make a new one. I will surprise and hopefully delight everyone who sits at our table —

Recklassly.

And this book is to encourage you to do the same.

Fire is good; fire is our friend! Cooking is a primal dance with the elements that we rarely get to experience in our dot.com, wifi world. So, when I can, I turn it up, all the way to eleven. *(Can you believe I got two obscure movie references in one paragraph?)*

Because I like it hot, very hot, I've learned to work fast. The higher the heat, the less margin for error and so my focus must become laser sharp — and usually with only three wheels on the ground at any one time. Sure, the risk of failure is exponentially higher but, and *if* and *usually* when you do "stick the landing," the results are fantastic. And working like this produces an experience for the cook that is the most addictive form of meditation.

The kitchen, figuratively speaking of course, is my sanctuary. Well actually, my temple. I say figuratively, because my kitchens have been under the last stand of pine at the timberline at 10,000 feet, making a hearty stew for my hiking companions, the back dock of a forgotten marina on the Gulf making dinner for my crew of 25, hotel rooms where I smuggled a crock pot and knives to make sure Mylove had our traditional "apple chowder" for Christmas morning, and my backyard where I bow down to the gods of the grill every chance I get. And when I say *temple*, I use that to encompass every use of that word from the place of Aztec sacrifice to the peace and subtle power of a Samadhi shrine.

Am I a little crazy? Well, hear me out, then you can decide.

But to do that, you'll have to follow me into the kitchen…

Let's get *Recklass!*

OVERTURE: A YEAR IN THE LIFE

I went around and 'round about how to present this book to you, and then I realized that the answer had been staring me in the face all along. In my first book, I laid out my general philosophy for cooking and that's that food is a celebration, and no celebrations are bigger than what I called "The Superbowl of Cooking" — the sacred time between Halloween and New Year's Day. *The holiday season.*

I realize that even today, a mere two years since I wrote that, even my metaphors and visual shorthand is changing right beneath my feet. "Superbowl" used to be a word I related to viscerally, which is why I chose it. As someone who had played organized football for 12 years, made varsity as a sophomore (a year ahead of everyone else) and was "scouted" by colleges as a potential "full ride" prospect, football had been the measuring stick/metaphor for just about everything. And *Superbowl* was the highest praise.

But now…? Notsomuch.

Because, for those of you who maybe haven't read my first book yet, GBTM (which I will reference throughout this book: "Getting Back To Me" — *from girl to boy to woman in just fifty years,*) I described the first years of my transition, and… well, a lot more has changed since then besides just the F on my birth certificate.

I'm aware that the way I used to describe and see things have additional elements that I don't necessarily want to bring to any table. And that's because I've chang*ed*. And now that I'm "on this side" of my life (finally) I'm re-examining everything. Every thought. Every belief. Every taste. Every opinion. Every feeling. Every *everything*.

But one thing that hasn't changed, is that the holiday season is still the crown jewel of the cooking season, however the air of competition, or victory, or conquest, and trophies and such, seems to tarnish its brilliance. So, instead, I want this time in my kitchen to be like the most precious of gems, the most valued of treasures: The heart of family and love and joy.

So, since I am also hoping to inspire you too to be Recklass in the kitchen, why was I holding back?

For starters, I really do align my kitchen with the calendar year. Everything, all year long is geared toward the sacred holidays, from balancing flavor palettes during the year so the holiday spice profiles will be enjoyed to their fullest, to allowing capital in the carb bank to grow so that when it is time to start cashing in, the experience will be enjoyable and won't take the first three months of the new year to work off the pounds.

I'm also picking up where I left off with my first book. One of the consistent and frankly surprising comments about my book and Mylove & my story is how inspiring and life-affirming the characters (and let me tell you, they are characters) were, especially with regard to my transition. Whether they were always on board, or suddenly had to skid left (I rarely use my turn signal), everyone grabbed onto the handrail called love and we all made it with minimal dents in our fenders. So that will continue in this, my second book.

I'll take you through a year starting in October and ending a year later. We'll go from both simple suppers to formal holiday gatherings, to romantic dinners for two, to casual brunches, family bar-b-ques and more dinner parties. Along the way, I'll introduce you to the amazing friends and family that make Mylove's and my life worth celebrating.

This will give us both something to hang onto.

A year of love as it plays out across our table.

You ready?

Cuz, I'm hungry just thinking about it!

Oh, one more thing as we fasten our seat belts … some basic thoughts and the foundational philosophy about the kitchen before we step into it like the TARDIS (Dr. Who, anyone?) to transport through a year's time and space …

A RECKLASS KITCHEN MAKES A RECKLASS MEAL. (THE INTENTION BEHIND THE CHAOS)

I post these thoughts for you to consider. You can debate me if you will, but you better bring your "A game" cuz I got results backing up my Recklass ways.

INSPIRATION *ONLY* –

If you're like me, you have a buncha cookbooks on your shelves and look at them like great reading books (okay, I confess, I have stacks in the bathroom library), but they're for inspiration only. I rarely follow them for anything other than a technique that I didn't know or a combination of ingredients that sparked a mindfire. But they are valuable for more than the sum of their parts. And that's what I hope you do with the recipes offered here. Sure, some cooks want to follow directions and replicate the dish (which is why I will connect the dots of each of my recipes) but if I inspire you to riff on my ideas then I've done my job — which is to know that somewhere, someone's lovin' their very own someones by cookin' it up good.

The only recipes I treat like Moses' tablets are baking ones. Baking is that wonderful alchemy that demands some modicum of precision — the difference between a biscuit and croissant is more than a pinch of salt, yes?

TOOLS –

I love to get lost in Williams Sonoma as much as the next gal. Aside from lusting after the killer set of knives that cost more than my yearly mortgage, I have almost everything I need. But, I will always buy more of:

CUTTING BOARDS –

I have about ten in various sizes, in a stack, waiting to serve me. I chop a vegetable on one and move onto the next one, that way I have an easy way to get the ingredients into the fire without losing valuable time, just lift, scrape and toss the board to the side. I can wash it later.

WHISKS –

I have about five at least at all times. They're the best for stirring and I can leave one in a bowl to give it a little stir if it's had to wait for its turn in the dance.

CAST IRON –

ANYTHING. I'm sayin' here folks, those fancy Silverstone skillets don't cut it for me. Gimme the old fashioned heavy cast iron. I can control the heat better. I keep them seasoned well so I don't have to use a ton of oil or butter to keep things from sticking. I use high heat — trust me, it's way better. I have two large skillets, one flat griddle, and about five smaller skillets. Plus, I have a five-quart Dutch oven and my south African potjie pot, oh, and two large woks. I am iron woman!

MIXING BOWLS –

Like my cutting boards, a bunch of various mixing bowls. I have both glass and stainless steel (thank you thrift stores!) They're great for storing your everything before, during, and after a meal.

THE RECKLASS KITCHEN –

Two things come to mind that make my kitchen work — Ingredients in progress and kitchen management. This is a fancy way of saying holding onto the dough you shelled out for your dough. I use mostly fresh ingredients (if it comes in a can, why did you buy a book to tell you what to do with it?). But, who has the time to go to the store every day? You gotta watch that the exotic vegetable you thought for sure was going into Sunday's showdown, *but didn't,* is not thrown out with next week's cleaning. So, there's lots of things that cooks throughout the ages have known. We have freezers, we have blenders, we have the technology. For example, what about that bag of corn chips you forgot you had until they're not so crunchy? Toast them in the oven to rejuvenate them and then crush them and stick them into the freezer. They'll make great crumbs for Aztec Chicken (recipe to follow). My point is you can puree things and freeze them to use later rather than trashing 'em. Also, with a little planning you can make ingredients that will be around when you want to really "throw down" — like pickled onions (onions, jalapeños, lime juice and salt). They're there when you get a wild hair, and they make a simple sandwich freakin' glorious.

SALT –

Use salt as a tool, not an ingredient.

I have family who suffers from high blood pressure so I have to be careful. But salt is essential to get reactions of the other ingredients. I have a pinch bowl (a large mason jar with the clamping, sealing lid that has a mouth large enough for my hand to take "pinches" of salt), and I keep it filled with kosher salt. I do have some fancy smoked salts that are used for garnish on dishes (like burrata with … gosh, anything), and/or sea salts that have a brinier tang.

I have found over years of being the salt monitor that I'm not offended (anymore) when someone salts my cooking. So, I have backed off making it part of the flavor profile altogether. There are exceptions of course, like salting the crust of baked savory dishes, or salting the hot cocoa … but other than that, I let others determine their own salt intake.

WASH AS YOU GO –

Okay, this one's hard. But it's the only way to stay out of your own way. You have to wash, or at least rinse, dishes and utensils as you go — which admittedly gets harder the closer you get to plating. But if you don't do it in the quieter moments at the beginning of your cooking session, you're sunk.

FRESH IS ALWAYS BETTER (EXCEPT MAYBE IN WINE) –

Wolfgang Puck always sez to start with great ingredients and keep it simple. I agree with the first part. And he's a gazillionaire so what does he know? You want that, go buy *his* book! So, get the ingredients that are going to make your dish a celebration. Why else are you cooking?

And this is especially true with herbs. Some are a little more hard core than I. There are snobs who think dried herbs taste like tea, but I *will* use my dried herbs in sauces and soups that will have high liquid content and high heat over a sustained period of time (like a marinara sauce). But I do agree with the snobs on this — nothing compares to the aroma of fresh herbs when you break them by hand and stir them in. I use herbs at all stages of a dish's prep, depending on what effect I'm looking for. I finish with them if I want that last "punctuation," (like Asian foods) but I don't hesitate to throw them in at the start (like Italian foods) if I want them to help color the foundation of the dish.

I do use bottled spices often, but if I have the fresh, they win. And many times, they are ready in a way that doesn't require hours or days of prep — like in the case of cardamom, paprika (smoked or not), cumin and curries. I keep both the whole and ground versions — and if I'm on my game, I reach for the whole version and grind it myself in a mortar (I have two, one for sweet and one for savory) — but when I'm moving fast, I don't discriminate against the ground.

STAPLES: THE SIGNATURE ON YOUR CREATIONS. EVOO – EXTRA VIRGIN OLIVE OIL.

Self-explanatory? Well, you can (and I have) spend a fortune on these — I basically have three types at all times. Basic everyday. I get the best quality for the lowest price. I try to stay organic when I can, and I try to stay single source. But… it's usually gonna be the means to an end, so if the above ain't happening for a the price, I don't stress.

I also have a better quality one that does conform to above for salads and any place where this will be eaten cold (like salads, or drizzles) this is one where I will shell out more scratch for quality. And then theres the special bottle that someone probably gave me for a present — this I save for special occasions, like a fine wine. BUT — I make sure I use all of the above within 6 months (usually not an issue) to enjoy it at its best. One last note I usually avoid flavored oils — I can make them better from scratch and that way I can control the flavor.

VIRGIN COCONUT OIL

What a time to be alive, amIright? Coconut oil went from being the scourge of the industrial food complex to new age nutritional savior. Here. In America. Elsewhere in the world it's retained it position as what it has always been — a great solution for recipes where olive oil and other vegetable oils won't cut it. Spend the extra buck-three-eighty (or whatevah) to get the good stuff to stay away from those free radicals. (Who should be out protesting, where they belong, right?) I use coconut oil for Asian stirfrys, East Indian curries etc.

VINEGARS

Okay, here's where I indulge — I have everything from rice and balsamic to coconut vinegars. I also usually have both a red and a white wine that I've let go to vinegar (rather than pouring it out), malt vinegar, apple cider, plain ol' "white" and whatever else trips my fancy. I also (thanks to my bestie Laurie) have several fruit flavored drinking vinegars that are very handy when dealing with fresh fruit for desserts) My point is — acid is an essential part of every dish and vinegars are often the solutions — I think of these like the shoes one wears fr a great dance, are you doing the cha-cha, some salsa or a waltz? Well, each requires a different dress, and that means different shoes, yes?

DIJON MUSTARD (ALL MUSTARDS, FOR THAT MATTER)

I'm sure I inherited this from my father — we love, love, love mustard, the richer and spicier the better. But as an essential tool in the kitchen, good old Dijon can hide all manner of sins and sew together flavors that are on separate orbits quite nicely.

CHIPOTLE (BOTH CANNED AND GROUND)

Nothing beats the sweet, smoky, bite of chipotle for turning up the heat. Canned chipotle (which are smoked jalapeños) are swimming in Adobo sauce (sweeter than it's European cousin, with sugar, vinegar, cumin, garlic & salt) are best in sauces and will come with their fire, but the ground version is great tool for merely "igniting" the taste buds, and used sparingly, can enhance without heating.

HOMEMADE...

I have a few ingredients that require some "nurturing" (or rather "mother henning") during the year so I have the last little bit of "p-cha!" or "z-ling!" that takes a dish over the top. These are simple ingredients that you have in your cupboard or spice cabinet that are handmade to give you a little sumpin-sumpin… like:

VANILLA SUGAR –

Stop what you're doing right now and get this going — the longer it sits the better it is. I use it for a lot of the recipes you're about to make. Take a clean jar, add organic granulated sugar and start it with a whole vanilla bean, split lengthwise. Bury the bean into the sugar, place it in your spice cabinet. Every time you go in there, give the jar a vigorous shake. Every time you use a vanilla bean (for anything) don't throw it away, throw it into your jar. Every time you need some sugar, add some back into the jar. Trust me. You will love me for this alone.

HABANERO SALT –

Just like the above method, but with kosher or sea salt (your preference — both are amazing and I usually alternate) and fresh chopped habaneros. In a quart jar, (filled with salt) I use 7 habaneros cut into rings. This is amazing on popcorn, or anywhere you want a little z'ling to tickle the tongue. (This won't turn a dish "hot" per se, it will just "make its presence known.")

THE MAIN INGREDIENT. YOUR HEART –

I think I learned this from my mom. She had a small repertoire to keep her family of 4 children and husband on budget, healthy and happy. She made the same things and kept the rotation. Every two weeks we'd see our old friends, BUT they were always amazing, because she cooked with heart, not her tongue. In fact, she never tasted until we ate, and never measured anything. But she always put her love for us into every pot.

In my kitchen, the heart wins. The brain will argue about this and that, citing science and physics and other facts, but the heart will know how much is too much or too little. And yes, everyone, whether or not they have the words to describe it, can taste your love.

Okay, enough talk — let's cook!

CHAPTER 1

·HALLOWEEN·

JACKIE-O-LANTERN SOUP

CHEESY JALAPEÑO CORN STICKS

DESSERT... ARE YOU KIDDING ME? GET OUT AND TRICK OR TREAT!

"BOO SCAWEY"

It's all just an excuse to eat candy, right? Halloween is, as I've written countless times, the gateway drug to Christmas. For me, it's the official start of the holiday season and that means cooking. Which, I will confess, is how I learned the first great thing about getting older — you know, and have the means to do, all the things you loved as a kid. Like candy. Amateurs would scarf a buncha sugar and feel like doo-doo immediately after and who thinks that's fun? Nah, professionals would lay down a base layer of nutrition to not only help process said sugars, but also to cleanse the palette!

For as long as I remember, Halloween came with a special comfy, dark, spooky, cloak of mystery and possibility that never happens any other time of the year. And I find it's best served with children. MUUHHA HAHAHAHAH!!!!

We have the perfect neighborhood for Halloween, but not so good for trick or treatin'. Let me explain. We're in the shadow (downhill side) of the infamous "dirt Mulholland." I say infamous, because only locals know that it's actually the dirt fire road section (and therefore closed to vehicle access between Topanga Canyon and east to Havenhurst) of the more world-famous Mulholland Drive. We're nestled under the oak trees in a rabbit warren of twisty, narrow streets that either look like someone's bad idea of a driveway or a semi-paved (and therefore potholed) foot path. There isn't a straight or level *anything* for miles.

We're perched on the last (or first depending on your outlook) paved street — there's nothing behind us but the Santa Monica Wilderness… thirty steps, and I'm away from any house. So, you can probably imagine (now that I've taken pains to get you this owl's eye view — which are abundant up here, along with coyotes, hawk, raven, mountain lion, skunk, opossum, and rattlers) that we NEVER get trick-or-treaters, tho' we can hear them braving the streets below.

Which made me a little sad, and one year I couldn't take it anymore. So, Marcy and I went as "our house" for Halloween. I cut the silhouette of our house from a refrigerator box, painted it with the actual leftover paint from our house, and put a bowl of candy on a "porch" I fashioned out of left over roof shingles. A flashlight peeked out of a cartoon porch light and Marcy and I could peer out the windows on either side of the door…

… then we went down to the trick-or-treaters and brought our house to them.

But this year is a bit bittersweet. We've become friends this past year with a fabulous woman, a single mom by the name of Gizi. But, alas, she is taking her 12-year-old son Marlon back to her native Switzerland at the first of the year, and this will be the last time we can celebrate together. She had bought one of the best houses in the neighborhood, (besides ours) a craftsman affair with a pool that the previous owner had allowed my wonderful Labrador Zuzy to swim in during the summer. (I used to take her daily to "Swimming lessons" just like a real suburban mommy). The previous owner had also been an amateur musician who used to stage a yearly birthday bash for himself and had built a huge "stage" at the end of the pool for just such an occasion. The property, with its house on the hill and the pool below nestled amid over thirty mature oak trees, gives an amazing three-dimensional environment for creating a super spooky Halloween party.

Gizi and I became friends when we first started passing each other every morning during my morning bike ride. She would hike "dirt Mullholland" after she had dropped off Marlon at school. One day, I invited her to one of my neighborhood book signings and she learned my story. We had her up for dinner and parties with her son, who is a charming young man who was very at home with adults (which really impressed me.) Gizi never knew me as anything other than Scottie, but working with a neighborhood contractor put her in the perfect position to hear the neighborhood scuttlebutt regarding me — a window into what people say about me when I'm not around. The headlines? Pretty much as you'd expect, everything from "I don't get it." To "Why does her wife stay?" (At least they get the pronouns right) but overall, nothing other than mildly amused or confused but no real hostility or discrimination… whew!

One morning, on one of our walks, Gizi confessed that she "may have done a bad thing." She had had a date with an art gallery owner a few years back, and found herself walking with her father past the gallery, and decided (serendipitously) to revisit the owner and say "hi." But when she walked in, she saw the owner dressed in business dress and heels, and instead of saying "hi" abruptly did a 180, and left. She said she "had no problem with the owner being transgender — it just *surprised* her. *Was that bad?*"

I was heartbroken immediately for the owner. I said, you can be surprised — but any human would feel her rejection — and I have faced this many times. But what can take the sting out immediately is to apologize. We (as trans folk) never know when situations like this happens if *we've* done something wrong *to* you. (And being transgender is not about *you* — it's about being *me*). She thought about it and decided to call the owner as soon as she got home.

That day I received an email from Gizi with a link to the "coming-out story" of the owner — who had months before taken control of her own story with a very public announcement to her clients and patrons. She has since become a good friend of mine and is very supportive and active in the LA community.

Oh… and she never even saw Gizi on the day she did a pirouette at her gallery.

So, there's that too.

Gizi and I have become very good friends since all of that, and we've been plotting since summer of having today's Halloween party. We have spent the entire week hanging "ghosts" high in the trees around the whole property. Marlon made these by stuffing filmy plastic sheets with white tissue. They are like an army of dementors hovering around the entire neighborhood, eerily wafting in the wind, catching the lights that we have strategically placed throughout the compound.

And the last ones are finally up as the requisite dark has descended for all Hallows Eve…

I race home to get my costume on — I always have a costume and in decades past have been everything from the mummy to a dragon high priest (I saw in an article in TV guide how Roddy McDowell was made into Galen each day with two key prosthetics — which I used as inspiration to create a dragon's face… but it backfired — it was alittle too good, and I ended up spooking everyone at the party! Nobody spoke to me all party long… oops).

But that was then. Since I've come out — I'm free! And yes, since you're wondering, I have done the sexy phase, making quite the coquettish vampire trollop, complete with petticoats and stilettos. No more drag(ons) for me. I don't have hide in ambiguity.

And tonight, I'm going all "Dia De Los Muertos" and have even bought magnolias and roses for my hair — but I have to work fast and.. this damn white foundation sucks!

Luckily, I already made Jacquie-O-Lantern soup and corn sticks — so, as soon as I can get my false eyelashes on, we're golden. Mylove has decided to opt out of the costume competition tonight — but she's lucky, she looks cute in anything, and has gotten into the spirit with her tights emblazoned with stars and moons and knee-high boots — she does have a costume, I realize — she's going out as a Goddess!

I ran right past the soup, didn't I? Do I have my mind on candy, or what?

Okay. Years ago, I thought, "what if we made pumpkin soup and served it *in* pumpkins?" Well, it's awesome. I roast sugar pie pumpkins to be the "bowls" and as you eat the soup, you can also scrape the roasted pumpkin flesh into the soup — I think Marlon will dig this idea.

When we get back to Gizi, Marlon's grandpa is there — despite having lived here in LA for three decades, he still has a thick Swiss baritone which adds gravitas to our outdoor Halloween feast.

I'm right about the soup — Marlon is loving it — Good thing too, cuz the only thing truly evil out here, is Gizi having put out not one, but *three* large bowls of candy.

If the rest of the neighborhood doesn't show up soon, we're all in trouble — Marlon and I are going to destroy these almond joys… Happy Halloween, MUAH HA HA HAAAAA, y'all!

(okay… so how do you make these recipes? Well, turn the page, silly)

JACKIE-O-LANTERN SOUP

I don't know what it is about using food as holiday symbols that intrigues me so... we've got Easter eggs, Halloween Jackie-o-lanterns, Thanksgiving turkey, etc. But I was always so sorry for the pumpkin — everyone else follows its life's destiny to nourish us as the foods they are, but not the humble autumn squash. It's gonna light the way up to and including the All-Hallows eve, but then, if it's been able to make it this far, will probably be sporting a blue beard (if 'n you know what I mean) by All Saints Day, and thus will be tossed out with the morning trash. Such a sad death...(and so... I dunno, Halloween-esque, for sure... but maybe a bit on the nose?)

And not that I've solved this completely, but... I did come up with a bridge to a solution, and that's this soup. And it's also a great way to coat the tummy for the onslaught of sugar that makes this day so wonderful!

---

1 baking pumpkin diced
(peel the skin off with a potato peeler — save the seeds!)
EVOO
Dash of chipotle
Dash of cinnamon
Dash of clove
3 cloves garlic
Splash(es) of apple cider vinegar
1 onion (diced)

1 pear (cored & diced — keep the skin on — we want this flavah!)
1 quart vegetable broth
1 tsp. ground ginger
1 tbsp. pure maple syrup (please God don't use imitation — you worked too hard to stain your dish with that crap!)
½ pound raw pecan halves (shelled)
1 tsp. of chipotle powder
Smoked salt

Preheat your oven to 400 degrees

In a mixing bowl
whisk the EVOO, spices garlic and apple cider vinegar, together, then toss in the pumpkin.

In a roasting pan
Dump in the pumpkin mixture — spread evenly in the roasting pan and roast for 40 minutes.

In a very hot, dry cast iron Dutch oven
Caramelize the diced onion and the pear — when the edges of the onion turn brown reduce the heat and stir in a tablespoon olive oil and a dash cider vinegar.

Sauté for 30 seconds.

Add one quart vegetable broth
bring to a boil and drop in the roasted pumpkin. Add the ground ginger and maple syrup

With an immersion blender
Blend everything until smooth. Reduce the heat to warming simmer.

In super-hot dry cast iron skillet
Toast the raw pecan halves — toss and shake the pecans to keep them from burning as you toast them — sprinkle in the chipotle and salt and continue to shake until the pecans are toasty brown and fragrant...

Ladle the soup into bowls.

Garnish with the toasted pecans.

CHEESY JALAPEÑO CORN STICKS

It seems like everyone has a recipe for this lil' wonder — but I have a rule about food — if you don't love it, (to eat it yourself) then leave it for others to do. The exception to this is of course my own mother. She made the best (and I've upset my Italian friends many times by declaring this) Marinara sauce ever. Bar none. The best. BUT she never really loved eating anything at all. (I think she had issues with her digestion that went undiagnosed) — even so, her sauce was consistently amazing. So, okay, she's the exception — I don't usually eat something from someone who doesn't love love love what they're serving me. I don't order the vegetarian plate at a steakhouse, and I don't order the "Asian Stir-fry" at anywhere. Where was I?...

Oh yeah! Corn sticks — corn bread, corn fritters corn muffins... go southern on any of the aforementioned — they loves them their corn, trust them. I stole the idea of throwing cheese in from Mr. Bam himself, I won't give him the credit for the jalapeño part — I threw them in before I even decided what to make...

Mylove and I were on the hunt for months for corn stick pans — we finally found a pair of cast iron beauties at a garage sale — and we finally had a happy (and pretty solution) to our dilemma — Mylove loves the moist fluffy center, and I like a bit of crunch. Done!

1 cup cornmeal	1 stick butter (melted)
1/2 cup flour	2 eggs, beaten
1/2 tsp. baking powder	1 cup beer or ale
1/2 tsp. baking soda	2 green onions (chopped)
1/2 tsp. salt	2 ears fresh corn (roasted & sheared)
1/2 tsp. chili powder	1 jalapeño (roasted & chopped)
3 cups shredded cheddar cheese	1 minced garlic clove

In a hot oven (350 degrees) oven — preheat your cast iron corn stick pans
In a medium mixing bowl, whisk together
the corn meal & the flour with the baking powder, soda, salt & chili powder.

In a separate bowl
Beat the eggs — whisk together with the butter & beer.

Stir the wet ingredients into the dry cornmeal mixture. Add the corn, onions, garlic and jalapeño. Add the cheese. Vigorously stir to mix thoroughly.

Carefully — grease your HOT corn stick pans.
Pour the corn batter into the hot pan and bake for 5 minutes in the oven. With a toothpick check to see that the center is cooked.

Turn the sticks out onto a wire rack to cool while you make your next batch — serve with more butter.

CHAPTER 2

· THANKSGIVING! ·

**ROAST TURKEY BRINED IN HARD CIDER
(WITH THE BEST GRAVY EVER!)
CRAB, MUSHROOM & BLUEBERRY SOURDOUGH DRESSING
ROASTED GARLIC & ROSEMARY MASHED ROOT VEGGIES
SAVORY PUNKIN' PIES
MAPLE GLAZED BRUSSEL SPROUTS**

DESSERT
**PUNKIN CHIFFON PIE
CARDAMOM PIE
PEAR APPLE RUSTIC TART**

"GET YOUR COOK ON!"

Thanksgiving is the one time during the year when everyone takes the time to cook. And not just any kind of cooking — we all reach back into our lives and bring forth something, anything that will give us a taste of "family" — if Christmas is for children (which I do not agree with, but I'm hearing myself out) then Thanksgiving is for family, with an emphasis on adult.

The flavors are complex — even the sweets are grown-up — there's no chocolate, there's green beans and brussel sprouts and if you're not careful broccoli and spinach will show up somewhere. Definitely not for kids...

At least it says so in small print. I have always loved the earthy, roasted, dark and complex flavors of November's Giving of Thanks. I use red wine instead of vinegar, I roast when I could steam, bake when I should boil, I want the natural sugars of every ingredient to caramelize into the warm and comforting palate of fall. You can always balance this with the crispness of salad and fresh berries, the tang of sharp cheeses, the snap of garden fresh herbs.

For years, Thanksgiving was for us, the homecoming. When we were first married, we were expected to split the time between our two families; being young and able-bodied we traded the time between Mylove's bay area family and my San Diego-based tribe, alternating locations with Thanksgiving & Christmas. But this meant that we were forever guests. And I missed out on the cooking — I would go so far as cooking a Turkey on the "Friday after" just so we could have leftovers! So, after Mylove's dad Malcolm and step-mom Marion passed from this world, we were able to turn it around and have our homecoming in our own home...

But... our families also had these obligations. My sister Lib had gotten married two years after Mylove and I, and her In-laws were part of an Ex-pat Minnesotan tribe who were so happy to be out of America's icebox that every year they would gather in a north San Diego County park and wear shorts and flip-flops for the Thanksgiving picnic (and send pictures to their snowbird family up north with captions that were variations on the theme of neaner-neaner-neaner).

Our middle sister KJ & and her partner Jan have been in merry old England for the last twenty some odd years, meant that our first course was usually facetime, and baby sister Shane has been in South Carolina for the past ten years...

Anyway… my point is, it's been really hard to get family back together for this once annual "no freaking way we'd miss it" holiday.

Yes, we've tried the various "orphan" thanksgivings and we've also accepted gracious invitations, but see above, I'm still gonna cook the day after… Because, if I hadn't made the point earlier, I'm not just a traditionalist, and a hopeful romantic (you expected the self-effacing self-less label didn't you, but see, I won't even cop to that) I still long for the comfort of a friendly gaze for the holiday… you can't beat home sweet home.

Or your sister's home — at this point, I'm not picky.

And this year, Lib and I will divide the chores and therefore the leftovers, what do I care if we have to drive three hours times two.

Not a freaking thing. Because, it's Lib. I had written lovingly and okay, a bit long-windedly because I want my sister celebrated in my first book, but it bears repeating, because I want the world to know that she and her husband Mikey have raised three of the most amazing humans in history. I want everyone to know how they, like Mylove demonstrated how incredible they are by staring into the face of society's teachings, their friends and other family's ignorance and their own fear and saw…

… me.

Her sister.

Lib & I have always had an amazing relationship and it never skipped a beat. Even as she was rewiring her own understanding of reality, she loved me first and asked questions later.

So, am I excited to be seeing her?

I'm out of my mind overjoyed. And after a twenty-minute phone call, where I talked her through my traditional brining recipe, she'll handle the Turkey. I'll bring the dressing and some pie, and together we'll make everything else.

This didn't relieve her duties as daughter-in-law in the park with the Minnesotan Tribe, so while we're fighting the six-lane wide parade south to San Diego, she'll pretend that shorts and flip-flops is a cool way to spend the holiday usually reserved for that comfy sweater and sweatpants.

Straight up? Lib is an amazing cook herself, inspiring her own family to be good themselves — her son Dane is the designated cook for his posse of skaters and might even pursue a career in the culinary biz. Kaylee has been feeding herself quite well in Portlandia and Mikey's roasted tomatillo salsa and chocolate chip cookies are legendary. The only one who hasn't come into her own yet is Hana but she's my favorite, so there. Lib's family is centered around the kitchen - case in point, their treasured Christmas Eve tradition is the entire family pitching in for the making of tamales (she's soooo, San Diegan).

After four hours on the freeway, (and Lib's obligatory picnic) the Madden girls can finally get to the real cooking!

Today, everyone hovers around Lib and me, pitching-in with chopping or slicing as we juggle the classics, mashed potatoes with toasted garlic and rosemary, gravy made with the classic drippings but thickened with a pear, an apple, and an onion that were happily roasting in the drip pan while the turkey was doing its thing. No flour or butter necessary — nay, this is the best gravy you will ever taste — I guarantee it.

Lib's got a killer technique for roasted sweet potatoes that we steal for the brussel sprouts and with a huge green salad, and Mylove's McVickar Family traditional cranberry salad, we sit down to an amazing feast.

We even raise a glass of Anchor Steam Christmas Ale to my pop. My dad had a toast that we joke was actually the Latin translation on the Madden coat-of-arms, *"Here's to those that love us and to those that don't… fuck'em!"*

This is usually shouted with such *recklass* abandon, even all of our friends will join in despite who's actually sitting at the table — priests and nuns have heard that toast at our table, my grandmother, aunts, nobody is too cool, too *special* or too anything, to come before that toast and its toasters.

But this year, it brings a tear to my eye — of gratitude. This family, my family has been a full enveloping hug of really intense acceptance. And I am forever grateful.

I should confess here, that like many trans people or anyone in the LGBTQIA+ community, I didn't expect this… in the years since I came out, I'm learning that we can track our evolution like this: first year, love first, ask questions later, second year, love *despite* the questions… this the third year, so it's, love and *ask* those questions…

Yes, there are questions. And there should be questions. This is, as Mylove is always reminding me, huge. For everyone, especially me. I do spend a ton of time making sure everyone is "cool" with this, with us, with me. There isn't anything that prepares you for being transgender — and let's be real — *there's nothing that prepares you for not being transgender (cisgender for those being academic) either* — but there is a shit-ton (emphasis on the shit part) of people who come after the fact, and try to slime the world with their fear and insecurity.

Hate is not inherent, it is taught. It is nurtured like a poison plant, fed with the bacteria of fear it festers into a toxic acid that erodes any vessel that contains it, slow enough so the hate can be carried to its destination like a parasite that doesn't kill its host. (Geezus did I really just bring that up in a cookbook?)

But tho' nothing can prepare anyone for either being trans or not there is little in society or in social mores that supports it either. In fact, the headlines everyday assume in their repeating that violence and discrimination are an accepted fact of our lives. That we, as trans people *are* the rare unicorns we are believed to be. We are a minority. (At present, we are guessed to be about 6 of every hundred Americans). So, yes. We know. We know. We know that all of this could be weird. It shouldn't be. But it is. So with those we love, it's important to take the time to get past the weird and get back to love.

What I didn't know was how hard my family was doing that *for* me. And completely out of left field, right before seconds are passed 'round (while others are starting to pine for pie) I hear Mikey say... *"you know, I... had... an... issue with... you, with this, with all of this... trans stuff."*

I am trying to make myself believe that I did actually hear what he said, when he repeats it. He goes on to tell me that right after my infamous first physical meeting with everyone as the divine Mrs. Scottie Jeanette, the one that I lovingly devoted many pages to in GBTM, describing that what I didn't know, was that right after I left, Mikey is right here, right now, confessing...

... that he lost his shizz.

He describes how he started actually ranting that he didn't give a shit, what I wanted. He didn't give a shit about pronouns. "I'm gonna call him a he, does he really think he can just walk in here and get us to change 20 years of life just like that????"

I'm stunned. I never knew any of this — he had been so polite and wonderful with me since that day. Asking questions — really trying to "get it right." And as I'm trying to catch my breath — wondering where in the hell he's going with this confession, he goes on to say that my niece/his daughter Hana, looked right into her father's bellicose belligerentarianism and says, "Daddy, that hurts my heart, that you would even think that about Aunt Scottie."

Now, both Mikey and I are crying. He confessed that not only did that his daughter's heart and mind shock him out of his own stupidity and arrogance, but that day he became my biggest champion, turning around every heart of those in my family who even hesitated in welcoming and accepting me. It seems that the transgender girl in the family may be the last to know what her family really thinks when she's not around.

I am surprised and just a tad annoyed to discover who Mikey has just given up in the tales he recounts, but the sting has been taken out by the fact that in most cases he was successful with turning them all around. And it shows that (DUH) the entire family, yes, the world transitions with us. And this work that he did on my behalf absolutely slays me, I'm speechless. I'm crying. But most of all...

...I'm grateful... and already a complete mess, I'm utterly toast when Hana comes over to hug me, her Aunt Scottie. She comforts me. Like that big Thanksgiving comfy sweater.

Did somebody say pie? *Why yes, please hurry — dear god, get me out of this before I melt completely.*

TURKEY BRINED IN HARD CIDER
(WITH THE BEST GRAVY EVER!)

Okay... this is the moment we've been waiting for all year — in fact, this is what separates the haves from the wannabes — your bird must stand on its own (a touch of cranberry and or a dollop gravy notwithstanding) this is where we want a bird to be a bird! Also, this is the time where the choice of the bird is important, (it's family, and it's only once a year, and its THANKSGIVING for crying out loud!) so I always go a little farther — and get an heirloom/heritage stock turkey — these are a bit darker, and a touch wilder in taste, even the breast.

I also put as much time into the brine as the roasting — and I've put mine up against all the other techniques, deep frying, pah! Oven roasted, come on! Brining smokes 'em all! I also discovered a cool trick — an apple, a pear, and an onion, (I know, I know, walk into a bar — but seriously) roasted with the turkey (in the drip pan) and pureed with the drippings makes the most amazing gravy you've ever tasted without flour. (You don't even need butter — but then again, does anyone ever really "need" butter?)

THE BRINE	THE ROAST/GRAVY
1 fresh turkey	2 sticks of butter
2 bottles hard cider (12 oz.)	Fresh herbs (I like tarragon and marjoram for this time of year)
3 quarts apple cider	
1 cup of salt	2 onions (1 quartered, 1 whole)
5 cloves garlic (peel'd & smashed)	1 large pear
3 cinnamon sticks	I large firm & crisp apple
7 stars of anise	
2 lemons	

We're making this (hopefully) at least a day before — 2 days is better, 3 is best!

The brining process is simple — for your turkey use a 10 : ½ ratio of liquid to salt.
Make sure you have the brining bag (I use "doubled" plastic, kitchen-sized trash bags. You want to put these in something strong with a lid (I have a perfect "12 pack" plastic ice chest/cooler) You want to have plenty of ice to keep it cool for the days of brining since you will most likely be loath to give up refrigerator real estate during this critical prep time before T-day!

In a large bowl
Pour the ciders in. Add the salt and whisk to dissolve the salt. Add the spices, juice of 1 lemon (we're saving the other for the turkey roasting) and then throw the

juiced halves in, add the quartered onion and the garlic. (Save the herbs & butter for later).

Pour the brine over it and let it bathe for at least 24 hours, but three days is ideal.
You may want to turn the turkey to achieve even brining every day or so. Keep also adding ice to keep it chilled.

When it's time to cook...

Remove the turkey from the brine, which you discard — *Sad, I know, but it's better for all.*

Allow to dry.
Take a stick of butter and gently stick your hand between the skin and flesh to create pockets. Fill these with butter and herbs. Also fill the chest cavity with the remainder of your herbs and the remaining lemon. Cut it in half and squeeze the juice into the cavity, then toss the halves in.

Roast in your favorite way.
If you are going to cook it old school in the oven or smoker, my McVickar by marriage contract requires that I implore you to start out breast side down for the first hour. Then (and only then) are you allowed to turn the turkey breast side up for the remainder of the cook.

In your drip pan
Peel the onion and halve it. Cut the pear and the apple into halves. Pour a thin layer of olive oil in the bottom of the pan and place the onion pear and apple cut side up to receive the dripping turkey juices during the cook. Watch them that they don't get too torched — turn them when necessary.

Baste your turkey with the natural juices every half hour.
I usually allow one hour (of cooking) per every six pounds. Since most turkeys use the 12–16 pound level as a baseline for selling, this is about right. I use a thermometer in the meaty part of the thigh to measure the internal temperature. When I get above 160 degrees I pull the turkey — I love a moist turkey even though most FDA guidelines are skittish with the low side of 165. You can be your own judge.

Let the baby rest!
I "tent" this baby with aluminum foil, while I take the drippings to make gravy. There's several tricks to get most of the fat, but I like using a slice of bread like a sponge to soak up the fat that is on the top. The bread then either makes your dog(s) extremely happy or can be used later as a thickener. (I won't use it today, because there's already so much extra filler/calories and don't need it here. But you do you. No judgment.)

Pour the drippings into a sauce pan

Over a medium high heat, add the roasted onion. Remove the cores from the pear and the apple, and add them to the pan. Using an immersion blender, puree the fruit and onion to make a smooth and AH-MAZING sauce that is a little sweet. You can adjust this to your liking. Depending on my mood and the other dishes I've made to this point, I have in the past added a dollop of Dijon, if I want it a little spikier, or butter to tone down the brightness. It may or may not need salt depending on your buds.

The saucepan will allow you to keep it hot until serving time.

Now go carve your turkey — they're waiting on you!

CRAB, MUSHROOM & BLUEBERRY SOURDOUGH DRESSING

I wrote about this in "Getting Back To Me" — and it's become a wonderful touchstone to a time where years of pain and confusions were starting to appear in my rear view mirror rather than in the road before me. It was a Thanksgiving away from Mylove, but it was, in many ways, the building of momentum to get back to her. Fully. It was a Thanksgiving with my crew in Alaska (not sure how I could be any further from home than there) and I was for some unknown reason (other than the She in me having filed the bars on her dungeon window and escaped) I was coming out without fanfare and maybe that was the trick — She didn't ask permission, didn't count the costs, didn't hesitate — she just came.

And I celebrated this by thanking the land of the free — Alaska. Land of the sourdoughs, (the name for those who've wintered more than 20 years in Alaska) of millions of miles carpeted by blueberries, and the eponymous crab — symbol of my zodiac birth, and of Alaskan Seas' Bounty... what ELSE would you make "Thanksgiving Dressing" from?

1 pound crab meat	**1 tbsp. dijon mustard**
1 loaf toasted sourdough bread (cubed)	**1 tsp. lemon zest**
2 pounds wild blueberries (these are smaller than their domestic cousins — and oddly daintier)	**1 tsp. sage**
	1 tsp. rosemary
3 stalks celery (with leaves)	**1 quart of chicken or vegetable broth**
1 red onion (diced)	**1 stick of butter**
¼ cup olive oil	

Preheat the oven to 350 degrees (who are we kidding! It's Thanksgiving and that puppy has been working since you got up this morning!

In a large bowl
Toss the dry ingredients with the olive oil and Dijon to mix.

Pour the broth over it
and continue to stir. Add the lemon zest.

Pour everything into a covered casserole dish
Dot with butter and allow to soak for ½ hour.

Bake for 30 minutes
it will bake during the time it takes to carve the bird. (approx. 30 minutes, unless you're O-Ren Ishii. I can't always reference my references. Google it… *tomorrow,* silly) Careful, this is very rich — soooo decedent, but your family is worth it!

ROASTED GARLIC & ROSEMARY
MASHED ROOT VEGGIES

Okay, I'll admit it here — I wait all year to eat mashed potatoes... which is kind of a shame really, I'm not proud of it... but there it is. I guess its 'cuz they will never taste better than on this day every year so why bother? And this is definitely a game of, if one is good three are better... Leave the skins of the root vegetables on — you can chop these during any lull in your cooking schedule and let them soak in the water until an hour before plating — bringing them all up from a cold start to boil will give you the latitude to juggle the rest of the dishes (gravy is always more time than you'd think) when everything is demanding your attention at the last moments before plating... these are the most forgiving, and they'll be nice and hot when serving.

---

1 golden Yukon potato per person (chopped into large cubes)

1 turnip (chopped into large cubes)

1 large brown onion (peeled and sliced into rings)

1 large carrot (sliced into rounds)

1 parsnip (chopped into large cubes)

1 head of garlic

1 tsp. EVOO

1 bunch fresh rosemary (strip the bristles off and chop fine)

1 stick of butter

In large stock pot of water
Toss in the chopped root vegetables and the onion. Light the burner during the last hour of the Turkey cook time.

Slice the top tips off the head of garlic — just enough to expose the cloves
Place on a ceramic roasting dish. Pour the EVOO over the exposed tips of the garlic and place in the oven beside the roasting turkey.

Boil the root veggies until "just" tender
turn the heat off and if you need more time — remove the veggies from the water but keep the water in the pot to reheat them just before mashing!

When you're ready to serve
Return the root veggies to hot water — when they're warmed up (about 2 minutes) drain the water. Toss in the stick of butter. Squeeze the roasted garlic into the pot (careful to get it all!). Add the chopped rosemary This is your call — depending on the freshness and the body of the rosemary.
Transfer to a serving dish or serve right from the pot - we're not judging... seriously, we're not. *We're not!*

SAVORY PUNKIN' PIES

This one is — admittedly "way over the top" but, it's also good when you are going to a pot-luck Thanksgiving — it's festive and fun — I'll betcha none of your guests have ever had this.

2 tbsp. olive oil	2 cloves garlic, crushed
1 tbsp. red wine or red wine vinegar	1⁄4 cup panko bread crumbs
1 can coconut milk	1⁄4 roasted pumpkin seeds
3 eggs	Dash of salt
1 large shallot	Dash of chipotle
Dash of cinnamon, allspice and salt to taste.	EVOO & sherry vinegar for brushing

Preheat your oven to 450 degrees
(This recipe makes pie for 8)

This can also be done with Hubbard or acorn squash if you can't find good pumpkins

Make the filling
Slice and peel a "pie pumpkin" or "sugar pumpkin" into cubes.
Stir to coat with olive oil and red wine vinegar with crushed garlic and your favorite herbs —

In a separate roasting pan
Add the pumpkin seeds (separate the "brains" or fibrous strands) and toss with a dash of EVOO and red wine vinegar.

Roast both flesh & seeds in a 450 degree oven
until the pumpkin is soft and the seeds are nutty. Let the pumpkin cubes cool, the seeds may take longer. When they are to your liking remove and set aside.

Meanwhile Make your "crust"
Slice the whole pumpkins
(at least slightly larger than a regulation softball) into 1 1⁄2 inch thick "rounds" for each serving. Cut out the center to make a thick circle of pumpkin flesh, (this is your "pie crust.")

Brush with oil & vinegar and grill these on your BBQ or a dry griddle
until they are just beginning to caramelize on the surface. Set aside to cool.

To your still hot griddle or grill
Add the shallots, brush with olive oil and cook until the edges begin to caramelize. Set aside to cool.

In a blender or food processor
Add the roasted pumpkin cubes. Add the coconut milk, eggs, cinnamon, allspice and salt to taste. Puree on low until smooth.

Build the pies:
Place your squash rounds on individual aluminum foil rounds (since they have no bottom). Set all of them on a baking sheet and divide the pumpkin filling into the centers and bake at 450 for about 35 minutes.

Make the topping
in dry hot skillet
Toast the panko "bread crumbs" until golden brown, add the roasted pumpkin seeds and toast all until fragrant — drizzle in a dash of olive oil and a dash each of the chipotle and salt.

Garnish each pie with the bread crumb/seed topping
Return them to the oven for an additional five minutes.

Remove them from the oven
Discard the foil and serve 'em up!

MAPLE GLAZED BRUSSEL SPROUTS

This one is what we in the kitchen call a "no-brainer" in that once you eat one, you lose your brain and can't stop eating! (Also one of the "Stupid foods" in the food Rhombus that bypasses your tummy governors rendering you incapable of exercising self-control.) Where was I? Oh, yeah. Maple glazed... anything — in this case, brussel sprouts.

And here's why these are dangerous lil suckahs that should be registered with the FBI — they are just little healthy green veggies, right?

Right. Roasted to a caramelized garlicky yumminess and coated with the heavenly mapleness that makes them almost as dangerous as a bowl of your favorite breakfast cereal. Put on your seatbelts...

2 lbs. brussel sprouts (washed and halved)	**2 tbsp. red wine**
3 cloves of garlic (pressed)	**1 tsp. coarse Kosher salt**
1 tbsp. fresh oregano leaves (minced fine)	**1/2 cup real maple syrup** (don't even bother if
1/4 cup EVOO	you'd even consider the fakie stuff)

Preheat your oven to 450 degrees

In a mixing bowl
whisk the EVOO, wine, garlic, salt and oregano. Add the brussel sprouts and toss to coat.

Roast in the 450 degree oven (stir every five minutes or so)
to roast until caramelized (about 25 minutes). Remove from the oven, and pour the maple syrup over and stir to coat.

Serve hot!

PUMPKIN CHIFFON PIE

I wish I could say Mylove's family invented this (cuz she'd be rollin'!) but really — like many of every family's recipes, this one is good BECAUSE it comes from the "The Joy of cooking" — which isn't the same online or even in the modern versions (call us old fashioned,) but if it doesn't have flour and butter stains from the last time you used it, what's the point? And I have to caution you — not every edition has the same recipes, we know this because I was doing a "satellite media tour" which is an odd marketing animal that used to roam freely in the broadcast jungle that entailed (see what I did there?) a host or subject, a Camera Operator & Producer (Moi), and an advertising Exec (or army depending on the project) stuffed in a little room (or a mobile truck) so that we could beam the camera's signal of the host to appear in as many individual local news programs across the country that the Ad execs had sold to accept the signal.

Mylove came with me the day (right before Thanksgiving in the early 2000's) when they were announcing the latest edition of TJOC... while the client, the ad exec and the host were wrestling over a few choice words, Mylove quickly rifled through the latest version to check if her beloved Pumpkin Chiffon pie was there...

... When it was not, she dropped the book in disgust. The client looked up and asked what the matter was, and Mylove didn't bat an eye, saying thanks, I'll keep my 1953 edition, thank you very much.

The client's shoulders slumped and she looked to the ad exec and said — "See, this is what I'm saying! It IS a problem!"

We love what we love.

So, in the interest of fair use and all, look it up in your edition of the TJOC and if you don't have it? Drop us a line and we'll talk you thru — trust me, it's worth it — you will never eat "whatevs" (old) pumpkin pie again.

CARDAMOM PIE

I saw this headline in a magazine I was flipping through at my dentist's office and could not get it out of my head. I didn't read the recipe cuz someone had ripped it from the mag, but that didn't matter cuz I love cardamom! So, I figured who would argue with a standardy, custardy pie flavored with cardamom and a flakey crust?

Since Mylove loves her beloved Pumpkin Chiffon's graham cracker crust, we balance the faire with a flakey one... and besides, somebody's gonna bring an apple pie (even when we tell them, we got this) so having this wild card brings an unexpected guest to the table.

1 tbsp. unsalted butter	**1/2 cup ice water**
1 stick salted butter (frozen — trust me this is amazing)	**2 tbsps. cardamom seeds** (crushed in a mortar)
1/3 cup sugar	**1/4 teaspoon salt**
4 cups cream	**1 whole vanilla bean** (split)
8 egg yolks	**1/2 cup of mascarpone cheese or crème fraiche**
1 egg	
1/2 cup flour	**1/4 cup shelled roasted and salted pistachios** (chopped)
1/2 tsp. salt	
1 tsp. sugar	

Preheat your oven to 350

Make your crust:
In a large mixing bowl
Whisk the flour, salt & sugar thoroughly. Take off your wedding rings to gently work the butter into the flour. With a cheese grater, grate the frozen butter into the flour, mix with your hands until it's "pebbly." I won't work it for more than 2:00 - ans don't be afraid to stick it back into the freezer if you can feel the butter getting too soft.

Add water a tablespoon at a time
Gather into a ball — again, don't "overwork" your dough. Wrap it in plastic and let it chill another hour. When you're ready, roll out the dough, and line your pie plate — spread the mascarpone cheese (or crème fraiche) on the crust to prevent it from getting soggy. Use as thin a layer as possible so as to not over flavor the custard.

In a medium nonstick skillet
melt the butter over medium heat. Add the pistachios and 3 tbsp. sugar; stir constantly until the nuts are lightly browned, about 5 minutes. Using a large spoon

or spatula, spread out the candied nuts on a baking sheet. Let cool completely.

In a medium saucepan
slowly heat the cream, cardamom seeds and the vanilla bean, (this should take at least 15 minutes — we are flavoring the cream, so take your time, the longer you go the richer/deeper the flavor. Remove the vanilla bean and scrape the inside pulp into the cream and put the pod into your vanilla sugar jar, then kick up the heat and allow it to come to a boil, then remove from the heat.

In your standing mixer,
beat the egg yolks, remaining 1/3 cup sugar, and salt until thick ribbons form when the beaters are lifted, about 2 minutes. Slowly pour the warm cardamom cream into the egg mixture, whisking constantly.

Pour the custard into the pie shell.
Bake for 25 – 30 minutes — check to see that the custard is setting up. Don't worry if it's little "jiggly" in the center, it will set up as it cools.

Just before serving, top with the pistachios.

PEAR APPLE RUSTIC TART

And just in case your guests didn't bring an apple pie… it's rustic tart to the rescue (we're still not gonna make the tradish apple pie that everyone expects because that guest who forgot to read might still come through the door). These rustic tarts the perfect solution to many dinner dilemmas — quick to make and real crowd pleasers. I learned the mascarpone/crème fraiche liquid barrier trick (that we just used with the Cardamom Pie) with rustic tarts and I realized that I never explained the difference — use the mascarpone if you like a milder flavor, the crème fraiche, if you like a little zing. To me they are interchangeable in these recipes for those who have a preference, and for those who are new, experiment — get Recklass!

This one uses a galette or puff pastry type technique (in fact since you've been cooking since yesterday, and still have bunch to go, there's not a jury in the world that would convict you if you got a frozen one of either) but if you're a mutant like me, you'll go scratch — it's still easy and adaptable — I make these savory or sweet for brunches or desserts and never strike-out filling them with whatever I have.

This stuff is easy, it just takes effort since the key is the series of rolling and folding to spread thin layers of butter between thin sheets of dough that will separate in the baking process.

5 cups bread flour	**1 splash Jack Daniels or Brandy**
2 1/2 teaspoons salt	**½ tsp. cinnamon**
2 cups water	**½ tsp. nutmeg**
2 cups unsalted butter, at room temperature	**½ cup brown sugar**
2 crisp apples (cored and sliced into thin wedges)	**1 stick of butter**
	1 tsp. orange zest
2 sweet pears (cored and sliced into thin wedges)	**1 cup mascarpone/crème fraiche**

Mix the flour and salt together in the bowl of a standing mixer with your dough hook. Gradually stir in water until the dough holds together. You may not need the full amount of water. Shape into a flat ball, and allow to rest for at least 10 minutes.

Place the butter between two pieces of plastic wrap using a rolling pin or other heavy object, pound into a flat disc.

Put this into refrigerator until firm, about 20 minutes.

On a lightly floured surface, roll out the dough into a large rectangle about 1/2 inch thick. Place your disc of chilled butter in the center and fold the two ends over it so that it is completely encased in dough. Roll out the dough again, to a ½ inch thickness. Don't let the butter break through. Fold again into thirds. This is your first "turn". Rotate the dough 90 degrees and roll out into a rectangle again. Fold this into thirds. This is your second turn. Again, rotate the dough 90 degrees, and repeat a third time. Put the folded dough into the refrigerator while you prepare your filling.

Preheat your oven to 450 degrees

In a dry, hot, cast iron skillet arrange the apple and pear wedges.
Get a lid ready, when the fruit starts to sizzle, hit it with a splash of brandy or Jack Daniels and immediately close the lid. Allow to steam for about 1 minute.

Lift the lid, add the butter and brown sugar.
Add the nutmeg, cinnamon, and orange zest. Cook until the syrup thickens (about 3 minutes) turn off the heat and allow to cool.

Roll your tart dough into a circle
spread the mascarpone/crème fraiche from the center out toward the edge — stopping about 2 inches shy of the edge so you have a wide circle of "naked dough" bordering your circle of crème.

Onto this circle of crème, arrange the apple & pear wedges in a concentric circles
(I like to alternate the direction of the circles, but this is YOUR tart, so you do you.)

Fold the naked dough in toward the center to make a crust over your circles of fruit.

Bake for 20 minutes
check to make sure the pastry is golden brown. Remove and allow to cool completely before slicing.

CHAPTER 3

"THE MOST WONDERFULL TIME OF... THE... YEAR!"

I wrote lovingly about how, um what's the word… sacred? Christmas is to me and Mylove. Each for our own reasons that (like everything else in a marriage) becomes fused together. But I never said why it is for me, nor did I tell you the whole story. Christmas is… my mom. She made this holiday literally stop time on the planet. She wove a crystal bubble of magic so spell-bindingly magical that I still feel every one of them to this day. She had boxes and boxes of Christmas decorations that would be brought out each year with reverence, treated as though they were made of precious gold and jewels — despite being made of Styrofoam and cheap felt. And the ornaments, holy relics that marked the time of a family weathering life's storms and bounty.

But more than the way our house looked, was the way it smelled. Cinnamon and Clove, Worcestershire & Garlic. My mom would wake up the day after Thanksgiving as if the Christmas Spirit had taken over her body and it wouldn't stop until January 2nd. It was hot and cold running cookies and "nuts and bolts" (hey it was the seventies!) right up until Christmas Day when the big guns came out. My mom had her repertoire: rocky road, fudge, and divinity, thumb print cookies, decorated sugar cookies stamped out of heirloom cookie cutters. She never made them all at once, but trotted out a new batch as the weeks between Thanksgiving and the big day got ticked off the advent calendar. This kaleidoscope of sugar and spice built the anticipation for Santa's arrival in a devilish tease that actually prolonged the Christmas spirit all year long.

So. Yes. Christmas is my mom. And I wrap myself in her lessons and love every year with great joy.

And I continue her traditions. But I have my own repertoire, created over thirty years of Christmas with Mylove. I start with the candies, we're putting carbs into our bank, so we have to start slow. I move onto cookies about December 10 or so. These are more time consuming, so usually it takes about two weekends. But like mom's "gradual roll-out" it helps with building anticipation, and keeping things fresh. If you visit during the holidays it would look something like this: If you come anytime between thanksgiving and mid-December, I'll probably serve you "cranberry jewels" (white chocolate bark with cranberries sautéed in cabernet sauvignon, toasted slivered almonds dusted with chipotle' and sea salt) toasted pine nut toffee and peppermint bark with your evening tea as we watch "It's a Wonderful Life." (BT-Dubs, we only watch Christmas movies from Thanksgiving on — this drives Mylove crazy, but I insist, sorry, them's the rules.)

If you come from mid-December until the Christmas Eve, you'll get all of the above plus our *Malcolm's Masterpiece Ginger Cubeds* (named for Mylove's father) *cranberry pistachio refrigerator cookies* and *Scottish Shortbread with lemon glaze.*

And that's just the sweet life…

The last week before Christmas, I'm cooking. I've got a marinara going, which takes 3–5 days. (I usually can't wait to start it, so I go five days. And if I've really got my mud together, I'm making croutons for the Caesar Salad, allowing them time to dry out perfectly. I'm also shopping. Picking up key ingredients along the way because I don't have the refrigerator space, and I want the vegetables to be perfect for this most sacred of meals.

'Cuz, I've been waiting all year for this.

Christmas is the time Mylove and I use to give back to our family & friends for the love and support they've shown us throughout the year. I am painfully aware of each time I say to our friends, "let's get together, call me" when really neither of us actually has the time for follow-through. In fact, I've trained myself to only say it, if I mean it. And many times, when I do, the other person either doesn't know I'm that serious, or doesn't know how to follow through. This human phenomenon drives me out of my mind. So, to remedy this, Christmas Eve is a five course (give or take) formal sit-down thank-you dinner for 10 of our closest friends.

I rarely accept help for this day. When I have, it was with two of the most amazing people God ever created, Lucy & Eleanor. But even then, having them over to help was for them, not me, and since they moved to the East Coast (still haven't gotten over, I see) I'll probably keep it a solo flight from here on.

Because I truly want everyone to have the dinner of their lives.

So, it starts with the formal invite going out in the first week of November, but really, we've started inviting people from as early as June. The regulars will probably always be there, but there is a rotation of some guests. And occasionally we get someone who is completely new to this extravaganza. One year a couple had made reservations for Hawaii well before they knew they were coming to our fête. When they saw that we were serious about the limited guest list, and how one can fall off the invite list if an invitation is declined (it's a rented table after all) they almost got divorced when one of the couple actually considered postponing the vacation in an effort to hang onto their seats at our table. I'm not so hardcore anymore. I'll consider each on a case-by-case basis. But in my defense, Mylove makes me swear that it will only be 10 guests, she doesn't want to dilute our attention.

One of the things that the invitation calls for is a dress code-

"Dress for the Evening is "Christmas Dressy" For further explanation our fashion consultant Mark Lyons is available."

I used to say this because I didn't want to spend a week's worth of cooking just to serve it to a bunch of people in shorts. This tradition started even before Mylove and I were married, in San Diego, where casual dress is deemed a birthright, "dressing up" is usually defined by anything other than board shorts & bikinis. I mean, we get so few opportunities no matter where you live to dress up, and I wanted an affair where women could wear dresses and that means the guys have to wear pants, and at least nice shirts. My dear friend Mark saw this and realized he finally had a place to wear the green corduroys that had been given to him. They were really nice slacks, but as a field audio mixer, he rarely had the occasion to ever dress up, and seriously, when would he ever wear green slacks? But since he took the invitation guidelines to heart, he was the best man to describe Scottie's dictum, hence his title as "fashion consultant."

As we get closer to the Christmas week, we bounce from joy to exhaustion, but I learned a long time ago, that the glow of Christmas is a yule log that is not just best when well-tended in the hearth, but more fun! Seriously, when is it okay to eat cookies and candy at night with a cuppa, except at this time of the year. Not even calorie guilt feels guilty about a second or even a third of anything. We'll work it out during tomorrow's hectic run-up to the holidays, or at least in the first weeks of the new year, so come-on, let's live a little.

Cause, besides making all of this goodness, we're probably going to the store... a lot. And not just any store — sure I'll probably live at Whole Paycheck err, I mean Foods. (Also, Trader Joe's is in my heavy rotation for key ingredients) but this is also the time I allow myself to go to the out-of-the-way Italian deli that I always swear I'm going to give my business. And farmer's markets (which I wish I had the time and patience to make it to every week — but sadly no). It's also the time I go to World Market for those weird edible trinkets and doodads that make everything you cook during this time just a little bit more special.

Cause this time is all about the glint in the eyes of those that you love when they bite into the crunchable, lickable, hugs & kisses that come from your kitchen.

I keep everything in special plastic treat containers and metal tins and every night after whatever supper we're having I serve them on the Christmas platters (that cost me 99 cents the day after Christmas last year) and are priceless kitsch that make everyone smile. I also always reserve (or make more when we've got more than the usual amount of guest traffic prior) a batch of everything for Christmas Eve and Christmas day — there is nothing worse than eating a normal anything on either of those days.

So that's the sweet world. As we get closer to Christmas week, I start the prep for things we discussed in the opening strains of this chapter. Marinara, croutons, a turkey is probably brining and I've started prepping vegetables for their time in a marinade (usually no more than two days.)

The key in the last days before ShowTime, is that you cannot be in three places at once. And the time you spend bringing home the freshest of the fresh is time away from the kitchen — so pre-planning is your friend.

If it seems like all I do is think about, buy and prepare food during this time, you're half-right. I'm also getting Mylove's Christmas gifts and… despite the 25 hour days I've written about above, I'm wallowing in the Christmas spirit. Sure, I've probably put off (despite my promise that this year I am going to get a jump on it) wrapping my gifts for Mylove, and will be wrapping them between doing the Christmas Eve dishes and trying to get to sleep before Santa comes, but…

… I really am having the most wonderful time of the year! (Thank you, Johnny Mathis — his version is best, doncha think?)

Okay, so let's focus up. It's now three days out and everything that could've been bought ahead of time should already be home and here. All that's left to shop for are the ingredients that should be bought as fresh as possible — even so, that still leaves me one last giant run around town tomorrow. Marinara is already on day 3 of a 5 day ever-so-slow cook. Croutons are air-drying after having been baked in a 250-oven brushed with olive oil and garlic and salt.

The one thing I don't have? Counter space. Yes, my kitchen is the size of a small closet. I've seen bigger galleys on row boats. I'm not kidding. I have one drawer. You heard me right. One. And it's one third the width of any drawer in your house. And don't get me started on shelf space. So, since everything is already on my counters the extra ingredients have to go somewhere….

Time to convert my dining room into my staging area. I push the table against the wall and stack the chairs in the corner — I need room to work. This is the world's best smelling Rubik's cube. I will constantly be methodically stacking and re-stacking on the dining room table for the next few days, and always trying to leave enough space for me to work as well. I've stacked things under the table and on the chairs that I've pushed into the corner. I will burn up the tread on a couple of pairs of shoes just going the six feet between these rooms in the coming days. I all ready for the big push which starts in the morning. I'm still mentally counting ingredients as Mylove and I snuggle in for long winter's nap…

Because tomorrow is marinade day. Which means I hit the ground running, I'll be going shopping for the last of my trips to the store(s) right after our morning fawkey.

But… something's not right. And that something… *is our septic tank.*

We could hear water draining inside the house. We could smell water draining inside the house… we just couldn't see it… until it came pouring down the walls of our master bathroom at about a few minutes past midnight.

In a blind stupor, Mylove and I are seeing things that should never be inside a house come down our wall onto the floor! As we struggled to figure what our move was, we shut off all the water to the house and got a plumber from our bestie Audie (our realtor mentioned in the Easter Chapter!) who graciously answered her phone in the middle of the night and had the right man for the job. He came out and after sussing out the culprit — the pump that pumps all the drains from the bottom of our house uphill to the septic tank (yes, we're the last streets in our rural neighborhood to get on the sewer lines — and not sure if that's going to happen anytime soon) so… two hundred fifty dollars and an agreement that the plumber will come back in the morning with the proper pump, later, we're trying to go back to sleep.

You know, with my first book, the first readers of the early drafts said that it seemed too easy, that people were unrealistically nice and supportive of my transition and that in order for it to be an "interesting read" it need more pathos, that there needed to be an antagonist. So, I recounted a few of those (my sister in South Carolina is one) who were, in essence the black hats that demonstrated that Scottie Jeanette didn't have a boring, uneventful, *uninteresting read* of a journey.

Which is what was threatening to be the case again for this book —

… and tho' I don't expect that a cookbook is necessarily *expected* to have an antagonist … it seems that we are off and running heading in that direction. Then, again, I didn't expect to be writing about raw sewage in a chapter devoted to sugar and spice and Christmas nice either… so, there you go.

The trials and tribulations getting to the Christmas Eve table start to take on more pathos than any cook wants connected to her holiday. And tho' our current candidate for antagonist has more of a smell than a face, it has definitely inserted itself into the narrative So, by all means, let's continue with this Holiday, cautionary tale…

Oh… did I say out loud that after the plumber left with his "don't use any of your toilets, sinks or showers" that…

BELLA GOT SKUNKED??????

I'll even include the recipe for the skunk juice. Get me, not only did I include a reference to raw sewage in a cook book, I even slid in a skunking. I'm either good or suicidal, and right now, there is no difference, so, moving on!

It's tomorrow.

I am jonesing to get started — as I said, normally, today is the day that I wake up and hit several of my favorite stores and shops to get the stuff I need because I'm going to be spending the whole day cooking. It's three hours of visiting the small shops (Like Cavaretta's — a groovy family Italian deli where hard core foodies like me are dancing with the construction crews that have come in to get their subs for lunch).

But no. I'm waiting for the plumber to come back and as soon as he gives the greenlight (and we have water — everything has been shut off, lest it comes back into the master bathroom), I can go shopping — he has said he will be here before noon.

And then promises he'll be there before 2:00 pm.

And swears it will be no later than 5:00 pm

Then absolutely swears it will happen by 6:00 pm.

I don't get out the door until 7:00 pm (I'll save the details and results for after Christmas).

I'm sweating now. My traditionally leisurely yearly gift I give myself has now become a mad dash to get everything while I'm frantically recalculating… everything. Who's still open — what can I get and what will I have to settle for — what substitutions will I have to make?

But, I finally burst through the door at 9:30 pm, sharpen my knives, and after a cup of tea, and three pieces of toffee, I am finally back in the saddle! Finding my groove.

Oh, and did I mention Christmas came early? I can't believe I buried the lead. Please forgive me. After years of "understanding" and begging, and then, out and out "writing it off," I decided to try my annual empty query to my sister Lib that since the kids are practically adults now, maybe she could come up for Christmas Eve dinner… She, of course, laughed (as she always has) in my face — I am still, despite estrogen's softening of spirit, her unrealistic and crazy big sister — the one who will never know how kids change everything.

Including their minds. Of course, they want to come have Christmas Eve Dinner with Aunt Scottie & Aunt Marcy.

What?

When I floated this idea, as we both were under Thanksgiving's tryptophan spell, and she said, "she'd look into it," I, of course, took it as her perennial deflection.

But it's happening. Since Kaylee and Hana will both be home from school, and Dane gets off work at noon, they'll be up from San Diego in time for dinner.

I am blown away.

Our table has swelled to 18 people. I mean table(s).

So, now you know why the plumber, bless his heart, despite saving us from a fate worse than sewage is only slightly worthy of my sincerest gratitude for getting us back to the world of the flushing only after stealing away my precious time with his "progressive arrival promises."

Okay, that's enough context — I am back on track and I still have less than 24 hours before showtime and that's with a night's sleep and a shower… but those come only after I get through this next stage. The Christmas marinades…

I will use a box of Ziploc bags, into each one, I pour a few tablespoons of an oil. Today, I'm using olive, grape seed and walnut oils. For the acid of the marinade, I will alternate between red wine, fresh squeezed lemon juice, balsamic and sherry vinegars, and I will flavor each of these with Christmas spices. Cinnamon, Allspice, Cardamom, Vanilla, Clove, Nutmeg. And of course, a variety of salts that I've collected over the past year from habanero to alder smoked. I don't measure these, I go by feel, and I vary the vegetables each year. What was good at the market? Which caught my fancy on the various shopping runs? What is a vegetable that I didn't know about? Or just made me think of Christmas? All are fair game. Have fun, this is your chance to play. What? You've never tried a grilled asparagus spear with vanilla and cardamom? Me neither. But you can bet I'm making that one this year. Over time, you'll develop some favorites and in the ten years I've been making this antipasti platter I've never duplicated a mixture. Not once.

Anyhow. Once I've put the mixtures in the bags, I start cutting vegetables — trust me do it in this order, cutting these later is big fat mess. Cut the vegetables with an eye toward arranging them on the platters for their intrinsic beauty. Grill marks will paint a delicious swath of color, but only if you give it enough surface area to work with. Once cut, add them to the bags in the combos your tongue and taste buds have already been discussing…

And stack them on the table in roasting pans. If you're like me you don't have any space in the fridge and the warm-ish temp will allow them to marinate perfectly. (remember this is December after all — and only my Aussie friends have to worry about the summer heat, yes?)

Okay that's done.

On the *usual* day before, (December 23rd if I hadn't made that clear) I'm making last minute runs to the store or I'm doing the above marinating because I couldn't get there yesterday. You know how people always say that Italian food is always better the next day? Well, I usually make more things today, so that tomorrow everything will taste amazing.

Today's usually supposed to be also the Meatball and Sausage & Peppers day. I'll also probably try to make the ice cream base and whatever else I think we'll make this year special. This is my last chance to dream up tomorrow, so it be a well-choreographed dance in the aforementioned galley kitchen, so most of my improvs will be with small details, anything else will either be a catastrophic necessity or a tiny derail.

As it *is,* it's midnight when I get to start making the meatballs.

The meatballs I make are made from dark and white meat chicken. You can substitute beef and pork if you like. What makes these so special is a traditional ingredient that started because our dear friend Maureen used to have a gourmet produce broker biz. She was the go-to gal for chefs wanting the perfect produce for their 5 star meals. One year, she gave something that changed my meatballs forever. Chanterelle mushroom Powder. Let me say that again, slowly. Chantelle. Mushroom. Powder. Dried Chanterelles pulverized into an amazing substance that reminds of those million dollar cocktails in Las Vegas where they salt the rim of a cocktail with powdered gold or diamonds. Only this is even better. And despite what it cost Maureen back then (Geezus where does the time go?) It's not cheeeeeap, but it won't break the bank and come on, it's Christmas! (Are you sensing a theme here?) To complete the extravagance factor, I add toasted pine nuts. Which do cost an arm and leg… that's how much I love my family! These get baked in the oven so that tomorrow all I have to do is warm them.

And it's almost 1:00 am when I start the Sausage & Peppers.

My sausage & peppers are made with turkey sausage (which I think are more amazing) but again, there's so few of my friends who eat the four-leggeds these days, and I say that so you'll be fearless in your cooking, and know that they're every bit as good as their porkier cousins. I use the ol' cast iron Dutch oven for this one, and I'll store them overnight in the same so I can reheat them tomorrow with little fuss later on… what am I saying?

… I don't have a *tomorrow* anymore.

Geezus that's right — even my body clock knows that it's already Christmas Eve. It's 2:30 am when I finally set the knives down. Oh, and turn off the flames…

I review my cooking times in my head as I pass out next to Mylove. The big factor when I get up is the "rising time" for the star of the show. I'm usually so antsy for tomorrow to begin, that I pre-measure the ingredients so that I can wake up tomorrow and get the ball rollin' (so to speak) so I'll have ample time to maneuver. But that will have to wait till I kick myself out of bed in a few hours. As my body starts to finally relax between Mylove and two sleeping dogs (none of whom were sure I was going to make it into bed tonight — sleepily making room for me) I start my endless backtiming. In order for the Timpano to come to the table *hot* but having rested for a half-hour, precisely at 7:00 pm means…. Seven o'clock minus the thirty-minute rest time, minus an hour cooking time, minus 30 minutes to build… minus 30 minutes to roll out the dough… minus second rising of 45 minutes… minus 2 hours of first rise… minus 35 minutes for sponge… minus…

DEFYING GRAVITY is the soundtrack to the dream that despite its all-star cast of those who will be coming to spend Christmas Eve with us is… SHIT!!!! It's also my alarm ringtone!!!!!

Time to get out of bed — luckily the adrenaline jolt of recognition that my alarm is ringing is also reminding me that it's *Christmas Eve* and you know what that is… time for coffee — I'm way too foggy to do what I got to do.

But the good news is that despite the false summit of yesterday's late start, I am now gloriously back on track so, no more wasted sentences in this chapter that start with "normal" or "usually" or what evs, cuz…

TODAY IS OUR DAY! CHRISTMAS EVE!

A quick note on timing. When we were first married, I loved, loved, loved cooking elaborate dinner parties for our Tag-Team friends. We were all going to take over the television and video production worlds and celebrated together every chance we got. But… sadly, my timing sucked. I was "swinging for the fences" as they say, trying complicated dishes with fresh ingredients and I can't tell you how many dinners got served well after the entire bunch of guys (and Ceege & me) were hamana hamana *hammered.* (okay we drank a lot of beer) I was lucky if I got a meal off before midnight. Luckily, they loved me and the wait was worth it… mostly.

But the worst of this crime was that I was usually in the kitchen trying to coax reluctant rabbits out of hats and that left Mylove to play hostess and she didn't like being a solo act.

She was right. This was no way to play. And it wasn't satisfying for me either. I barely had any time with the people who I was practically dying for in the kitchen … so I changed my game. I learned to time everything so it got to the table at showtime and I got the results I wanted and the meals became everything I hoped they would be.

This night starts promptly at six o'clock with hors d'oeuvres, and a relish platter. Which gives everyone a chance to settle in and get ready for showtime. The funny thing is there's not usually anywhere to sit, since for this occasion, Mylove and I push the living room furniture to the sides and set two rented tables in the center of the room so we can have the Christmas tree (once you go to 9 feet you'll never go back) and the fireplace. The table probably already has porcelain platters (that I bought about ten years ago once I finally locked the menu) of antipasti — grilled vegetables, each in an aforementioned Christmas spiced marinate: carrots in orange zest and cinnamon, zucchini in basil and cardamom, cauliflower and broccoli in lemon-zest nutmeg, portobello mushrooms get cabernet and allspice. Arranged in rows, drizzled with olive oil and garnished with olives, cherry tomatoes, marinated garlic and preserved lemon.

During my morning, I had time during the Timpano dough risings to get the rest of the ingredients for the Timpano assembled, cooking fresh pasta, marinara sauce, pesto sauce, grating the four cheeses (smoked mozzarella, fresh mozzarella, parmesan, Romano) sautéed mushrooms, grilled onion and roasted garlic.

In addition to making sure dessert is on track (Figgy pudding is mostly chopping and soaking — it will go into the oven after I pull the Timpano — the ice cream base was made yesterday so all it has to do is go for an hour in the freezer and then cure during dinner). I'll toast onion rings in a super-hot cast-iron skillet, and when they are the perfect caramelized translucent, I shut off the gas, add olive oil, capers and freshly grated nutmeg. I'll de-glaze the whole shebang with some Jack Daniels and pour the mixture over a beautiful three-pound, wild caught (worked too long on a fish dock to ever eat farmed fish!) salmon filet that's waiting on a cedar plank that's been soaking in water and Jack Daniels all day. It's not going on till a half-hour before showtime, so any time it gets to "get to know" it's nutmeg and caper coating is all good.

I'll also get the vegetables grilled and plated, as a project that I get to in small "time crumbs" — the point is to make them pretty, and garnish, garnish, garnish... I can futz with these, right up until showtime with a little something here and there, depending on what time I don't have.

I also have made this more complicated by adding in the Scottie factor. And that means at some time, well before the last phase before, I'll slip away and shower and get my makeup on, this is best when I'm on the other side of the "heavy lifting" (and sweating) so, certainly, I need to make sure everything is done with the exception of building the Timpano, so I shower at 4:00 and get my make-up and hair done... I'll save getting into my party dress until after the Timpano goes into the oven.

When it gets to be 5:00 pm — I'm ready. The Timpano is the most cherished guest of honor at tonight's fête. I first saw it made in Stanley Tucci's, "The Big Night" and I've modified it and perfected it after 13 years of Christmas Eves. His called for a giant pasta noodle, but I find the pizza dough makes a way more elegant dish. Pastas are layered with cheeses and the vegetables and sauces into a pizza dough-lined ceramic bowl. A pizza-dough top seals it all together into a drum. After baking, it is inverted onto a plate and sliced into wedges (like a slice of wedding cake) so that the layers are revealed. We will pass more marinara and grated cheese, *magnifico*.

After I pop it into the oven, I run down stairs for the last-minute touches on my hair and make-up. This is such a dream-come-true night for me (as I wrote about lovingly in GBTM) that looking my absolute frilly Christmassy best is part of the day.

I have barely enough time to get back to make sure the hors d'oeuvres hit on time.

Mylove has been working hard this whole time too, setting the table — this is her domain. She's a warrior tonight, sucking it up despite fighting off the seasonal sniffles that she probably picked-up from the hundreds of hugs she's given and gotten in the last few days… But she looks radiant (as always) and only I know the extra effort she's making to stay in the game. She makes the centerpiece, while I place the antipasto platters, the table looks abundant!

Tonight, Donny & Vanita are the first to arrive. Donny is here and he's packing. Handmade dark chocolate truffles and white chocolate and pistachio candies. And he's not only brought a dozen for each guest, but he's giving me several dozens, vacuum-packed "for the house." These usually go straight into the freezer, but I always pull out two for the after-dinner coffee. Donny is my dear friend. A fellow foodie, but unlike me, who is self-taught, Donny took a God-given talent for cooking into a real UCLA extension course for chefs. He is very scientific with his cooking, with a keen eye and patience toward texture and temperature. His truffles attest to that. They are not for the faint-of heart to ever try to make. And they are show stoppers. But then, so is everything he makes. He turned me on to the sous vide technique for cooking (and by turned on, I mean not only did he inspire me with his "work," but he also bought me one as a present) and always pushes me to really take my love for cooking to the next level.

The next guest to arrive is my brother-in-law Macky. It's amazing having family "just down the street." Macky takes his "big brother" role to heart, gently watching over Mylove (his seester) and me and jumping in whenever and wherever we ask, from doggie sitting to picking us or dropping us off at the airport. My relationship with Macky has changed more dramatically as I've transitioned than anyone else. Because of him. I was the "man" who was going to take care of his little sister forever. We both took this role seriously. When Macky was going to come and live with us for six months after relocating to Southern Cal (it would be for another 3 months past the agreement) it was…

… right as I was transitioning fully in the world. He was the first in the family to actually see me as I told him the truth. I was, and always had been a woman. Since he was going to be living in our house, he needed to know what was going on. He actually started to tear up as I was telling him and that made me cry too, which made him cry. He said he cried not because I was coming out, but that I had suffered for most of my life. He was and is beautiful about this.

And he's all in with Scottie Jeanette, as his sister-in-law. Sometimes more and faster than me. I hadn't ever kissed a boy. Sure, I kissed my father all the time. But Macky kisses me on the lips, like all the other women in our family without a second thought. I have to stand on my toes (he's six four) and I've caught my leg kicking up in back like a girl in a 1950's movie. It's something you don't really ever think about before transition. You think about the big things — how your lover and you will be (or change) how the government will have to change how you live, how your career and those with whom you work will deal with the change. But you rarely think about how you will be in the little things; how will you kiss the man you used to only shake hands with, or at best, bro-hug?

We try to invite couples to our event but Macky, and our dear friend Duncan and now our recently divorced Mark (he got us in the settlement, sorry Jennifer) are all three wildcards. If I'm going to honor Mylove's stipulation that it we keep it to ten, Macky and Duncan will be a "couple," which means we need to pick-up another solo-it's (kind of like a ski-lift line.)

But Duncan is a vegetarian. And this is an important point. I used to, as Chef, be worried that I couldn't make "what *I* wanted," when trying to accommodate all of the various-itarians. Which is, let's face it, completely *ego*-based cooking. It's why I switched the intention of Christmas Eve from being a party (where I was going to blow everyone away) to being a Christmas Present, where we (Mylove and I) would be giving our dearest friends love on a plate. It was the same people, on the same night, but the main ingredient *love* would replace ego. And thus, "*Recklass*" cooking as a concept was born.

I started this idea while cooking for Mylove. I like it waaaaaay more spicy than she does, so I started putting the chilies on the side. She wanted to eat less meat. So, I started putting that on the side too. For dishes where it's better for the meat to simmer in the other ingredients for long periods of time, I do that in smaller batches on the side and add that to my main bowl after I served hers. It also made me realize that too many times meat is added as a way to make a bigger statement with a dish (caterers always add "bacon" to something to make it feel more extravagant like bacon mac & cheese. But really, can your tongue discern the extravagance after the first mouthful redlines your taste buds?) And the good news is that, separating out these components is really no big deal, but it goes a long way to making those in your life feel loved and special — and really, why are you doing this other than that?

Guests are arriving! One incredible guest today is truly only making a cameo. Dr. Mark Katz sadly, has to work tonight — manning the emergency room at a busy hospital and his shift starts right when we're going to sit down. But since he read about the "Empress of Holidays" in my first book, he wasn't going to let a silly old thing like work or saving lives get in the way of at least sampling a little of this sacred time in our home. And rumor has it that he won't go away empty handed, or stomached (I'm preparing him a to-go feast that will be a miniature version of our feast that he'll be able to eat in the Doctor's lounge — complete with a "timpanito" and Donny's truffles.)

I'm able to give him hugs and love between slicing and dicing and he's enamored with our guests especially my nieces and nephew whose bright spirits light up the whole room.

Mark is also hitting it off with another special guest and newcomer to our annual feast, my agent Susan. Susan saw the staged-reading for a drama based on my book that I've teamed up with my dear friend Valerie C. Woods (whom you'll remember, those of you who read my first book, inspired me to not only write that book but we went on to develop a television series based on it called, "The Other Woman") anyhow, Susan was invited by Kelly Mantle the actor I had cast to play me, and when she heard during the audience Q&A session after the reading, that I had parted ways with my old agent, hit me up. We've been friends and agent/client ever since.

Susan has been looking forward to this dinner for a whole year and has brought a dear friend Randy as her "plus one" and together they are filling in my family with tales of my professional career that only an agent could know.

Me? Well, I'm blissed out of my mind with the buzz of those I love, loving others that we love, while I putter and flutter about the kitchen trying to land a space shuttle of foodieness on this good ship lollipop on the sea of love… (yes, I am blissed).

The last thing I get rolling is the hot apple cider. Two quarts of the best apple cider I can find (and each year is different — I suspect with the hard cider craze hopefully continuing, apple cider of all kinds will up everyone's game. I go old skool here, and spike a gorgeous orange with cloves and then float it in the cider with a few cinnamon sticks, a chunk of crushed ginger root, three-star anise and even a little coarsely ground black pepper. This will probably only have two to three takers but it will be a key ingredient later on… you'll see.

As soon as the Timpano comes out of the oven — the meatballs go in. They'll warm in the still hot oven, giving me time to get the water boiling for the coddled egg for the Salade Ceśar. The sausage and peppers are (still in the Dutch oven) put onto a flame and re-heated. The salmon plank goes onto the grill outside.

I start to make the salad in the family heirloom "Moses' boat," a hand carved, rectangular, wooden bowl that is so perfectly seasoned it just begs for a great salad to be laid into its bosom. I pour EVOO into the bottom, and squeeze fresh pressed garlic into the oil, and work the garlic into the oil. Next, comes fresh squeezed lemon. I keep working every ingredient lovingly into the next. Dijon mustard, Worcestershire, a sprinkle of salt. I keep the anchovies out (tho' I love them, remember, we still have some veggie-terriers in our crowd) next is the coddled egg. When everything is just so, I dump the croutons in, then the torn lettuce, and sometimes some cherry tomatoes for color. Lastly, I grate fresh parm onto the top and toss. The croutons have had a head start in the dressing, but not so much that they soak up all the dressing (a mistake I've made before). As I carry the boat around the table it's a special time to see everyone's smile lit by garlic's glow!

We sit and toast everyone with Christmas wishes and Grace, conversation will invariably take us back to Timpano's past. Which is good, cuz it gives me time to Flip the Timpano — I have a special "cake plate" that we bought several years ago just for this occasion. It's the perfect size, and I lay it upside down on the Timpano and invert the affair so the "bowl" is upside down…I take the Salmon off the grill and transfer it to a platter for serving on the table. I take the meatballs from the oven and build them into a five-story pyramid. I drizzle marinara sauce over the hot meatball mountain, and dust with grated parm for that "Matterhorn" effect. It goes to the table, followed by the sausage and peppers. By now, everyone is done with salad, and already Mylove has organized the clearing of the plates to make room for… Timpano!

I've just taken the bowl off, and it is beautiful, golden brown, and dusted with cheese and smoked salt, the aroma of baked bread, smoked cheeses and Italian spices is intoxicating. I get the same reaction every year that Mr. Tucci got in his seminal scene.

Amid applause and delight, the Timpano takes its seat at the head of the table where Mylove and I preside. As the meat and antipasti platters are passed, everyone knows to clear an LZ (landing zone) for the main attraction. I carve the Timpano and place a little slice of masterpiece on each waiting plate.

At some time, somewhere between singing Christmas Carols and everyone sharing their favorite Christmas memories (even our Jewish friends can play along having now been to several of these dinners) I will slip away and begin building dessert. Mylove will see me go and start to take coffee orders. When we're sure that the savory portion of our show has finished, out comes the Figgy pudding. Years ago, I bought cheap oversized martini glasses at Pier 1, and these are used once a year for this night — we are missing a few of the original red (they look so pretty and Christmasy) but the blue is nice too. In goes a still hot scoop of the moist classic figgy concoction. Each is topped with egg nogg ice cream that's been happily churning in the background all along.

When the second round of coffee is ordered, out will come Donny's truffles and a platter of the cookies and bark. Donny will use this time to go around the room and hand a package of his sorcery to each guest. I have set a platter of them out so they don't need to dip into their own stashes to nibble, along with pine nut toffee and cranberry gems.

Sadly… at some point everyone realizes that this starts all over again tomorrow, only this time, Santa will have come, so the coats are put on, the hugs and kisses are passed around and to all a good night is bid.

I've got dishes and presents to wrap…

And apples to cut up for tomorrow's breakfast!! Years ago, in the early part of our marriage, Mylove & I would volunteer for a yearly video production that would have us waking up on Christmas day in a hotel room (the production was on the road). But did that stop us from having a tree and a bit of our traditions? You remember who you're talking to, yes?

Well, I invented a Christmas morning breakfast called *apple chowder*. I'll save the story for later, but the part you need to know now is that I need to cut up about 10 really good apples. I have tried all kinds — it can be your personal favs, I like to 'speriment, and go with ones that will make a great apple sauce for this stage. I core and cut them into cubes, throw those into my slow cooker and pour 2 cups of the cider that was happily maturing on the back burner all night long. I even toss the clove spiked orange in for good measure and turn it on high. It will turn into magic while Santa's doing his thing, and we're all fast asleep. We're getting up early (it's Christmas, right) so it'll be cooking for about a max of 6 hours.

PS — we can do dishes tomorrow... or the next day. I've boxed them all neat and pretty-like in milk crates so I can keep them out of my way tomorrow — who wants to wake up to see that, when all you want to do is keep Christmas rolling!

Now where's the scotch tape — it's time to wrap

Okay, so turn the page and let's get into how all of this is made.

MALCOLM'S GINGER CUBEDS
(CHRISTMAS COOKIES)

Okay, I know (and so do you by now) that I can be prone to a bit of hyperbole, but I have tried to "tone it down" about my cooking lest the adjectives get in the way of clarity — but if there's one recipe in this book that I feel comfortable putting up against ALL comers, it's this one... And I don't do this lightly. Gingerbread is of course a kingdom that some may simply choose not to visit, so indifferent are they to even understanding why it's citizens doth lose their minds for the stuff...

... and that's okay. I guess that if you are one of those, we can't be friends anymore. I'm kidding of course, because even if you are one of "them" — chances are, one of us is in your immediate family, in which case I'm about to bequeath to you the holiest of grails... (Marcy & Scottie Jeanette's recipe including heaping tablespoons of fresh hyperbole).

But don't just take my word for it. It's a recipe Mylove and I have been perfecting for as long as we have been married — almost three decades, so when I made these for Mylove's father, Malcolm, he took a bite, tilted his head to the sky in ecstasy and took his sweet time to finish chewing. When he was done, he opened his eyes and said... "Could I buy a dozen of these from you?"

Henceforth, they were renamed in his honor, Malcolm's Ginger Cubeds (since they rock with fresh ginger, powdered ginger and crystallized (candied) ginger... I may not be very good at algebra, but I remember at least the power of exponents!

This is better with time and this is "double batch" because these are always a way to ring in the holidays starting December 1. I make the dough and keep it in the reefer until I need to "Restock the cookie jar" and take out only what I need to bake them a dozen or so at time — this is, I'm embarrassed to admit, a system I only figured out three years ago after having my heart broken that we'd eaten them all before Christmas Eve...

---

4 cups of all-purpose flour
3 cups almond or cashew flour
2 tsp. baking soda
2 tsp. salt
2 1/2 tsp. powdered ginger
2 tsp. cinnamon
1 tsp. ground clove
1 tsp. fresh grated nutmeg.
1 cup (2 sticks) salted butter
1 cup brown sugar

1 pound crystalized ginger (chop these into small chunks)
6 tbsp. fresh ginger juice (grate about 1/4 pound of fresh ginger root and squeeze it)
2 tbsp. apple cider vinegar
1 1/4 cup Blackstrap molasses

GLAZE
1 1/3 cups maple sugar
1 cup half & half
1 pound chopped pecans (toasted)

In a large mixing bowl
whisk the dry ingredients thoroughly. (Ahhh… that smell!)

In a standing mixer
cream the butter and brown sugar, toss in the crystallized ginger (don't be afraid of also scraping in any sugar crystals that sometimes flake off, it's Christmas, right?) add the flour mixture one cup at a time to form a stiff dough.

Transfer the dough to a floured board
form it into a ball. Wrap in plastic wrap and refrigerate for at least one hour (and as we said, up to two weeks).
Preheat your oven to 400 degrees.

Wet your hands
roll small handfuls into balls the size of golf ball. (These are very robust cookies — so smaller is better.) place the balls on an ungreased, non-stick baking sheet.
Bake for about 5–7 minutes
Using a spatula, smash the balls into a thick cookie — the cracking on the edges is the mark of classic ginger cookie. Bake for another 5–7 minutes.

Cool on a rack while you make your maple glaze
Now, here's where years of perfection paid off — this last bit of detail makes these world class elevating these from the honorable ginger snap into high art. (Yes, these are the Mona Lisas of cookie — not quite sure why she's so beautiful, the smile, the radiance, the overall Mona Lisa-ness?)

Get out your candy thermometer and high heat tolerant saucepan and spatula.

In a saucepan
pour the sugar and cream and stir to prevent from boiling over or burning. Bring to 230 degrees then remove from heat. Allow to cool enough to whisk into a creamy glaze.

Place parchment paper or foil under your cooling racks to catch the dripping gold!

Dip the cookies into the glaze
(it doesn't need much) and place onto your rack — sprinkle the chopped toasted pecans on half the cookies and keep the other half without nuts for those that are. (Seriously, there are those who don't like nuts in their cookies and we have to understand them, we do. We seriously must try to make room for them, we must. we must… how am I doing?)

I have a plastic cookie keeper that I put them into after allowing the glaze to dry. The nuts allow them to be stacked on top of one another without sticking to each other...

I created this symbol, based on the American Sign Language, for "I Really Love You" and had it embroidered on clothing for Mylove each year at Christmas... This was her personal logo and the hand gesture was how we waved goodbye to each other...

CRANBERRY, PISTACHIO ICEBOX COOKIES

Okay... I'm (obviously) not a professional cook. Nor do I pretend that I invented any of this stuff (except of course Malcolm's Ginger Cubeds as previously crowed about) because that's what home cooking is — an oral tradition (okay, I'm getting all misty eyed for the past, but still — for girls especially like me, who rarely had the mother-daughter relationship that commercials and sitcoms tell us, "you" all had.) What I love — especially about holiday cooking, is that each recipe becomes the trading cards we all swap to connect as humans. After all, they are all just variations on butter, sugar and love, right? Why am I telling you this, here? Because this recipe fell into my holiday canon, from a subscription that someone gave me to a gourmet magazine — and tho' the subscription lapsed long ago, this dog-eared, ingredient-stained special double holiday issue is one of the treasured pieces of our family bookcase.

These are the perfect cookie for the holiday repertoire, in that just like the Malcolm's Ginger Cubeds, you can keep a dough chilling in the reefer and bake them on demand when the cherished friend or family comes to call during the holidays and you are that magical being who turns a simple cup of tea and chat into a magical holiday affair in a seemingly effortless wave of your wand.

The key to these little jewels is that they actually are like little jewels! Square and crispy, they sparkle with sugar crystals, ruby red cranberries and lime green pistachios and their flavor is uniquely celebratory — not like any of the other flavor combinations that surround the holiday palette. If Malcolm's Ginger Cubeds are the blue-collar dad who puts on a tie for midnight mass, these are the girl next door who got a new dress for the party after!

---

1 1/2 cups all-purpose flour	1 tbsp. fresh orange juice (juice of an orange)
1/2 tsp. cinnamon	1/2 cup shelled, roasted pistachios (whole)
1/4 tsp salt	1/2 cup dried cranberries
1 1/2 sticks (¾ cup) unsalted butter (softened)	Parchment paper or plastic wrap
1/4 cup granulated sugar	1 large egg (beaten)
1/2 tsp. orange zest	Muscovado sugar (or other decorative large crystal sugar)

In a mixing bowl
whisk together the flour, cinnamon, and salt.

In your standing mixer
Cream the butter, sugar and orange zest and juice. Whip at medium high speed until fluffy.

Fold in the pistachios and cranberries
add the flour in small scoops, mix on low speed until thoroughly mixed.

Gather the dough and place on the parchment paper
Divide the dough into two and roll each into a log about 8–10 inches long about 1 ½ inches in diameter. Wrap the log into the parchment paper and flatten each side to form a squared bar. The sharper these edges, the prettier the sliced cookies will look on the plate.

Refrigerate for at least two hours or up to two weeks.

Preheat your oven to 350 degrees

In a shallow bowl
whip your egg.

In another shallow bowl
pour your decorative sugar.

Line two baking sheets with parchment paper.
Unwrap the bars and using a very sharp knife, slice thin cookies about ¼ inch thick. You want to slice right thru the pistachios and cranberries, to expose their brilliant Christmas colors.

Square off the edges that may get misshapen during cutting
try to preserve the sharp edges as much as possible. Roll the top and each edge in the egg, then roll thru the sugar to coat. (Don't coat the bottom.)

Bake for 15 minutes until pale golden.

Allow to cool on racks.

ICED SHORTBREAD SNOWFLAKES

Newsflash! Scottie Jeanette Christine Madden is a proud Scottish Lass! (and a proud Irish Lass — what's your point?) And Christmas for her is not complete without Shortbread. Now, I wish I could say I grew up with this lembas-like manna (LOTR anyone? Anyone? Waybread of the elves? Galadriel's Gift? Still nothing? Were those Tolkienites going to be at this show?) anyhoo… My mother was Polish and Finnish and Swedish. Her Christmas repertoire was sugar cookies, rocky road and thumb print cookies with jam — but that's in my next book!) No, I discovered my Celtic culinary past <u>after</u> I started running my own kitchen — and shortbread became a Christmas staple about the same time that Malcolm's Ginger Cubes took the stage — I was looking for a balance to Malcolm's gingery commitment and found it wearing a kilt!

Shortbread has many different personalities and like most Scottish lasses, can dress up or down depending on the circumstances — since these Bonny Lassies are competing with the Holiday lights, I glaze them with a lemon glaze that makes them spectacular.

I've had some family recipes that are very complicated and others that are just as happy coming from a brightly painted tin of my Great[10] Grandfather, Robert the Bruce freeing Scotland from England's Tyrannical reign (sorta) and I like them all (good Scottish Lass am I) but these are a surprisingly simple version that fits in well if you are building up a cookie bank to get through the holiday entertaining. I also vow every year to make them very pretty, but have yet to follow through — I cut them with a traditional snowflake cookie cutter and glaze them brilliant white, and they stand on their own. If you are able to muster a way to run a spine of white frosting to define the snowflakes edges or add silver sugar beads, would you please send me a picture? I have thought about doing that just about every year since I first starting making these, I just haven't been able to keep from eating them before adding the last details!

THE COOKIE DOUGH	THE GLAZE
2 cups Irish Butter (Shhh… just do it — when the Scots start marketing Scottish Butter you can use it)	**1 1/4 cups powdered sugar**
4 cups sifted all-purpose flour	**1/4 cup lemon juice**
1 cup powdered sugar	**1 tsp. lemon zest**
1/2 tsp. salt	**1 tsp. vanilla**

In a medium bowl
Cream your butter.

In another bowl
Whisk together the dry ingredients.

Add the dry ingredients into the creamed butter — mix thoroughly.
Refrigerate for ½ an hour.

Preheat your oven 325 degrees

Roll out on a floured surface — cut with your favorite Christmas Cookie Cutters
Place on baking sheets lined with parchment paper. Bake for 20 minutes or until just this side of golden.

Make your glaze
Whisk the powdered sugar, lemon juice, zest and vanilla together.

Allow your cookies to cool on a rack until they are cool enough to pick-up, but still warm.

Dip the cookies tops into the glaze and place on racks to dry.

This is a double batch. I make the whole shebang because some yahoo always eats these by the handful and I want some too!

TOASTED PINENUT TOFFEE

I have always, always, always, loved, loved, loved, toffees & brittles. I will confess that other than a good ol' Heath Bar, I never understood why brittles and toffees were only a Christmas food. Until I became an adult and realized how powerful these are at eroding my self-control. Maybe it's the way it crunches perfectly against your teeth giving an amazingly satisfying "bite." Maybe it's the way that it's the perfect delivery vehicle for dark chocolate opening up the taste buds with the caramel "fulcrum" making the chocolate goodness go straight to your heart? Whatever it is, it takes about a month to pull out of this glorious tailspin... I'd never make it eleven more months!

When it came time to develop a house recipe, I was making brittle and toffee at the same time, and was really keen on making almond brittle, so almonds were already "taken" — what to use for toffee?

I remembered a good friend of mine in fifth grade, Doug who had gone on vacation with his family to New Mexico and came back with "Pine Nuts" we cracked them from their dark shells and feasted on these during Mr. Newton's class, the buttery nut that seemed like God loved what She had done over in the islands with the macadamia so much She reprised it, but this time with feeling... and pine needles. So, I went with them. Costs be damned, it's Christmas after all.

One thing that makes candy making (barks and toffees) a joy in our house is an ingenious gift from my beloved Donny. A "corner piece" of a granite counter that fits over my counter top that I keep outside to chill. It's the perfect surface for allowing candy to cool.

1 lb. Irish butter	**14 oz. fine dark chocolate** (I like 62%-71%) **broken into small chunks**
2 cups sugar	**Parchment paper**
1/2 tsp. bourbon or whiskey	
1 lb. pine nuts (toasted)	

Put a piece of parchment paper onto your granite surface or a chilled cutting board. (flat surface)
Arrange half of the pine nuts in a rectangle about 9 inches by 12 inches.

In a saucepan
mix the sugar and butter and stirring occasionally bring to 290 degrees (this takes longer than you think, until all of the sudden you're at temperature — so be vigilant!)

Pour the hot mixture onto your arranged pine nuts
I try to keep the candy in a defined rectangle. Christmas Candy is about aesthetics, right?

Sprinkle the chocolate evenly over the hot toffee
As it melts, take a blade spatula and spread it evenly, giving it some dimension by making swirls, and spreading it to the edges.

Sprinkle the remaining pine nuts onto the chocolate
Gently tap them into the soft chocolate to hold them as the chocolate cools.

Stick the toffee into the freezer for about thirty minutes.

With a large sharp knife cut into a distinctive shape (I make diamonds) and store in a tin in the refrigerator.

CANDY CANE BARK

I am a sucker for all things peppermint — it just tastes like Christmas — in fact I don't eat it at all during the rest of the year, so sacred is this flavor to December. Peppermint Bark is so easy it's almost a crime but it always brings a smile to everyone's face.

Don't skimp, go old school! And really, just get over it, say this with me — Whole Foods is just not going to have the perfect crunchy canes. You want the kind that Santa's elves made at the North Pole Candy Kitchen Annex of the Workshop. I always buy the kind that are medium-sized and the ones I don't use will decorate our tree.

Contrary to urban myth (or what grabs headlines every Christmas from Buzzfeed or HuffPost) — White Chocolate IS Chocolate as long as it has cacao butter. Look for the real stuff not that BS that gives WC such a bad name.

14 oz. fine white chocolate (Lindt makes a good "go to")	**1 lb. candy canes** (crushed — and save the dust!)
14 oz. dark chocolate (I like to go a bit higher here 71%-85%)	**Ziploc bag or other strong transparent bag**
3 drops peppermint extract	

In a Ziploc bag
put the candy canes and crush them with the flat head of tenderizing mallet. Using a screen sieve shake the dust from crushed pieces into a glass bowl. Set aside.

In a saucepan
Slowly melt the Dark Chocolate. Chocolate melts at between 96 and 90 degrees (which is why it melts in your hand not in your mouth!) so, it doesn't take much. Stir with a spatula.

Pour the melted chocolate onto a parchment-lined flat surface (cutting board)
I try to keep the candy in a defined rectangle. Again, Christmas Candy is about aesthetics, right?

Sprinkle half of crushed candy canes over the hot chocolate
Place the chocolate slab into the freezer.

In another saucepan
Slowly melt the White Chocolate. White Chocolate melts faster (higher milk solids content). Stir with a spatula. When it becomes a smooth liquid remove from the heat.

Keeping stirring as you pour in three drops of peppermint extract
stir to dissolve — don't worry that it'll be enough — it's very strong. Take your dark slab out of the freezer.

Spread the remaining crushed candy cane onto the dark chocolate.

Pour the hot White Chocolate onto your dark chocolate slab (covered with crushed candy cane)
Using your blade spatula to spread it evenly — but don't be afraid to leave some of the edges of the crushed candy cane exposed — it's like half-buried sleds left in the yard after a snow. Give it some dimension by making swirls, and spreading it to the edges.

Sprinkle the reserved candy cane sugar dust on top
Return to the freezer for 30 minutes.

Slice your slab into 1 ½ inch strips and cut these squares.
Store them in a tin in the reefer until serving.

CRANBERRY GEMS

(CRANBERRIES MARINATED IN CABERNET, WITH SLIVERED ALMONDS, WHITE CHOCOLATE, DUSTED WITH PINK SALT & CHIPOTLE *BARK*)
{NOW YOU KNOW WHY THEY'RE JUST CALLED GEMS...}

I'm proud to say that tho' I wasn't the first girl to make cranberry bark, I think mine will blow minds. I made these as Christmas Gift for my bosses at High Noon Entertainment in Denver, Colorado (after Dude You're Screwed was picked up for series) and got one of my greatest compliments ever of my cooking... That year I wrapped two "gems" in elegant gold boxes and left them for each of the owners and my two direct bosses in their offices as a surprise.

The woman that became my champion in hiring me, Pam, was however, an LA girl like me and I wasn't sure which office was hers when she visited the Denver HQ for the annual employee meeting Christmas Party. When I saw her that night I asked her if she'd received them and she said, "Oh my God, was that you? I saw there were two and I was happy to take one home for my husband, but after I ate the first one I stared at his and said, "Fuck him!"

The secret to these is the elegance of presentation and sophisticated party of flavors — tart cranberries mellowed by the red wine, seductive creamy white chocolate ignited by a spark of chipotle and salt, and the satisfying crunch of toasted slivered almonds!

2 cups of dried cranberries	¼ tsp. powdered chipotle
¼ cup of cabernet sauvignon wine	¼ tsp. pink Himalayan salt
1 lb. slivered almonds (toasted)	
14 oz. good white chocolate	

Soak the cranberries in the Cabernet Sauvignon for about 30 minutes.
Don't you dare throw this out! You can reserve this for your next marinade or sauté (and you are welcome!) Strain them onto a paper towel to dry.

Onto a parchment-lined flat surface (cutting board)
Sprinkle half of the almonds onto the paper and arrange in rectangle.

In a saucepan
Slowly melt half of the White Chocolate. White Chocolate melts fast (as we just discussed). Stir with a spatula. Pour onto the almonds to cover them. Sprinkle half of the cranberries onto the slab. Place the slab in the freezer.

In a saucepan
Slowly melt the other half of the White Chocolate.

Take the first slab from the freezer
Pour the melted white chocolate onto the slab and spread with a blade spatula.
Sprinkle the remaining cranberries and almonds onto the warm white chocolate.

Dust with the chipotle and salt.

Return to the freezer for thirty minutes.

Cut the slab into 1 ½ inch strips and chop these into triangles.

Store in a tin in the reefer.

MOM'S MARINARA

This is the legendary recipe for my family... there's lots of dishes that made-up our childhood but this one defined it and (dare I say, us, as women.) Many consider it sacrilegious, profane in fact (which, Scottie-dear are the same) to claim to make Italian food better than Italians, but I'll put my mother's sauce up against Mama Coppola, Mama Scorsese, even Mama DiMartino's (you know where to find me). As I wrote in GBTM, my Aunt Marie, the oldest daughter of twelve in the DiMartino clan was trying to make friends with her fiancé's (my uncle) Rob's Polish-Finnish-Swedish sister (my mom) and taught her how to make this Sunday Night staple for every Brooklyn/Queens Italian family.

My mother made it one Sunday and her soon-to-be-sister-in-law suggested they not tell anyone who made it. (I'm sure figuring that there's no way this Polak girl was going to hold a candle to hers) but Aunt Marie's family remarked that it was the best Marie had ever made... and their relationship slid downhill from there...

The truth, as everyone knows, is simple. It's time and patience that make this sauce so magical. So, give yourself time. I try to make it at least a week before Christmas eve... low and slow will be the Philosopher's stone.

---

5 lbs. ripe heirloom tomatoes (chopped)

1 large brown onion (diced)

1 head of fresh garlic (peeled into cloves and crushed)

1 red bell pepper (cored & chopped)

EVOO (lots)

1/2 cup red wine (cab or merlot)

1/4 balsamic vinegar

1 small bunch (1/4 cup) **fresh oregano**

1/4 cup maple syrup (less depending on the sweetness of the tomatoes — remember you're late in the season — some traditionalists insist on sugar but trust me, it blends better and is easier to control)

Salt to taste

Minimum cooking time 6 hours (better if overnight — better still, 2–3 days)
In a dry, hot, large cast iron Dutch oven
Caramelize the onions. When they are golden brown add the garlic, and have the EVOO standing by...

Add the red pepper — pour in the EVOO to sauté
Stirring quickly so as not to burn...

Add the wine...
Add the tomatoes...
Add the Balsamic Vinegar...
Stir vigorously. Let it come to a bubble, add the oregano and taste. You're not ready to season, you're getting a reading of how far you might have to go (again, this is how you gauge the ripeness/sweetness of the tomatoes.)

Is it:

Too tart? (You're going to — but not yet — but, soon add sweetness)

Too bland? (You'll start with salt — let's see if the tomatoes perk up after bathing in the wine)

Too wine-y? (Again, time will help this — let's give the tomatoes time to stand tall)

Okay... let everything cook vigorously for an hour. Careful not to let it burn.

After one hour, reduce the heat to low simmer and check it after two more hours.

Is it:

Still where it was on first tasting? Then stick to your plan for one more hour.

Has time helped? In what way?
Use the above choice and adjust accordingly. Err towards baby steps — you're going to let this cook for a minimum of 6 hours but low and slow over a as many days you can stand is better, you'll always be able to adjust as you go. Remember you can't take salt out, you can only correct (by adding time, heat or other ingredients).

So be patient and allow time a chance.

I let mine rest for an entire day before giving it more heat and/or flavor adjusting — technically, it's done when you can't stand not eating it anymore. I use bread to dip and taste — it's the best way to judge.

TIMPANO

Okay, I've written extensively about our Christmas Eve Tradition now almost 2 decades in the making. As I said, my life changed the day I saw Stanley Tucci raid his mother's recipe for a dramatic turn in his masterpiece the "Big Night." And over the years, I've refined it to this current "blueprint," (because it is like building a home). And like any home, once it's built or remodeled, while you're enjoying it, you're already fixing it or changing it. I will say that I've settled on the basics from my study of this wondrous "event" (calling it a "dish" seems so... inaccurate), but I'm always looking for ways to improve this structurally that won't impede the overall taste or place it has in the meal...

... tho' it is the Empress, it must still play well with others.

Because I've made the other "meat dishes" (Salmon included) and the grilled antipasti, I continue to make this a "vegetarian" version — but you can add whatever you want to your layers. Stanley's was more of pasta noodle "shell" — but it was too crunchy (and not in a good way) so, I've made mine more of a pizza shell that veterans of our table, tho' they don't have anything to compare it to, agree that they prefer. And that's good for me, 'cuz I already did the leg work. The construction of the star of our Christmas Pageant defines my whole day and the rising & resting of dough has become, over the years, the times when I get the rest of the meal or myself "done" so that I can be at the table at precisely 7:00 pm as the invite states....

1 ½ cups warm water	**"FINISHING CRUST"**
1 tsp. dry yeast	1 tsp. granulated garlic
A pinch of sugar	1 tsp. Kosher salt
4 cups all-purpose flour	1 tsp. ground chipotle
½ cup wheat germ	1 tsp. fennel seeds
¼ cup barley malt	
2 tbsp. + a "splash" olive oil	
1 tbsp. red wine	

The "Shell" Dough

I love the "sponge" technique, that in our house we call the "Tassahara Trick" after the Buddhist Monastery in Northern Cal, that uses this trick in their baking — spoiler alert, I've changed it to suit my needs. My current method uses three risings plus the yeast starter (15 minutes of the yeast in a warm bath): a 45 minute sponge, 2 ½ hour rising and a 45 minute punch-down recovery. So, plan accordingly.

NOTE: This requires the "perfect" bowl or pot. In "The Big Night" Stanley and Tony use an old enamel pot that looks like it was used by their mother "and her mother before her, and her mother before her." I use a ceramic bowl that I got when I walked into Sur La Table the day after seeing the movie and before I could even finish describing it, the woman boredly sent me to "Aisle 17." I was the fourth person that day to come in with the starry-eyed look. It's a Mason Cash "Original Cane" No. 9 — almost 13 inches in diameter and 6 ½ inches deep.

To the warm water, sprinkle the yeast and whisk together
Feed your yeast with the sugar and allow them to eat for 15 minutes.

Make your sponge
Gradually pour 2 cups of the flour into the yeasted water, stir to mix thoroughly for a minute and let stand for 45 minutes.

In a standing mixer with your dough hook
Add the Barley Malt, wheat germ, salt, oil and wine. mix thoroughly. Gradually work in the remaining two cups of flour to make a soft dough.

Turn the ball onto a floured board and knead for five minutes

Put the ball into a large bowl, and pour a splash of olive oil.
Cover with a damp cloth and put it in warm spot for rising. Allow to rise for 2 ½ hours.

Punch down the dough
and divide it into two balls one ⅔ the dough and the other ⅓. Allow to rise another 45 minutes.

Meanwhile prepare the Timpano "Filling"

2 quarts of "Mom's Marinara"	6 eggs (beaten)
½ lb. pasta shells (cooked al dente')	**Pesto** (we'll leave the cheese out since this whole thing is held together with cheese)
½ lb. pasta wheels (cooked al dente')	
½ lb. pasta ziti (cooked al dente')	2 cups fresh basil leaves
1 lb. smoked provolone cheese (grated)	¼ cup EVOO
1 lb. mozzarella cheese (grated)	½ cup walnuts (toasted)
1 lb. romano cheese (grated)	2 cloves fresh garlic
1 lb. parmesan cheese (grated)	1 lemon (juiced)
1 lb. mushrooms (sautéed in garlic & EVOO)	

Construction — **preheat your oven to 350 degrees**

Roll out the larger of the two dough balls.

Prepare your Timpano bowl
Mix the spices of the Finishing Crust (salt, fennel, chipotle) together in small bowl. Pour a splash or two of EVOO into your Timpano bowl and tilt and spin the bowl

to coat the inside, then sprinkle your spices evenly to coat the inside of the bowl, then sprinkle the cheese — don't worry if it starts to slide to the bottom, because this will be the top of your finished Timpano when we invert it.

Line the inside of the Timpano bowl with the rolled-out dough
Allow the excess to hang over the side — don't trim.

Begin to layer the ingredients
Start with a layer of cooked pasta. Sprinkle a layer of smoked Provolone. Add a ladle full of marinara. Don't make it too soupy, the upper layers will draw down during baking. Continue to alternate pasta-cheese-sauce until your bowl is filled to the half-way mark. Add the sautéed mushrooms in place of the Marinara — having defined layers is the key here. For the next layer go for the Pesto in place of the Marinara — it's a great strip of green goodness in the middle of your masterpiece. Continue to layer pasta, sauce, cheese until you reach the top.

Using a large chopstick or long blunt stick
Poke holes into your layers to allow the beaten eggs to run down through the layers of sauce and cheese and noodles.

Beat the eggs
Pour the beaten eggs into the holes you just poked. This will help to bind the whole dish together. Time to close the lid.

Roll out your smaller remaining dough ball.
Lay the rolled-out dough top onto the top layer of filling and fold the excess from the bottom dough over the lid and pinch to seal.

Bake for 45 minutes
The top can brown quickly so be prepared to lay a piece of foil to prevent it from getting too brown.

Remove and allow to rest for 30 minutes.
Time to get ready to reveal your masterpiece!
I have a wrought-iron cake service that has a ceramic plate that fits into the wrought iron frame, that was bought specifically for this — but alas, last year I was rehearsing to make this for my friend's Cooking show — estrogen had changed my upper body strength so dramatically that the "flip" I had been doing for over 20 years, went horribly south! I was able to save the Timpano, but my beloved plate broke! So, I now have a new (lighter) version that is large enough to extend past the edges of the Timpano bowl which acts like a lip to contain the juices during flipping and serving.

Take your plate and place it on top of your bowl and quickly (and deftly) invert your Timpano onto your plate BUT DON'T LIFT OFF THE BOWL YET!

Allow it to rest an additional five minutes
Now you can reveal our masterpiece. Carefully lift the lid.

I usually make as grand a show as Stanley and Tony did — and I generally get the same reactions they did — take a bow, girl, you made this!

Slice it as you would a pie, using a sharp knife and a good wedge spatula to support the slice as you cut — it will begin to lose "structural integrity" fairly quickly, so serve everyone — it is the star of the show. Pass more warmed marinara sauce.

And, like most Italian food, it can be "just as good" (some claim better) the next day, and you probably won't eat it all. Simply put the same bowl you baked it in back on as a "cover," then invert it so the bowl is back upright — — this will allow it to keep its shape for Boxing Day and other meals during the stolen week between Christmas and New Year's when you're getting a well-deserved rest in the cooking detail. To reheat, simply cover with foil, put the whole affair back in a 350 degree oven, and forgo inverting (you can slice it right out of the bowl).

SAUSAGE & PEPPERS

I think I fell in love with these when my mom made them on cold winter nights — I now know that this is something that my Italian Friends (especially the East Coasters) take for granted in the way we take getting burritos for granted in the City of Angels. They're just always going to be there, so why make a big deal?

When I stopped eating so much red meat and pork, this was the only thing I truly missed, even more than bacon — until of course, the great revolution of the late nineties when everything good was chicken again — now it's possible to get great Italian sausage made from Chicken or Turkey and I think they're better — lighter and less greasy, they don't fight the marinara but dance elegantly, leaving room for the sweet red pepper to solo like a Prima Donna. But don't get me wrong — I ain't judging, you can (probably should, to avoid mutiny) use your favorite Italian Sausage pork or no.

1 lb. hot Italian sausage (sliced on the diagonal)

1 lb. sweet Italian sausage (sliced on the diagonal)

4 large ripe red "bell" peppers (cored, halved widthwise and sliced into 1 inch wide slices)

2 large brown onions (peeled, halved, and eighthed into separated layers)

3 cloves garlic (sliced)

¼ cup EVOO

¼ cup red wine

1 cup marinara sauce

In a cast-iron covered Dutch oven
Brown
the sausage slices, then remove but keep the oil.

Sauté
the onions, garlic and peppers until caramelized.

Return the sausage to pot. De-glaze with the wine.

Add the marinara,
stir, cover the shut off the heat. Just before serving, fire up the pot again to rewarm if needed.

CHICKEN MEATBALLS
ROLLED IN CHANTERELLE POWDER

One of my fondest memories of my mother involves Monday Night Football, a big bowl of homemade Meatballs (there was some sausage in there — she combined them in her version) and her hug. I was playing Varsity football and was trying to slim down (hence the "sans pasta" serving) to stay at my "flanker" position — a running back position that was also a wide-receiver when we used a fullback... I used to join her late to watch the MNF in progress, because my own football practice went till 6:00 pm and my school was an hour away from home. My mother was a rabid football fan, and Monday nights were our sacred time together.

Not your typical Mother-daughter memory, but there it is.

These are another of the many details of Christmas celebrations in our house that are a hug and kiss to her memory. In this case, another remarkable woman in our life, Maureen "I go to all of Marcy's Weddings" Booth used to have a specialty vegetable wholesale business and gave me a jar of dried powdered Chanterelle mushrooms that I decided to use one year... the rest is history.

I actually make these the night before and warm them before serving — I traditionally make Mount Judy stacking them on a plate in five story pyramid, pouring hot marinara over them and giving them a snow line of grated parmesan cheese.

1 lb. ground chicken (white meat)	**3 cloves garlic** (minced)
1 lb. ground chicken (dark meat)	**1 tbsp. red wine**
1 cup fine bread crumbs	**¼ cup dijon mustard**
¼ cup EVOO	**1 cup pine nuts** (toasted)
1 cup shallots (minced, lightly sautéed in EVOO)	**8 ozs. dried powdered chanterelle mushrooms**

Preheat your oven to 350 degrees

In a large bowl
Mix all of the ingredients with your hands (lose that wedding ring — it's time to get sticky!).

Clean your hands and while they are still wet, grab handfuls and roll them to form golf ball-sized beauties.

Pour the Chanterelle powder into dish
Roll each meatball in the powder to coat them and place them on a baking sheet.

Pour EVOO between each ball.
Bake for about 15 minutes

Use a toothpick to check that they are cooking through. You don't want to dry these puppies out. If you are cooking these the night before, pull them out now. If you are serving them now, cook until they are done in the center.

Pour some marinara over them, dust with grated parm and serve.

CEDAR PLANKED SALMON

This is my go-to way to cook salmon flawlessly — I use two different approaches — savory & sweet — both use the cedar planks that I cut myself at Home Depot — A whole board yields 8 planks for the same price you pay for one plank at any store's meat market — Thank you Alton Brown!

Soak the plank for at least 1 hour (2–3 is better) in water and some bourbon/whiskey.

1" thick 1-2 lb. wild caught salmon filet (I work in TV and unfortunately, I've done a few fishing shows — farming aint' where it's at — go wild!)	**GLAZE** (The secret here is to "protect" the fish when the flames start to rise.) **2 tbsp. of olive oil** **I large brown onion** (slivered) **1/2 cup capers** **1/2 tsp. fresh grated nutmeg** **1 healthy dash of Jack Daniels or other whiskey**

In a dry hot cast iron skillet:
Caramelize the onions — after they go thru the "mealy" sweet stage and start to toast,

Turn down the heat and add:
The EVOO, capers and nutmeg.

De-glaze them with the Jack Daniels and turn off the heat.
when it's show time… preheat your grill to medium high heat.

Remove the plank from the water,
Put the salmon on it and spoon the onion glaze onto the fish.

Put the entire plank onto the hot grill and close the lid.
You want the flames to lick up around the plank and for it to catch fire — it will release the cedar smoke to do its magic. This is also a great way to not overcook the fish. We like ours rare, but you can leave it on for as long as you like, just inspect both the ends and the middle with a skewer to make sure the flesh is cooked to your liking.

Remove the fish from the plank onto platter and make sure you serve each piece with generous amounts of the onion glaze.

AUNTIE PASTI
(MARINATED VEGGIES IN CHRISTMAS SPICES)

This came about because the very first time I tried to make the Timpano I went all in (surprised?) I had several layers of veggies, and even made the pasta noodle type...

This was a teachable moment as they say (read — almost a complete disaster) but being the hard-headed Irish Lass that I am, I was not to be thwarted — and if Stanley could do it (despite having a food styling team and props dept.) well, I had to at least try. Besides switching to a pizza dough, the other leap forward in EVOOlution was taking out the veggies — they were releasing too much juice in the baking process. But I didn't want to take veggies off the banquet menu...

So, I came up with this — large platters of grilled veggies arranged like bouquets of abundance as centerpieces on the table that are edible! I wish I could say I did it the same every year, but the truth is this is very gloriously flexible part of the menu that leaves room for how I feel that particular day and is great place to give your meal that sumpin-sumpin that a day of prep reveals is nessa... I take all day to build these, not because they're hard but because they are easy and I can juggle all the other processes that might need my immediate attention and when it's time to "send them out" they are ROCKSTAR quality elevating the banquet to legendary. You can also be open to what looks good when you go shopping — realizing that Italian cooking is about allowing veggies to be their truest selves, and here they're just getting dressed up for Christmas Eve.

VEGGIES
1 lb. fresh zucchini (sliced lengthwise)
1 lb. Japanese eggplant (sliced lengthwise)
1 lb. green beans (remove the stems)
1 lb. snow peas (remove the stem and vein)
1 lb. asparagus (remove the woody end)
1 lb. cherry tomatoes
4 large yellow peppers
5 large beets (coat these in kosher salt and char them on the grill)
3 cups fresh baby spinach (washed)

MARINADES
EVOO
Walnut Oil
Avocado Oil
Balsamic Vinegar

Red Wine Vinegar
Sherry Vinegar
Coconut Vinegar
Fresh Squeezed Lemon Juice
Fresh Squeezed Orange Juice
Dijon Mustard
Honey
Maple Syrup
Fresh Tarragon
Fresh Oregano
Fresh Rosemary
Ground Nutmeg
Ground Cinnamon
Ground Allspice
Ground Cardamom

GARNISH

1 cup fresh basil leaves

1 pint balsamic onions (get these at the deli/olive bar)

Preserved lemon (see page 190)

Pickled garlic

1 cup Italian olives

1 cup sliced pepperoncini

Ziploc bags (you need as many of these as you have types of vegetables)

Okay — it works like this — It's like a gourmet marinade bar — arrange all of the options and all of the rinsed and cut veggies in front of you — you are going to decide each flavor combination according to your tastes, and really you can do no wrong here. Come on, it's fun! You're going to start with an oil, pour a tablespoon into a Ziploc, followed by an acid — you have several — vinegars, and citrus juices, and then add a sweetener that will compliment one spice and one herb. With each vegetable envision, (entaste?) what makes it special? And which of these spices will help it shine? Now which acid will do that? Which sweetener will do that? For example — you can't go wrong with Asparagus, EVOO lemon, tarragon but which spice? Is it Cardamom — not a jury in the world would convict you, but how about cinnamon? You decide. Try to mix it up and try to surprise your guests — sometimes going against type is a pleasant surprise.

I do all of this overnight and allow each veggie to truly marinate.

Grill them — we're going for pure aesthetics, this is all about the grill marks they're already practically cooked by whatever acid you used.

Arrange them on plates

Some years I keep them all separate so everyone can find they're favorites, other years I used them like "colors" and arranged them in pleasing "floral "arrangements. Drizzle more EVOO over them — then garnish with the various pickled thingys — purple balsamic onions, green olives, bright red cherry tomatoes, white pickled garlic, bright green basil — let your inner Georgia O'Keeffe shine.

SALADE CÉSAR

Mylove's family has a giant wooden salad bowl they call Moses' boat (you could float a prince downstream to be hidden among the slaves until he leads his people to the promised land) that we take out once a year. Rarely, do I make this much salad at one time — it's that big. And it has that been used with garlic and EVOO for decades (we never use soap to wash it) that it seems that any salad will come out legendary.

The key here is "room to work" 'cuz this salad is all in the wrist. And to make it Christmasy, I add bright red cherry tomatoes. Ideally this is a table-side show — and you can decide if you're a "with" or "without" kinda César, anchovies that is. I'm not judging. I'm a "with" girl, B-T-Dubs, but many of my guests are not, so we skip it for Christmas Eve.

2 cups homemade croutons (take good bread and cut it into cubes. Let it dry out then toss with EVOO and granulated garlic and bake at 200 degrees for 30 minutes.)	**1 egg** (coddled) — see below
	3 cloves garlic (pressed)
Romaine lettuce leaves (for 12 people I used three heads)	**1 tbsp. dijon mustard**
	1 tsp. worcestershire sauce
1 lb. cherry tomatoes (halved)	**1 lemon** (juiced)
1/2 cup EVOO	**1 cup parmesan cheese**

Boil Water
Pour into a mug and gently add the egg — careful to not crack the shell. It will coddle while you work.

In your salad bowl
Add the EVOO and garlic — whisk together. Add the lemon juice. Smell THAT! Ahhh.. Okay, come back.

Crack the egg into the oil mix, continue to whisk,
add the dijon, worcestershire sauce and tomatoes (we want the tomato juice to mingle)

Add the croutons and stir (you want them to get a jump on the lettuce, then add the lettuce and finish with the cheese.

Toss and serve!

FIGGY PUDDING WITH EGG NOGG I'SCREAM

I get great joy out of blowing my guests' minds and this may very well be the first time someone has actually had "Figgy pudding." English steamed puddings are a breed unto themselves — there's very few desserts (besides Donny's truffles) that could possibly cap this feast except for good "jolly Ol' Figgy Puddin' indeed.

The other good thing about this is that it can be happily steaming in the oven while you're eating dinner and the aroma of cinnamon and allspice won't begin to compete with the Timpano's garlicky goodness until everyone begins to push back their chairs to literally make room for dessert. I have a ceramic cookie jar that is cylinder shape that makes the perfect 'bowl" or mold. But you can use a Bundt pan that will give you the more traditional "ring" like presentation, that's fit for Tiny Tim himself.

The same goes for the Egg Nogg I'Scream — because it seems to be the perfect jewel in the crown.

2 cups dried figs (chopped)	**1 tsp. salt**
1 cup dried dates (pitted and chopped)	**3 eggs**
1 cup raisins	**1⁄2 cup melted butter**
1 3⁄4 cups cream	**1 1⁄2 cups breadcrumbs**
1 1⁄2 cups all-purpose flour	**1 tbsp. grated orange peel**
1 cup sugar	**EGG NOGG I'SCREAM**
2 1⁄2 teaspoons baking powder	**3 cups good quality egg nog**
1 tsp. ground nutmeg	**1 cup vanilla sugar**
1 tsp. ground cinnamon	**1 tsp. brandy**

Preheat oven to 350 degrees.

In a medium saucepan,
Heat milk and chopped figs over medium-low heat, but do NOT bring to a boil.
Cook for 10–15 minutes stirring occasionally.

In a medium bowl
mix flour, sugar, baking powder, nutmeg, cinnamon, and salt.

In a standing mixer
beat eggs at high speed for about a minute. Reduce speed to low and add butter, bread crumbs, orange peel, dates, raisins and warm fig mixture. Slowly incorporate flour mixture. Beat until just blended.

Pour the mix into a tall ceramic bowl or Bundt ring
Cover the bowl with a piece of aluminum foil greased on one side, greased side down.

Place the bowl in a roasting pan and place on oven rack.

Fill with hot tap water 2 inches up the side of the mold. Bake for 2 hours or until the pudding is firm and it is pulling away from the side of the bowl pan. Remove the pudding from the water bath.

Remove the foil and cool on a wire rack for 10 minutes before serving.

Now here's where I divert from the classic presentation —

I slice my servings and put them in a martini glass and add a dollop of Egg Nogg I'Scream — the hot pudding and cold I'Scream dance beautifully!

EGG NOGG I'SCREAM

3 cups good quality eggnog
1 cup vanilla sugar
1 tsp. brandy

Whisk the brandy into sugar add to the egg nog until completely dissolved.

Freeze in an ice cream maker.

Scoop onto warm Figgy pudding and stand back!

SKUNK JUICE

I seriously considered moving this to end of the book. But why start decorum now? This is readily available on the interwebs, but I am a woman who keeps her word. So here you go. I recommend you get these together now and keep them wherever you will bath your pet — most likely you will be doing this like we do, out of a deep sleep and in a blind frenzy of chaos — you don't wanna have to search for the ingredients when your eyes are tearing and you're trying to breathe.

2 cups hydrogen peroxide

1/4 cup Dawn dishwashing detergent
(good enough for the Exxon Valdez/Gulf Deep Water/Horizon wildlife, good enough for Bella)

1⁄4 cup baking soda

Mix the above ingredients together in plastic pitcher
You could use glass but it will be chaos — your pet will be freaked-out, the water and stink is everywhere — go for ease and safety here.

Get your pets fur wet
Pour a good dose of the Skunk juice over your pet

Work it into their fur like you would shampoo and get in there!
And hurry! The faster you react the better it will be and the sooner you can go back to sleep!

Rinse and repeat until you can stand it or your pet will tolerate you spraying them with water.

And don't forget to repeat aloud — living in the country means living with wildlife — living in the country means living with wildlife.

And fix that hole in your fence! Go to bed.

CHAPTER 4
• CHRISTMAS! •

CHRISTMAS MORNING
APPLE CHOWDER WITH GRILLED SAUSAGE

CHRISTMAS DINNER
KING CRAB LEGS WITH DRAWN BUTTER
ROASTED CHESTNUTS WITH APPLE, PEAR & ONION
RICE PILAF WITH DRIED CRANBERRY & SPINACH

"THE DELICIOUS CALM."
(THE MOST WONDER*FULL* TIME OF... THE... YEAR, CONTINUES!")

No matter how late we do end up going to sleep, Mylove and I usually wake no later than 5:00 am. It's an unspoken (until now!) joy between us that no matter how "old" we get — Christmas is still a giddy rush of childlike excitement that just won't let us sleep in. And we love it!

Even when we don't have guests, we always rise to open presents in the still dark air of a glorious morning. It's a special gift that Mylove gives me every year — the experience of someone sharing a quiet special joy that only the two of us truly knows.

And the house smells AMAZING! Cinnamon-spiced apple chowder has been working it's magic while Santa got his toys on and we can stand it no longer... up we go!

The kettle goes on for fawkey, (what you would call coffee), the tree lights plugged in and the fire is lit... it's TIME! Mylove and I open presents! Since I came out, this has been a time for us each to celebrate our journey together in innocent ways that make our hearts wrinkle with happiness or sometimes to outright sob with joy. This is the time, three years ago, that she had demonstrated how she had made giant leaps in her acceptance of my femininity by making me handmade earrings, or choosing a blouse that brings out the color of my eyes. I use it as way to show her that she is the sun in my universe, surprising her with answers to even the smallest wishes she has uttered aloud over the past year. It's Christmas — when time stops. Our bubble of "us" is celebrated in the most amazing way.

After presents, (and a couple of cups of fawkey and whatever goodies Santa brought) we will eventually get around to feeling "peckish." This is usually after we've had our traditional "nap" (is that what the kids are calling it these days?) under the Christmas tree. This is something we started early in our marriage and it is one of our favorite times and places to "nap," there's just something irresistibly romantic about fresh pine, the yule log burning brightly, cinnamon, the new nightgowns we probably bought each other and the utter abandon we have — as we christen our Christmas tree.

Which will make us finally hungry for something a little more food-like than each other. (Although as I write this, nothing is coming to mind.) Oh yeah, this is a cookbook. Sorry.

And I expected this. And I'm prepared. All I have to do is pull the orange out (that has been spiked with cloves) and stick the immersion blender in. This will be the base of the chowder. Next, I chop two apples (this year, they're Black Marias — never had 'em, but they are beautiful — a bit less crisp than one I'd smear chunky peanut butter on, but perfect for sautéing) a pear, and two cups of golden raisins.

In a cast iron skillet, I toast pecans, pull them out add the fruit to skillet and a stick of butter (come on, it's Christmas!) and sauté them until soft, add a healthy pour of maple syrup, add the toasted pecans, and pour all of this into the chowder. I fry-up some chicken sausage and serve them alongside the steaming bowls of the chowder with a healthy dollop of good mustard. Mylove likes to pour a splash of heavy cream on her chowdah when she eats hers, but I'm a purist.

Now, back to the Recklass Philosophy, cuz, there will be some chowdah left over. It will keep until New Year's Day when I will make chowdah buns. See, everything plays its part in this grand symphony of food!!

All day long we'll snack on a variety of finger foods and hors d'oeuvre and then it's time to get our Dinner on...

Now... I have, by this point, spent literally a month cooking. And I've taken those who've been at our table from the rich abundance of Thanksgiving's harvest flavors, through the utter fuck-it indulgent decadence of Christmas Eve Childhood Sugarplum Faerie Fantasy... at this point, I need to take a breath... where do we go from here?

Elegance.

There is a mysterious, quiet elegance to Christmas day, after the fever pitch of the morning — after a year's worth of anticipation has found it blessed relief, that I like to describe as "the delicious calm." It's like the graceful crystal stillness that comes when I cuddle with Mylove. It's so quiet that I could dissolve into blissful sleep, but this crystalline brilliance gently sparkles with awareness that keeps you from missing a moment. Even the Christmas Carols in the background are quieter... they are richer, and everything seems just right.

Which is why I am choosing elegance as the palate. The big bold sauces and rich complex flavors were so, yesterday. Everything today is chosen with the utmost care to have as few ingredients as possible so that they each take their turn in the culinary spotlight. In the same way that pure gold and precious jewels require very little filigree, so too, does tonight's palate.

The rest of today's menu will be mostly nibbling until dinner — but I want this to be elegant and tho' I don't have to, I want to dress-up. We have, in years past, had another houseful of guests (as I wrote about in GBTM, we had two of Mylove's brothers with

Doug's daughters our nieces, Sophie & Rosie — it was an epic Christmas) and it is where our next tradition comes from — King Crab Legs.

Before this, I had always brined another Turkey for Christmas Dinner. But one year, I had been working in Alaska and had sent home 30 pounds of King Crab Legs... (yes, I was in Nome doing what Nomans do) and Mylove loved it so much, we decided to make it our new tradition.

And newsflash, they're almost stupidly easy to prepare so they are the perfect solution for an elegant fête. The other dishes are oven affairs with almost no "mother henning," again, the perfect low pressure — high elegance dishes for the day...

... all this is to say that I won't have any problem serving dinner whenever Mylove is ready, with only a half-hour's notice. My point here is, I have no stress whatsoever. I'm golden. I'm good. I will, of course, finish standing up... You can already feel the banana peel materializing under my foot as I walk, can't you?

I am going to take my shower — a long luxurious one that I rightly deserve after almost a month straight of culinary backflips. I think back over the successes of this year's offerings — truffles were an unexpected coupe, timpanito for not only Mark, but my niece Hana (who doesn't eat cheese). And this year's visit from Santa was one of the best ever, Mylove showered me with her love and gifts, and I made out like a Queen...

Wait what's that sound... never mind that... WHAT'S THAT SMELL????

Oh shit. Literally. The second time that raw sewage makes an appearance in a cook book. And in our Master bathroom. And our Christmas. The good news is, I got my shower before the shit hit the fan. The bad news? Mylove didn't get hers.

This will mean that I've got to close off any drain of water. No toilets, no showers, no sinks.

I will have to make an elegant dinner as if we're camping out. I have experience doing this, but never when dealing with a paychecks' worth of ingredients (35 bucks a pound for Crab legs this year).

But it's Mylove. And together, we can do anything. This is nothing!

The plumber is scheduled to come tomorrow. We still have some of Mylove's dowry fine china that we didn't use last night for tonight's feast, and if I place buckets in every sink, I can still make it all as if nothing had happened...

Which is what we do.

With a cheery fire roaring in the fireplace, the Christmas tree all aglow, our velvet dressed Victorian Christmas Angel watching down on us, and steaming King Crab Legs (that had been flash boiled in white wine and served with drawn butter and our plates full of pilaf, and oven roasted chestnuts with pear & onion and a light green salad… we are in bliss.

NOTE FROM THE GHOST OF CHRISTMAS FUTURE: Tomorrow, Boxing Day for you Anglophiles, I will spend washing the two days of dishes (remember Christmas Eve was a five-course dinner for 18 and the pots & pans for two days of feasting) in our carport — ferrying hot water in tubs onto a portable table next to Mylove's Convertible Celica) then laying them all in the driveway to rinse them with our garden hose. It is an amazing event that will take me over three hours, but it's also so worthy of recording for posterity sake, that it actually makes the "WTF?" factor fade instantly It's, okay, slightly romantic? Certainly, a great chapter in the legend that is our marriage. It's also a way better place to do dishes — I'm outside, the sun is shining, the breeze is cool, the birds singing… as long as I don't chip the gilded Lenox china dinner plates, it will remain a very cool story…

Now, about those recipes… turn the page!

APPLE CHOWDER
(& BREAKFAST SAUSAGE)

Deceptively simple — and oh so freaking good — this is Christmas morning in our house and as I said this was actually created bringing Christmas into our hotel room when we were on the road, and like Mel Torme's famous (and successful) attempt to recreate Christmas out of whole cloth, this does the trick. Especially, because the day is so special, why would we eat any old breakfast on this one day of the year?

If I had no other reason to have a slow cooker other than Apple Chowder I would always scour garage sales for one.

Trust me — it's that worth it. Also — I always have a pot of hot apple cider going for Christmas eve and it's been hit-or-miss whether anyone has any from year to year — but I will always make it cuz it gives me a super-rich apple juice that can only help the morning chowder and it gives me the orange that I had spiked with cloves that makes all the difference.

Oh, and that story I promised you? The origin of apple chowder? It goes like this; Our friend Jack was an aspiring actor — who was a production assistant on the biggest production of the year, and who got his big break one day when an actor called-in sick... Jack's only line was supposed to be, "Hey man, things will turn out all right, you'll see. Let's go down to the diner and get a nice hot bowl of clam chowder and I bet when we get back to work everything will be okay — you'll see."

Well... under the hot lights and the director's stare, (and the rolling cameras) Jack, chuffed his line, saying instead, "Let's go down to the diner and get a nice hot bowl of apple chowder..." and feeling embarrassed, and worried that he'd missed his chance, Jack proceeded into a ten-minute monologue about how in the world, could he chuff his one shot at stardom?! Especially in his neighborhood's vernacular, "to chowder" meant to really blow it! My heart broke for him, as the monologue continued, but the light bulb went off... Apple Chowder? Like a kid's dream soup? I kept mulling as he sputtered and spun... the entire recipe exploded in my mind! Don't fret for Jack, after he calmed down, he nailed the next take with no issues and won a spot in the production — a happy ending and now a great breakfast tradition... only in Hollywood!

10 apples of various varieties (core and chop 8 of them)	**1 stick of butter**
3 pears	**1/4 cup maple syrup**
1 "spiked orange" (with whole cloves)	**1 tsp. cinnamon**
1 cup apple cider	**1 tsp. cardamom**
2 cups pecans	**2 tbsp. fresh grated ginger**
1 cup raisins	**Heavy cream** (for passing)

Tis the night before Christmas, in a slow cooker on low
Add 8 for the chopped apples, the spiked orange and apple cider and go to bed, Santa's coming!

The next morning after you've opened presents
Who are you kidding! If it wasn't for that amazing smell around you, you probably would've forgotten that you even made breakfast. Okay, but you're here now and you're ahead of the game because now you and everyone else is hungry! stir the apple mixture in the slow cooker and using an immersion blender, blend the apples into a smooth chowder-like consistency.

Chop the remaining apples and pears.

In a super-hot, dry cast iron skillet
Toast the pecans — remove them from the fire, and set them aside — add the apples and pears, and a splash of apple cider, cover with lid — allow them to steam for a minute or so.

Meanwhile chop the pecans.
Add them to the apple/pear mixture — toss in the stick of butter. Squeeze the grated ginger into the butter and reduce the heat.

Sprinkle the cinnamon and cardamom over the mixture
Add the maple syrup, raisins.

Add all the apple/pear mixture to the chowder mixture and stir to incorporate.

Serve with cooked breakfast sausage with a generous dollop of hearty mustard, and piping hot coffee.

And save the leftover apple chowder we'll use it to make the chowder buns for New Year's Day!

KING CRAB LEGS

This is another of Scottie Jeanette's "set the bar higher" kinda thingy's (which in other languages would translate to "careful what you start"). In the reality TV world, all roads lead to Alaska. It seems that cable networks in the lower 48 regard Alaska as a genre unto itself, and I've been there for 4 different shows and am currently helping to develop two more. And since I've been there, it makes sense to have wanted to bring back the "spoils of war" (which I started early in my career — with Black Pearls from Tahiti, gold and diamonds from the Amazon, and Opals from Australia) and nothing says Alaska more than the legendary King Crab. So, that's what I did one legendary Christmas, which coincided with the very first Christmas where Scottie Jeanette shined with ALL of my glory (and which I wrote about in GBTM).

And a tradition was born. Mylove was the one who said, "Why can't we have King Crab every year?" She's forever asking these questions which at the time feel like a 2x4 to the head. I had no retort — but if you look deeper it actually is the perfect solution. By now, if you've been modeling even a tenth of my example during this season, you probably have already set your bar very high and so how would we top one of the most crucial meals of the year, but King Crab Legs? And really, they are affordable cuz few people can (at this stage of the holiday eating season) eat their fill. Two legs and a claw will put most under the table. And almost nothing, save for even the mighty LOBstah can match it for the height of elegance.

Oh, and one last note — there really is no such thing as fresh King Crab, unless of course you're on the Time Bandit or it's brethren — King Crab is flash frozen at sea by the vessels that catch 'em, the cargo is way too precious to let them spoil on the way back to market. It takes longer to prepare the drawn butter and cut lemons than it does to heat them. So, cooking them is a snap (literally) you really are just "heating" them up and maybe flavoring them — but how can you improve on this, save for generous dunks in butter? Well... read on...

2 legs and one claw (per person) **of King Crab**	**A half stick of butter per person** (melted to liquid)
A big pot	**1/2 a lemon per person** (people like to squeeze their own — just cut it & put it on the plate)
A buncha water	
A splash of white wine	

Boil the water
And I mean boiling, big rolling bubbles, bursting!

Rinse the crab.
Make sure they are "defrosted" (they were on ice since they left the North). Throw them into the boiling water.

Add the splash of wine
Count to 30.

Stir the legs
Count to 30 again

Pull them out and serve.

BAKED RICE PILAF WITH DRIED CRANBERRIES, SLIVERED ALMONDS & SPINACH

It's elegant. It's colorful. It probably will only get eaten (if you serve this with the crab) by the heartiest of eaters. That being said, I love this for breakfast the next day too. Years ago, Gerhard (my mentor whom I wrote about extensively in GBTM) gave me a ceramic Dutch oven that is absolutely foolproof for baking grains. But with any recipe that mixes veggies with grain, I find that parboiling the grain gives you the latitude to not overcook the veggies.

1 cups red rice (parboiled — bring to a boil for 3 minutes and shut off the heat)	**1 cup dried cranberries**
	2 lbs. baby spinach
1 cup basmati rice (same)	**2 tbsp. fresh tarragon** (minced)
1 quart chicken broth	**1 tbsp. orange zest**
1 onion (diced fine)	**1 splash red wine**
2 tbsp. EVOO	**1 tsp. dijon mustard**
3 cloves garlic (pressed)	**1 dash of ground chipotle**

Preheat the oven to 400 degrees

In dry hot skillet
Caramelize the onion, add a tablespoon of oil, throw in the spinach, stir quickly, add the wine -- shut off the heat.

In a mixing bowl
Whisk the oil, the Dijon, garlic, tarragon, chipotle and zest. Add the cranberries and toss to coat.

Mix the rice and add half to a covered baking dish
Spoon the spinach mixture onto the rice. Add the cranberry mixture and cover with the remaining rice.

Pour the chicken broth over the rice.

Cover and bake for 30 minutes.

Reduce the heat to 350 and bake for an additional 20 minutes. Serve.

ROASTED CHESTNUTS
WITH APPLE, PEAR & ONION
(TOSSED IN DIJON VINAIGRETTE)

This one is another no-brainer — I love the idea of chestnuts and open fires and all but seriously that nut is amazing when truly roasted with something acidic to bring out it's nummy goodness. They are also elegant as all get out in a silver dish with some dainty serving tongs. It's one of the dishes that, like a fine pair of pearl or diamond stud earrings calmly whispers "sophistication." And this dish delivers in the taste department. It's also light to stand with the King crab legs — I rarely have leftovers of this, no matter how many candy canes everyone ate today.

1 pound chestnuts (shelled — you can buy these already shelled or shell 'em yourself, it's your manicure. I've done both depending on whether I saw the prepared ones before or after I saw the barrels of nuts heralding the season)

1 pound pearl onions

1 large crisp apple (cored and diced)

1 large crisp pear (cored and diced)

2 tbsp. EVOO

1 tbsp. balsamic vinegar

1 tsp. dijon mustard

¼ tsp salt

Preheat the oven to 400 degrees

In a mixing bowl
Whisk the EVOO, balsamic, dijon and salt. Toss the chestnuts first, then add the onions and fruit.

Pour into an open roasting pan
Don't forget to scrape the sides of the bowl for all of that vinaigrette we worked so hard on.

If you're making these with the Rice Pilaf recipe you're already there! Put them both in at the same time and remove them when you drop the rice down to 350 — then pop 'em back in at the last five minutes to serve them piping hot)

Roast for 30 minutes. Serve.

CHAPTER 5

· NEW YEAR'S DAY ·

NEW YEARS' MORNING
APPLE CHOWDER BUNS

"LINNER" OR IS IT "DUNCH"
"FORTUNE & WEALTH" (SHRIMP) POTSTICKAHS

"HOPPIN' JOAN"
(black-eyed peas with chicken & root veggies)

"CHRYSANTHEMUM HAPPINESS SALAD"
(daikon & carrot slaw)

"FULL CIRCLE"

Oddly, tho' NYD is traditionally the jumping off point into the great unknown of a brand spankin' new trip around the sun, I have always looked at it like the great Greek God Janus — one face looking back, as one looks forward. As a cook, it's the last day of a solid month of nonstop cooking, an important denouement of weeks of shopping, planning, prepping and preparing, that needs to be something "old" and something new, something borrowed and something...

Whew! I had no idea how to get out of my reverie and that's really what this day is. In our spiritual lives, it's a day most sacred, that started very early (actually last night) with Mylove and I toasting the new year with the crystal champagne flutes that my Godmother and aunt Mish gave us on our wedding day. We use them every NY Eve and since Mylove has not "drank" since before we were dating (some thirty years ago) we have always filled these with either sparkling apple cider or mineral water. After we ring in the new one, they are washed and put back into their satin lined box to wait for another 364.9 days...

We devote the morning, to learning the course our spiritual lives will take in the coming year, then we break our fast with our newest tradition. The rest of the day is actually almost a calm before the storm, a priming of the pump, a chomping at the bit of the possibilities that await, while actively reminding each other all day long of the blessings we have or currently enjoy. It's a subtle practice that always sneaks up on me — one, I forget that we're going to do, until we're doing it, but it deliciously takes all of our energy and focuses it in the most powerful way.

After we rise up from our spiritual practices, we are hungry and I'm really looking forward to breakfast — partly because I'm excited that I finally created a way to celebrate the past, namely our leftover Christmas morning apple chowder. I rarely eat breakfast on weekdays and eggs are saved for the weekends (such a child of the seventies — when eggs went to jail for cholesterol and never quite shook their rap sheet despite several surgeon general's attempts) so, it would break my heart that I never got around to wanting a bowl of something (our apple chowder) so identified with "last Christmas" that I would finally surrender and throw it out when it did become "something blue." Yes, I had tried stirring into oatmeal, which is great and maybe you'll do that with yours, but (and if you haven't done so already) hear me out — this will make you a New Year's Day rock star!

I make a galette/puff pastry which is a pastry dough that is puff pastry on steroids — spreading softened Irish butter on a rolled puff pastry dough, then folding it over and spreading it again, and repeating this procedure until it's mathematically still possible but physically impossible (most I usually get is three folds). Then you carefully roll it out again into a 9 x 12 sheet… if you can do this without the butter squirting all over your pastry board, then, in the immortal words of Kwai Chang Caine's Blind Shaolin Master, Po, "it's time for you to leave." After I've rolled out a nice thin(ish) dough, I spread the leftover apple chowder over it, and roll the pastry into a log. Then I cut into individual 1 inch thick pastries, and set them into on their sides (so you can see the swirl) into a buttered glass baking dish and bake for about 40 minutes.

After it cools, let's be real, these puppies have already got us salivating, but why stop here? I smear a maple sugar glaze on top (as if they needed it — but hey, once a year, right?) and then we indulge.

Later on, today I will try to stick as many cliché New Year's Day traditions into the food schedule as I can — Hoppin' Joan (which is a lighter, more refined version of "Hoppin' John" the traditional Black-eyed pea dish from the south) which is cooking in the slow cooker with roasted chicken thighs and root veggies, Chinese Potstickahs, Japanese Chrysanthemum Salad … we're not really sitting down to dinner so much as sneaking up on it.

If you're wondering how a southern dish could get stuffed between two Asian dishes, it's cuz I really like the idea of eating traditional "good luck foods" for NYD, and for a while, all I could find were articles about black-eyed peas, so that has always been there — I haven't always cooked for NYD and for many years, we were on tour with an annual television broadcast/production, and so our meals were catered. But New Years in America seems more about recovering from a hangover than eating celebratory foods, except for the Asian side of the world, which has always revered the turning of the calendar's page.

And besides — Chinese Potstickahs actually mean something to us. They remind us of the first time I went to "Meet the Parents." We had driven from San Diego to Marin county, and pulled off the road after a 7 and ½ hour drive at "Larkspur Landing," and went to a Chinese restaurant that Mylove loved when she had lived there. Since we were really just trying to refresh a little before meeting her father Malcolm and step-mother Marion (Mylove's mother Mardie had passed some 20 years before), we just got some jasmine tea and some pot stickers. Since then, they have always had a sacred place in our hearts!

As for the Chrysanthemum salad, as I said, I collect recipes for just such a day.

Mylove is still under the weather, so we're taking it slow today. The cold she was fighting at Christmas is starting to win. She's usually good at shakin' these things — so I'm hoping that the fresh vitamin burst of a fresh salad, and the roasted comfort of the Hoppin' Joan will do their respective tricks.

The day will be, what it will be, and unlike other days when we say that — there's a special crispness to that emotion that really is anticipatory — I always have my plans, but I want to see what *this* year is going to be, and I'm hoping that those first gentle breezes of the winds of change will carry a clue as to how the infant New Year is going to blossom in our lives.

So, turn the page to get the recipes — while I'll go back to taking care of Mylove.

APPLE CHOWDER BUNS

These are as simple or as complicated as you feel at the moment. I keep a puff pastry in the freezer for when I ain't feelin' it, so no one (here) will judge you if you want to cruise today — YOU DESERVE IT! And Honey? If you need someone to give you that latitude, I'm your girl!

But... and when... you do decide, use the same recipe that I laid out for the Pear & Apple Rustic Tart, And remember that last bit of Apple Chowder I told you to hang onto? Now's the time...

> **1 galette/puff pastry dough**
> (see Pear & Apple Rustic Tart in the Thanksgiving chapter)
> **1 cup of apple chowder**
> **1 cup of maple sugar**
> **2 tbsp. heavy cream**

Preheat the oven to 350 degrees

Roll out your galette to a 9 x 12 rectangle
Spread the apple chowder evenly to leave a 1 inch naked at both ends. Fold the naked end over to start your roll, and roll the dough to a log.

Grease a 9 x 9 glass baking dish
Slice the log into rolls about 2 inches wide. Place them face up in the baking dish. Bake them for about 20 minutes. This will be a slurpy juicy gooey affair so makes sure the dough cooks all the way through and then allow them to cool.

Whisk the maple and cream together
Take the buns out of the baking dish and allow to cool on your serving plates.

Spread the maple glaze and try, try very hard, (we've all been there) to wait until you just can't stand it anymore for the glaze to set up. (And like the Tootsie Roll Pops' Mr. Owl, I never made it very far.)

"FORTUNE & WEALTH" POTSTICKAHS
(SHRIMP & VEGGIES)

You could, (and I have) try to make your own potsticker, wonton, and egg roll wrappers... but should you (other' your own edification) really compete with the world's oldest civilization? Here's one place where you could after decades of practice achieve mediocrity, when instead you could, focus on the filling — ah, there's time well spent!

So, surrender — it's New Year's and you've got some serious chillin' to do. The difference with this recipe and mere dumplings is the fried bottom. So, I use a cast iron skillet and some good rice wine for the steaming (see, there are some places to express thyself).

To the Chinese (on New Year's) the Shrimp symbolizes Fortune and Wealth — and dumplings, abundance. My wish for you!

---

1 pound fresh shrimp
(peeled, de-tailed & deveined)
1/2 cup scallions (minced)
1/2 cup fresh snow peas
(cut into matchsticks)
1/2 cup fresh bean sprouts
1/2 cup fresh celery (matchsticks)
1/4 cup fresh cilantro (minced)
2 tbsp. peanut or nut oil

1/2 cup + "1 generous splash" rice vinegar
1 1/2 cup filtered water
1/2 cup toasted sesame oil
1 tsp. fish sauce
1 tsp. Ponzu sauce
1/4 cup fresh ginger juice
1 tsp. red pepper flakes
Sriracha sauce (optional)

In a dry super-hot wok
Put the scallions, bean sprouts, snow peas and celery — turn off the heat and pour in the peanut oil and stir fast, pour in half of the rice wine vinegar, half of the sesame oil. Stir and work it. Add the shrimp, stir to coat. Sprinkle in the pepper flakes and cilantro and allow to cool.

Preheat your skillet and have a lid nearby

In a mixing bowl
Whisk together the ginger, remaining rice wine vinegar, fish sauce and Ponzu for a dipping sauce.

Remove the Shrimp from the mixture and chop it fine
Stir it back into the filling.

Have a bowl of water near a clean cutting board.
Spoon a teaspoon of the mixture onto the middle of a dumpling skin. Run a wet finger along the edge. Bring one side over to the other and and pinch it closed.

Bring the corners toward each together which will stand the edge up like a spine in a half-moon shape.

In your heated skillet (with a lid)
Pour in a thin layer of oil and place the dumplings in with the spines up like a stegosaurus ridge. Fry them for about 3 minutes. Get your lid ready, pour a generous splash of rice vinegar and the water in and close the lid — allow the water to steam away (about an additional 3 minutes). Check that the dumplings are done. If there is still water, you can pour it off to allow the bottoms to crisp back up and then remove to paper towel to drain.

Serve with your dipping sauce.

"HOPPIN' JOAN"
(BLACK-EYED PEAS WITH CHICKEN & ROOT VEGGIES)

Born Hoppin' John, this traditional pork-based version is made with Chicken (which the Vietnamese like for their New Year's Day festivities) so I renamed it Joan. Hey, it worked for me, why not her? Black-eyed peas are eaten in the south on New Year's Day for "Good Luck" which seems like the blue collar version of good Fortune... but seriously can you have too much of either? As an Irish Lass, I vote no. You can't have too much of luck or fortune — may you have them both.

This dish is also "good luck" because it makes use of the Cajun "Holy Trinity" — Onion, Bell Pepper and Celery — the base of all the Cajun dishes you know — creoles, etouffee, gumbos. So, it can't hurt on the first day of the year to make offerings to your version of the Holy Trinity (which seems to show up in many of the philosophies of the world.) This dish is a meal in itself, so it's perfect when you want to be festive and you also want to chill... it's got your protein, legumes, rice and root veggies... with all that, you can call it macaroni! In a slow cooker

2 cups black-eyed peas (rinsed)	**1 red pepper** (chopped)
2 cups rice (cooked)	**1 tsp. granulated garlic**
4 chicken thighs	**½ tsp. of salt**
1 bottle dark ale	**1 tsp. sassafras leaves**
1 stick of butter	**1 tsp. oregano**
5 cloves of garlic	**1 tsp. smoked paprika**
1 onion (chopped)	**1 tsp. cayenne**
3 stalks celery (chopped)	

Place the chicken thighs skin side down. Add the garlic in whole cloves. Turn the slow cooker on high and allow to cook dry for about 15 minutes — Add the ale, close the lid and allow to cook for six hours at high — or if you are making this night before (you might be on your game on NYE who knows?) then go 8 hours on low.

2 hours before serving
Cook your rice in the normal way.

In a dry skillet
Add the onion, bell pepper, and celery. Add the butter, allow to melt and add the spices.

Add all to the slow cooker and allow to cook for an additional hour.

Serve.

CHRYSANTHEMUM - "HAPPINESS" SALAD
(DAIKON & CARROT SLAW)

I was looking for a salad that would balance the Hoppin' Joan and be pretty without much trouble. This is a beautiful "solution" and the super cool thing is that the Chrysanthemum is both the Japanese symbol for the Imperial Family (and thus Royalty) and Happiness!

It's light and looks amazing and I guarantee that maybe you had something like this but it will delight and surprise everyone on this day. Make this a few hours or even the night before (HA!) before serving — the longer it has to marinate the better.

1 large daikon radish (shredded)	1 tsp. sugar
3 large carrots, shredded	1 tsp. salt
1/4 cup fresh ginger juice	1/4 cup fresh lemon juice
1/4 cup rice vinegar	1 tbsp. toasted sesame seeds

In a glass bowl
Whisk the dressing ingredients together.

Divide the dressing between two glass bowls.
Add the shredded Daikon to one and the carrot to the other. Chill in the refrigerator until serving.

To serve — use individual plates for each guest
Using Tongs take a scoop of the Daikon and arrange into a circular mound. In the center of the mound place a scoop of the carrot to make a beautiful blossom — garnish with the toasted sesame seeds.

CHAPTER 6

· VALENTINE'S DAY ROMANTIC DINNER FOR 2 ·

SHRIMP COCKTAIL

PARVATI PÂTÉ WITH POLENTA COOKIES

CUPID SALAD
(avocado, mango, strawberry & fresh basil salad)

WARM LAVA CAKE

"BE MINE(S)"

February is here and we are so freakin' happy to say goodbye to January. We had a rough start — Mylove's cold turned into full blown pneumonia and the trip to the emergency room won her a one week stay on the respiratory ward… then three weeks of self-injecting antibiotics three times a day — She is only too happy to have that in her rear view mirror… We are both ready for a little celebration.

But really? Go out with the amateurs? Please … Seriously. Puh-leeeeze. I used to get all worked up for Cupid's high Holy day. I used to try to "get my digs-in early," to "beat the competition" to score "the" reservation. Now, sure, I've been a snobby foodie from jump. And, let's be real, I wasn't always necessarily vying with the next "guy" to get the killer table, since Mylove's and my idea of "the most romantic" dinner wasn't everybody else's. But, since every restaurateur has finally figger'd out (what took them so long?) that this is a high-volume day, second only to Mother's Day in both stress level and the cash people are willing to fork out, *any* option is also usually "booked up" in advance. Including our favorite little holes-in-the-walls, and really what's the point?

Romance.

That's the only point. A crowded restaurant, stressed-out waiters and being rushed out so the next "romantic couple" can get your table can't be anybody's idea of the perfect date. But, like the rest of the adult world, I thought this was the only way to celebrate Cupid's aim, and it took me about 20 years to get over it.

But that does not mean I'm over Valentine's Day by any stretch of the imagination. It's one of my most favorite times of the year. I usually start plotting about mid-January, sketching in my mind, the latest installment of an on-going performance art installation known as "Ninja Valentine." I wrote obliquely about this in GBTM, and it's one of the things that both helped create the legend of the perfect husband that was "Scott," and that made the transformation to Scottie, what many have called, "unbelievable." I don't think they're using that as a superlative. Even today, many people still have a hard time even believing that being transgender is real, (mine or anyone's). My own sister Shane was one. Maybe it's because the dude I created called Scott, had such mad skillz in the "Mr. Right Department," that I became a victim of my own PR. Of these, my killer Valentine chops were one of the things that made many husbands actually hate Scott, for "setting the bar too high." And these are the same husbands (and boyfriends) who breathed a collective sigh of relief when I came out, apparently because now the pressure was off since they now knew that they had been competing all long with a woman. This is one of the weirdest backhanded compliments I have ever received... sorta. It not only makes me scratch my head, but also if I think too hard on it, it makes me sad... for those wives and girlfriends... oh, well, I hope their sex is good?

But, here's "Ninja Valentine" spelled out: every Valentine's Morning, Mylove wakes to find a new, and hopefully, mind-blowing riff on the classic "handmade" Valentine. The very first one that started us off on this wild tangent was when she opened her eyes to see that I had strung a canopy of 150 red and pink felt hearts on golden cords over our bed. Yup. That was a tough act to follow! But follow it I did. For over 20 years.

The criteria for each "piece" are these:

1. It must be made in the spirit of the classic handmade Valentines of our elementary school days. I loved, loved, LOVED the giving and receiving of these paper hugs from every kid in class every February. Over time, the classic materials of construction paper, glue stick and glitter have seen modern materials, including video used, but the best ones have riffed on the traditional paper "card."

2. It must appear out of nowhere. This is getting trickier as we both get more mature. The engineering of them is getting trickier as I burn through the obvious solutions. And doing this in the middle of the night requires not making noise, which would spoil the surprise.

3. It, of course, must have a certain wow factor. She's been getting these for over 20 years, so I've got to surprise her. As I said, I set myself up for a tough act to follow!

Over the years I've:

- covered the 60 panes of our sliding glass doors in the living room with pink, red, and purple acetate hearts, transforming the entire side of the room into a stained-glass Valentine's mural,

- made a twelve-foot long giant cupid's arrow with heart shaped point & flight as if a giant cherub had used our backyard as a target,

- constructed a three-sided, four-foot tall spinning "chandelier" with backlit acetate heart patterns,

- and one year, when I wasn't going to be able to be there for the "day of," I hid a pull-down window shade on which I hand-painted Valentine hearts and a message, and hung it on the office curtain rod. Rolled up, it was hidden-in-plain-sight, as if it had always been there. You had to be looking for it to see it. I was able to make it while I was at work, and wait until the last possible moment to hang it when I went to grab my purse as I left for my flight. But I panicked. What if it was hidden too well and she missed it on Valentine's Day? Telling her to go looking for it seemed to spoil the wow factor. So, I strung a red cord to the blind's pull cord and attached it to a heart shaped note that read, "Do Not Pull Until February 14th."

I got the best of both worlds. Three days before Valentine's Day, I was in Virginia, and I got a call on my cell. She had found the note and the rolled-up shade, but now had three days of anticipation, and three extra days to know how much this Cupid loves her.

But this year, I want to celebrate my "Superhero" honey.

I like the Superhero metaphor. It fits Mylove like a shiny spandex uni-tard & cape. The strength that she musters every day to deal with having cancer. The superhuman mental flexibility to stare her own fears in the face and choose love for the real me over the fears of losing her albeit beloved, but still imagined, *husband*. She's the *"you"* I wish everyone one of us could be — the best we are capable of being — the lovingest we hope we could be, the noblest we aspire to be. She is her better angel every moment of every day.

I asked her, if she were a superhero, what would her costume look like? Surprisingly, she had a very specific look. This made my job easy. I'm getting pretty good at Photoshop, and I was able to create a perfect comic book alter-ego of her, *"The Sabre,"* with black yoga-like tights and laser-flame "sword of wit." She was accompanied by our leaping dogs, her sidekicks, Aria and Bella, and her "familiar," a raven. I was even able to get the highlights in her hair that she was getting pretty fond of, and finished it with some sparkle to her leotard. I printed the image onto acetate and painted the backside like a real animation cel.

But there were still two problems to solve:

1. The background. The image I created was of *"The Sabre"* and her sidekicks all flying from a zero perspective (from the center of the background) toward the viewer. What background would be worthy, not too busy, and possible to pull-off?

2. Where was the traditional paper and glitter hearts of a classic Valentine? (criteria number 1 from the above.)

I decided to dig back into our "archives" for inspiration. Years ago, my production partner Mitch & I made a short video segment where we took video of our own heads singing to her, (and Mitch to his wife Karen) and superimposed them onto a hand-drawn animated body of a cherub complete with fluttering angel wings. This go-around, I'm not going for the cute factor so much, but video is good idea. I found a video clip of a supernova exploding from within a crown nebula. I was able to edit them on my desktop to create a repeating loop, and wirecast that to our living room TV via "Airplay." I'm thinkin' that if I hang the clear acetate image with Mylove's Superhero self on it in front of the screen and the background video loop of the supernova would show through.

And if I hang it by fastening the acetate sheet to a frame made from foam core onto which I add hearts and filigree…

Well, yes. It made quite the statement. She, of course, teared up and loved it — noticing every detail and marveling at how I pulled it off during the night.

And that's something that makes our marriage fun. We have this little game called Valentine's Day. I make something out of paper, crayons, finger-paints and glue stick and she pretends she didn't hear me banging around upstairs in the middle of the night. All night.

But this installment of Ninja Valentine helped me figure out what to cook. Actually, what to *serve*. While I was in the archives of Valentine's past, it reminded me of one of our most memorable Valentine's Days ever. The one where we spent the entire day in our fold-out couch bed. It was *breakfast-lunch-and dinner* in bed.

We don't have all day this time as my love has a few appointments, but we will meet back in our bed in our sexiest lingerie for romantic Movies and "Dinner" in bed. And you thought getting that reservation at "Chez whatevs" was the call?

One thing that's the key on this night is that the food shouldn't take me away from the fun for any longer than it has to. So, nothing's complicated and everything is prepared ahead of time. It's not about volume, it's about fun, spicy and interesting….

I've got finger food that isn't too messy, a nice salad, and killer dessert that finishes us off.

But the main entrée tonight is each of us. Romance has always been my strong suit, but I'd be lying if I didn't tell you that I'm keenly aware of the changes in my playbook. And personally, I am trying to thread the needle between "different" and "real."

I'm not sure if other trans women go through this — the difference between us girls who were raised by wolves and girls who transition as children and teens, is that we have had to reconcile our feminine instincts with testosterone's push and shove. The longer we live with testosterone distorting our view, coupled with society's schooling for our behavior and/or expression, the more we develop habits that become, well … *there*.

One of the hardest things for me to reconcile was that, as much as I hungered to be accepted as a woman in Mylove's eyes, it was still awkward for me to *act* as a woman in her arms. I had been taught by the women in my love life how to be with them. Like any lover teaches her lover how she wants to be held, kissed, touched, I had brought learned behavior to Mylove and she had, over twenty years plus, modified that behavior to suit her needs.

And I need to remind myself that I did *willingly* try to be "her man" in her arms. I never allowed myself to even act on my feminine instincts, and really what are those? Intimacy is listening, feeling, connecting and cluing in, but, it's also a trying things and getting feedback thingy. An, "I like it when you do that," or "I don't like that so much" and a "I LOVE it when you do that" kinda thingy. But I'm realizing, I never turned any of that feedback on myself. I never said those things to Mylove, because anything that might seem like I wasn't "being a man" would trigger questions that would lead to the truth of who I was. So, I just always concentrated on making her feel good, and loved and cherished.

But there was a price to be paid for all that. It took away 180 degrees of my "just be me" options, it required constant monitoring to make sure I never strayed into that area of "feminine" and thus, I had no choice but to hold back.

But also, I was stunted, so to speak, in even knowing what I, as a woman, wanted *from* my lover. I didn't even know what it would be like to act as a woman. Complicated eh? It's one thing to say you are, but when the lights are out, I only know how to hold Mylove. I never thought about how I wanted to be held myself — I wouldn't allow myself to go there.

But Mylove is helping me discover this. This is something that we as a community don't usually talk about. The transgender person is forced to be so declarative in their coming out, in the explaining of just what in the hell they're talking about, that it sounds like they have it all "thought out," been so sure about everything, been so convinced about a hugely mysterious aspect of being human, (that every human just pretends to have figured out for themselves) which is, "one's identity," that they can, with confidence, step out on a limb and actually "go against society's norms."

This "one's identity" thingy is so mysterious that we have come up with all kinds of ways to describe it; *"finding one's self," "coming into one's own", "getting all one's wheels in the same direction,"* all of these are metaphorical ways to describe the indescribable — the thing that many people never ask of another, nor hope to have to completely answer for oneself: *"who the hell are you, in 25 words or less"* because it simply can't be done.

BUT the transgender person is expected to have this answer ready for whomever demands it of them — like a border patrol official at the gates of respect. We train ourselves to have this answer — we are schooled by society and hard knocks and trial and error to have this answer, our papers or passport stamp, if you will, and then we are held to it — so it had better be a good one. But the cis-gender world (those who identify as their "born" biological gender) would never dream of having to answer that question themselves. And nobody asks about it of them. But they ask us.

We have to spend so much time declaring our identity and have all the answers that when we finally get everyone on board, we're not about to start asking our own questions. But how else do we learn about sex, let alone real deep intimacy?

Mylove's and my intimacy has always been mind-blowingly deep — rich, healing and satisfying (that seems so base a word, like saying that getting a breath of air after swimming to the surface from the deepest depths is "satisfying"), but it never really depended on my gender. The physical act of us coming together was only ever about male and female parts while we were inches apart. But, as we came together, we became one and there was no longer male or female anythings. There was just us.

Before I transitioned (medically), we tested out different ways of being together. I went slow and let Mylove call the shots. Dictate our pace. Steer the direction. Yes, I held my breath, hoping this would go well. Our intimacy depended on it. Could we be two women together? Could we find new ways?

Once we knew we could, she could, I felt I could say I wanted to medically/surgically transition. She wouldn't be losing anything. She would be gaining a fuller me. And it worked.

Now, if there's ever an issue, it's me. I have different wants, I want to be held as much as I want to hold. But I also want to hold her differently. Since my behavior was learned before, I now am allowing myself to want something, a way of being that was me without the lessons learned under testosterone's sway.

And Mylove is helping me with that.

And what a perfect night to practice that. While one of the most romantic couples in history — Cleopatra and Antony, played by one of the most romantic couples in history, Liz and Dick play out on our television, one of the most Romantic couples in present day, Mylove and her Scottie Jeanette sip sparkling water with strawberries floating amid the bubbles, nibbling shrimp and each other's ears ... between kisses that is. And love is not only in the air, it's all there is.

Happy Romance day!

SHRIMP COCKTAIL

Just the thought conjures up elegance and romantic evenings but for Mylove and me, this was what was waiting for us when we "stole away" from our own wedding reception to begin our official life together in the "honeymoon suite" my father gave us as one of many presents: a night in the local B&B because we weren't leaving on honeymoon until the next afternoon. (That, and three of our out of town relatives needed our bed at home.) But our dear friend Maura arranged to have shrimp cocktail, sparkling water and chocolate-dipped strawberries to greet us — and so they will forever remind of us of our day.

The secret here is the cocktail sauce — so simple to get right, and so easy to chuff. So, let's break it down, you want a tomatoey sweetness with a slightly acidic base that plays well with the subtle briny sweetness of chilled shrimp.

And as usual nothing beats the bright sparkle of fresh!

4-5 large fresh raw shrimp per person (peeled & deveined — leave the tail on)	**1 tsp. sugar**
2 large ripe heirloom tomatoes	**Pinch of salt**
1⁄4 onion	**2 lemons**
1 clove garlic	**1 quart of water**
1 tbsp. fresh horseradish	**Bowl of ice cubes large enough to hold the shrimp**
1 tsp. dijon mustard	

Rinse the shrimp. Set aside.

In a blender
Puree the tomato, onion, garlic, horseradish, and Dijon. Add the juice of 1 lemon, sugar and a pinch of salt. Blend together and chill for at least an hour — you want this cold.

When it's time to serve:

In a 1 quart pot
get the water boiling…

Add the shrimp to the boiling water
Count to 10. Take a breath. Count to ten once more. Pour the water and shrimp into a sieve or strainer. Immediately rinse with cold water. Add to the bowl of ice and cover the shrimp. We wanna stop the shrimp from cooking any further.

Spoon the cocktail sauce into one martini glass.
(You're sharing — it's romantic, yes?)

Hang the shrimp on the rim and garnish with cut lemon wedges.

PARVATI PÂTÉ
WITH SAVORY POLENTA WAFER/COOKIES

We first made this at our nascent Christmas Eve feast as an appetizer — we were looking for a dish that Mylove and I created together — I came up with the pâté and she invented the Polenta cookie. She loved the Corn Pone of her childhood (I know, I know, weird for a Yankee Girl, but there it is) — and when we found a corn pone pan in an antique store she went crazy with nostalgia. I, on the other hand, had my world rocked — I had pictured a thicker corny-kinda cookiesque-thingy but was surprised that the pan itself was very shallow and at best was capable of making something no thicker than a crepe. But that's their magic. Thin and crispy they are the perfect counterpoint to the pate — and elegant and savory. The perfect romantic finger food.

You don't need a special pan, but it's more fun. The real key here is that they are rolled like a bugle ('member them?) which creates the perfect edible spoon for the pâté. These are not the traditional hard crunchy southern belles, but a thin and elegant, more refined Northern Lady made with Blue Corn meal. They are twice fried, the first to make 'em into a wafer, the second to form them into a cone.

1 cup blue corn meal	1 lb. blueberries
1/2 cup pastry flour	1 large onion (diced)
1 egg	3 stalks celery (chopped with leaves, separate and reserve the leaves)
1 tbsp. melted butter	
1 cup buttermilk	1/4 cup EVOO
1 tsp baking soda	1 tbsp. red wine
1 tsp. salt	1/2 tsp. salt
1 tsp. granulated garlic	½ tsp ground chipotle
1 lb. of mushrooms (chopped)	

Make the Cookies

In a blender

Blend the cornmeal, flour, egg, butter, buttermilk, soda, salt & granulated garlic to a smooth batter.

In a skillet

Pour thin pancakes. Cook on one side until all the bubbles that appear, burst. Turn and allow to fluff up. Press them with a spatula to make a thin wafer and transfer to a parchment lined plate to cool. Place a piece of parchment paper to separate the layers. Allow to cool completely.

Make the Pâté

In a dry hot skillet

Caramelize the onion. Add a splash of EVOO and the mushrooms sauté until soft, deglaze with red wine and add the blueberries. Add the salt and Chipotle.

With an immersion blender

Grind the mushroom mixture. Transfer to a bowl. Add the celery. Stir and transfer to a serving bowl. Garnish with the celery leaves.

Heat up the remaining olive oil in a skillet.

Roll the polenta wafers into a cone and place the seam side down in the hot oil to seal. Cook until "golden blue brown." Transfer to a paper towel to drain.

Dust with salt and arrange on a platter to serve with pâté.

CUPID SALAD
(AVOCADO, MANGO, STRAWBERRY & FRESH BASIL)

So… this whole romance thingy… for us, began with a mango….

I can say that I never really had one until Mylove showed me. In fact, all of the good things in our life, with the exception of my family and Gerhard, came from Mylove. When we first dated, she always had one of these magical fruits around and one morning she sliced the "cups" off of both sides (lengthwise) ran a knife along the slice that still held the pit to remove the flesh that remained and handed one end of the "strip" to me. She took the other end into her mouth and I mirrored her, and like Pongo & Perdita on their first date, we ate toward the middle… mango juice on our chins, we laughed as she showed me how to scrape the tenacious fruit that still clung to the pit and handed it to me to try… We were locked in an embrace and the slippery fruit shot out my hands like the cartoon bar of soap and landed on our chests — Orange smiles and sticky fingers later… we learned that day… to eat mangoes in the shower… which we did. Again, And Again. Courtship never tasted sooo good!

1 ripe mango (diced — instructions below)	**1 dash of ground chipotle**
1 ripe avocado (diced)	**Pinch of salt**
1 cup ripe strawberries (halved)	**Pinch of sugar**
¼ cup fresh basil leaves (ribboned)	
1 tsp. balsamic vinegar	

In a glass mixing bowl
Whisk the balsamic, chipotle, sugar and salt. Toss the strawberries and basil in the mixture and refrigerate for about 30 minutes.

With a paring knife — dice the mango
Hold the mango on "Edge" (they are slightly flattened, yes? And pointier on one end, than the other, yes? Good). Take the mango and let it rest on the cutting surface. Hold the fatter end (with the pointier end pointing away from you) and roll it a quarter turn onto the edge. Inside that edge is the edge of a flattened pit/seed — it's about ¼ to ½ inch thick. Place the blade of your knife parallel to this pit and slice "the cup" from that half of the mango. Do you see the pit? If not it's thinner than you gauged which is okay you can trim that precious flesh off (or gnaw it off yourself — you're the cook and you get some perks!) Repeat this process on the other side. Trim the "ring" of the remaining skin and flesh from the seed to remove as much fruit/flesh as possible without cutting into the seed.

Trim that fruit into cubes.

Take the cups — we're *not* going to cut all the way thru here

Place them skin-side down so you can cut into the flesh without cutting the skin. Carefully cut three or four slices lengthwise, then four or five widthwise. Do the same with the other cup. Then grasp the cup with your fingers on the edge as poke your thumbs into the back of the cup to turn it inside out. The flesh will jut out like the back of an orange horny toad, creating perfect cubes of orange heaven. Slice them off the flesh and add them to the strawberry mixture.

Dice the avocado — *with almost the same techniques as above...*
Only we can skip the inside-out poke — and instead, use a large spoon or your blade spatula to lift the cubes from the shell. Add these to the strawberry mango mixture.

Toss.

Chill for an additional 30 minutes and serve.

MOLTEN LAVA CAKE
(THIS RECIPE MAKES 6 ½ CUP RAMEKINS – CUZ YOU'RE GOING TO WANT SOME BREAKFAST AFTER LAST NIGHT!)

Two dramatic things happened after I came out. First, I got a discipline to my eating that I had never needed to have before (without throwing womankind under the bus with another classic and tired trope, I will say that getting into my little black cocktail dress is incentive enough to reconsider that second piece of anything). And desserts are better when they come from the less is more hard-drive. The less weight, the more enjoyment. Suddenly, my taste shifted for intense bold flavors rather than space fillers. And nothing is more intense in the flavor category than Molten Lava Cake — which doesn't even have enough flour (yay!) to call itself a cake. It's really pudding with an attitude.

These are best piping hot — you can make the batter ahead of time so you'll be ready for that perfect moment — just allow the batter to return to room temp before pouring it into buttered ramekins. Since they only take 10 minutes to bake (ignore what they tell you in those fancy-schmancy restaurants!) they're ready when you are. And with one ramekin pretty enough to share, you can have your cake and eat it two!

1/2 cup unsalted butter (plus more for buttering ramekins)

6 oz. (2 high quality gourmet bars) **bittersweet chocolate** (chopped)

2 large eggs

2 large egg yolks

1/4 cup light brown sugar (packed)

1 tsp. vanilla extract

1 pinch salt

3 tbsp. all-purpose flour

1 tbsp. powdered sugar

Preheat the oven to 450 degrees

In a saucepan
Melt the butter. Turn off the heat and add the chocolate. Whisk together until smooth.

Beat the eggs in a separate bowl.
Add the sugar, vanilla and salt. Add two tablespoons of the flour. Add to the chocolate and stir.

Butter your ramekins
Add some flour to each buttered ramekin and tap to coat the inside of each completely. Divide the mixture between the ramekins.

Set the ramekins onto a baking sheet and place in the oven for 10 minutes. Remove.

Let set for 5 minutes, then serve Hot. Place the serving dish on top of the ramekin and invert the ramekin, then lift it off. Dust with powdered sugar, you romantic little devil, you!

CHAPTER 7

GRAMMA MADDEN'S IRISH SODIE BREAD

CORNED BEEF

KOLKANNON

ROASTED ROOT VEGETABLES

(white & purple carrots, rutabagas, & long radishes in a garlic vinaigrette)

"IRISH AYES"

I'm a lot of things, but I identify as Irish (until it's time to be Scottish, Finnish or Polish.) The only part of my heritage that I never really tap into is my Swede. It's cool. I just don't ever really feel Swede... maybe just Swede-ish? ...

But Irish? Put it like this: the Gaelic spelling of my name is O'Madhain. I know this from my dad doing one of those ancestry searches, back before every spit-in-a-tube company sprouted up, there were door-to-door salesmen, and one must've been let onto a car dealership lot on a slow day when my father was one of the top closers in the Inland Empire back in the day. But we didn't need a piece of paper to tell us that we were fiercely, fiery, irreconcilably Irish with a capital Aye! My dad's mom, Gramma Madden was the repository of all the legends and myths and stories of who we were. And the legends were many — an Uncle who "went over the wall of a monastery to protect his sister's virtue" (and then fled to America). My Granpa wearing a gun until my father was seven years old, you know... stuff like that. These "snapshots" were charged with drama and intrigue and pride and were repeated like mantras by us all.

I asked Gramma one time if were related to Owney Madden, the infamous gangster and head of the "Murphia" in Hell's Kitchen. She lost her shizz screaming at me to never, ever, even breathe that name in her house again. I wasn't sure if I should take that as a "yes."

Gramma was many things, but we remember a fiery white-haired gracious, magical sprite who, my father swore, was "almost" five-feet tall, but who my sister, Kimm, swore was more like fifty feet tall. Because when she was angry? The North Sea Storms were no match for her fury.

Sure, I wore green on every St. Patrick's Day growing up. But it wasn't till I got out of college and started to settle into my calling of being a filmmaker that I realized what *being* Irish really meant. We are the poets, the singers, your storytellers. We are the lovers, the fighters, and the resilient ones. We have put up with so much shite for centuries and we always bounce back. And we are proud. So, proud that it isn't that we think we're better than you, it's simply that you are here to be our audience. We love you.

This explains me to myself so much. But what I celebrate more than anything else on this day is my dad's side of the family. My mother's side never makes the effort. Except, of course, my beloved Godmother, my mom's sister, Aunt Phyl, who is the exception to every rule. But my mother's brother and his family? They want to be estranged. They want to forget us. And they are the Polish, Finnish, Swede side. There's no green over there. (This wasn't so when my Gram, my mom's mom, was alive. But after her funeral, we haven't spoken to my Uncle's side of the family. My mother would be heartbroken.) Nope, not one whit of the green over there, whatsoever. Sigh.

But my dad's side of the family is fiercely loyal. They are hardcore Irish and I wrote lovingly about them in GBTM. They are mostly working class; there are a lot of tattoos. But there are also a lot of nurse's licenses and badges with all that ink. There were some bikers, a couple of NYPD (both Detectives and Rank & File), a fireman or two, and a sh*t ton of love.

So, this is what we celebrate when I get up early every March 17th to make Gramma's "Sodiebread." (Yes, one word. I actually had no idea it meant soda as in *baking soda*). I actually started this tradition a few years back. I wanted some way to make this holiday more than telling my friends that green Budweiser was just not cool. I suddenly remembered how much I loved the caraway perfumed crunchy crusty sweetness, still warm and slathered with rich creamy butter.

This humble combo was a seminal experience in my culinary growth. I used to stay away from this side of the flavor spectrum, preferring the bombastic explosions of hot and spicy. But having stayed away for decades, coming back older, wiser and slightly nostalgic, the softness of this comfort food politely snuck up on me. It was weird, as if someone took a set of blinders off my taste buds! So, every March 16th before I go to bed, I measure out the ingredients and let the butter soften while I sleep, so I can put it all together and let the aroma wake up My Irish Rose (Mylove) with a smile.

I have to play air traffic control with aroma today. Already the house is filled with the powerful aroma of corned beef that went into the slow cooker last night. Tonight, we're having dear friends and sisters of the emerald isle over for a sorta-spontaneous celebration. I say "sorta" cuz this is, after all, a celebration looking for a place to happen. Mylove and I were always going to have all this stuff anyway, and it's a bonus to share this with those who will find it particularly special. This is the perfect time to remind you of my main points for writing this book, (and for cooking in general) and that's that cooking is one of the richest and most profound ways of expressing love for someone, namely your dinner guests. I can't say it enough. *Love actually* is the most important ingredient.

With St. Paddy's Day, it's a time to keep tradition alive even for those who may not be celebrating their Irish roots. Like I said, they are our audience…

But tonight, I am going at this concept in reverse: my guests are going to have to trust me, because we're going some places that modern American taste buds rarely get a chance to go. I'm talking caraway, dark ale, cabbage and, wait for it — we're letting an old friend out of dietary purgatory ... butter.

Now I can hear your head shaking from here. But we use butter all the time. Not like this. The Irish use butter as a side dish, condiment, and entrée, all in one. It's really the bedrock of the flavor profile. It's not an add-on coverall like Southern cooking, not a guilty pleasure like the Nouveau-American cuisine, or a catch-all like Indian ghee ... no. In Irish cooking, butter is the star, and you have to clear the stage with each bite lest you crowd its delicate presence into merely a supporting role. But we'll get to that in a sec.

So, what I'm saying is that I usually care very much for everyone's dietary restrictions and mores, but for this meal, it's one of those rare times when in my kitchen, you know what's coming. Tonight, we all are along for the ride. I mean in today's world, how many times, with all the gluten-free, vegan, plant-based, low-carbon footprint restrictions do you get a "hall pass" to not only eat, but celebrate red meat? And not just any red meat, but the lowliest, fattiest, seemingly never-admit-in-polite-company-that-you-actually-like-it, red meat of all — corned beef? Salt curing? (Which is presumably the technique required to make this cut edible. And maybe that's why it's the symbol of the Irish American Experience — blue collar, hardscrabble, silk purse from cow's (help me out here my metaphors are colliding), whatever ... it's what the Irish have always done. Make something *Ah*-mazing from something so humble.

Even when Mylove and I were hardcore vegetarians (a period of about 14 years) I still longed for the corned beef of my childhood. And let's be real, my Polish, Finnish-Swedish Mom, who generally mastered every cuisine from Mexican to Italian made a corned beef that made my Irish-Scottish father swoon with ecstasy, but....

.... well, let's just say that he had a very, very low bar.

I, on the other hand, have little tolerance for blanching flavor from an ingredient and the thought of boiled anything makes my heart shrivel. How could you do that to something that was so beautiful just minutes (usually hours) before you decided to kill it?

Did I digress? It's the Irish in me, taking any opportunity to wax poetic ... for this corned beef, we're taking another staple from the Irish American cook lore, namely Guinness Stout, to bless this humble cut. It's a key to the Irish-American philosophy of life — if one is good, ten are better. If you could use water, then use beer. And if you could use beer than why not stout? And since there's really only one stout, Guinness, well, there you go. And, since I am, as my father would say a "California Sunshine Girl," I of course, add a chipotle in adobo for good measure — not enough to turn the flavor profile all the way south to Mexico, but just enough to give it a SoCal flair. So that's how I improve on mom's technique. I did start off right with an organic brisket (no nitrates, nitrites, no ni-anythings), chopped large brown onion, a handful of garlic cloves, and two tall cans of Guinness draft. I set the slow-cooker on low and that's the aroma that fills the house right now. I'll add more seasoning later.

Back to sodie bread and tonight. Sodie bread taught me a lot about the ways I had lost control of my taste buds, as I alluded to at the start of this chapter. In a sense, my buds had become arrogant. Almost snobby. If they didn't have the verve of mango or chipotle, lemon or cardamom, then they couldn't be bothered. It was as if the brashness of hot and spicy flavors seduced me from appreciating the subtlety of butter, lavender, apple, zucchini. This revelation is one of the most significant turning points in my cooking. It changed my approach from using spices to make flavor to using spices to draw out the flavor of the ingredients.

Soda bread is great example of that interplay — without the caraway, it would just be a really rich, large raisin scone. But something magical happens with the combination of caraway, raisins and butter that never happens anywhere else. So, I toast the caraway seeds and throw them while they are still hot into the dry ingredients the night before to allow them to thoroughly "perfume" the mix. I also leave the egg and buttermilk and butter out so they are soft and room temp when mixing. Of course, this must be done with sufficient precautions in place to prevent any of Aria & Bella (our furbabies) midnight snack raids.

I have a cast iron skillet that has a removable wooden handle. It was an off-to-college gift from my father. Odd choice, but cool and strangely prophetic. After mixing the ingredients together in my Kitchen Aid mixer, I butter the sides of the skillet and spoon the mixture into the skillet. It should be dry enough that when you dip a knife in flour you can make the "St. Paddy's cross" into the dough ball and it will stay. A lot of websites like to say you cut a cross to let the devil out. But seriously? I don't know about you, but there's no devil in anything I ever bake. Now, I put the kettle on and make sure there's a ton of good Irish butter softening while the aroma of toasted caraway and sweet buttermilk dances with corned beef that has been happily bathing in Guinness in the next room.

While it is baking, I brush more buttermilk into the trench and across the top to make the perfect crunchy crust. Toward the end, I cover the bread with foil to make sure the crust doesn't burn while the inside is still baking. The cool thing about the cross is that it makes it easy to divide the bread into four pieces to share with those you love. Mylove and I generally eat one as soon it's cool enough to cut, though most times we don't make it that far before we can't stand it and eat it piping hot, slathered in butter.

After a breakfast feast, Mylove and I get dressed in our green, which is, in itself significant. Mylove's family is the Scots-Irish which, if you remember your history, are not the kissing cousins of the Irish but rather the Protestant bulwark that the English used to keep the hot-headed Irish Catholics in check. Hence, they wore orange to signify allegiance to the Protestant Crown. Over time, Mylove has given up her mother's way (who wasn't even Irish, but since she married into the McVickar clan, loved a chance to go against the grain of Irish Catholic conventional wisdom). This un-talked about chapter of history is usually never acknowledged in your local green-beer-serving-capitalizing-on-any-excuse-to-sell-something, pub, nor your elementary school pot-of-gold art project, because it doesn't jibe with Leprechauns and/or Saints ridding islands of snakes or doling out miracles, like potatoes. But then again, the same could be said for Cinco-de-Mayo, which is a great excuse to sell gringos cerveza & guac, but ain't Mexico's Independence Day. So, there you go.

But tonight, will be a real get together for Mylove and me with our tribe. Our dear friend, Mena Kerry Kehoe, who sounds like she's Hawaiian but couldn't have a more Gaelic name if she tripped over a sheleighlee, and Nitti, two friends who share the path of yoga Mylove and I have practiced for over 30 years, are coming for dinner. Mena is a still photographer who was on many of the sets of television projects under my direction. Hence our names for each other, Video Girl and Still Girl. And side note here, Mena shot the cover for this book you now hold in your hand — so again, there you go. Keeping it the family, Aye!

Now, those of you who've followed my story, will know that my nickname wasn't always Video Girl, but was rather Video Guy or Video Dude when Mena wanted to be cute. And she was there when it officially changed to Video Girl, and was amazingly and joyfully supportive, including slipping her favorite camera-ready concealer into my pocket with a kiss on the check for luck. Through her lens, Mena documented one of my first and largest book signings which happened in the Berkeley Firehouse Art collective. (Thanks again, Tommy dear!) This served as an un-official Northern Cal coming out party. It was an amazing celebration of many things, from the unveiling of the original painting that graced the cover of the first edition of my book, (painted by our Godson's mom, Sally Joy) to the embracing by a huge community of our friends, the transition not only of their friend, but of our marriage. But one of the most significant things that happened is that Mylove went from a supporter of our LGBTQ activism to a full-fledged participant. She found her voice and stepped forward as not only my honey, but as an ardent and articulate ally — fully leading by example, for true equality, diversity, and tolerance.

And oddly, tho' Mena has been there with us and for us, tonight truly will be the first time she will be a guest in our home, and we are excited that she spontaneously decided to celebrate her favorite day of the whole year in SoCal.

Nitti is herself a still photographer and old friend of Mylove's with whom, despite her relocation to the SoCal area, we had yet to break bread. I am anxious to turn what had been a mostly professional relationship with this amazing woman into a friendship, and what better night to do that.

But as you can guess, I am also taking a chance. What would cooking be without my seemingly second favorite ingredient, namely adrenaline?

I had been planning to experiment with something that I've mulled for years … and this brings us back to the tease I laid for you a few pages back …

… butter.

Years ago, when we were vegetarians, I was researching alternatives to corned beef to celebrate St. Paddy's day when I came across a dish I had never heard of — Kolkannon.

This dish is made of smashed (not mashed) potatoes, cabbage, and as many varieties of onions that you can lay your hands on. Oh … and butter. In fact, some of the women who wrote lovingly of this dish as the Irish comfort food of choice, wrote that it is really an excuse to eat butter legally. A mound of this amazing concoction is served really more as a vessel to hold a half cup of melted butter — an edible bowl for serving butter that would be slightly more gracious then chugging the butter with a straw or beer bong.

Okay, I'm being extreme to make a point, but the point is made. And if you are able to A.) get really great butter (Irish Kerrygold works in a pinch) and 2.) truly appreciate the sweetness of this golden nectar of the Goddess without a stitch of guilt, Kolkannon will become your go-to St. Paddy's day dish.

It is quite simple: potatoes and cabbage are boiled with onion, herbs and salt. Then the cabbage is chopped, the potatoes are smashed and fresh raw spring onions and scallions and more butter are all stirred together. They are served, then, using the ladle to make a well in the middle, filled with more melted butter…

But, and here's where I was standing on the precipice of gambling, corned beef is usually CornedBeefandCabbage, and in some homes, CornedBeef&Cabbageand&BoiledPotatoes, so, how do I make that and Kolkannon which is virtually the same ingredients?

Duh, (to myself) use Irish math. Just add Guinness.

So, this year, just after the puttin' on of the Green, I add two quarters (of a head) each of red and green cabbage, and two pounds of potatoes (creamy golden and red rose) cut in halves, and one large brown onion cut in large pieces to the bubbling brisket happily bathing in Guinness in my slow cooker. Now those of you able to follow me through the bramble and ramble of my anecdotes, parentheticals and asides would say, "But the brisket has been cooking with onions all night," and you would be right. They have two different textures and therefore subtle flavor profiles that we want, and two different uses.

We will let this all cook for about two-three hours. This time variation depends on the size of your brisket and the amount of people you are feeding, so check the cabbage and potatoes to make sure they're soft and then we'll pull them out of the slow cooker until we're ready to serve. In fact, tonight Kerry and Nitti miscalculated how many beers they'd want at their local pub's St. Paddy's day celebration and therefore got on the road with everyone else in the south bay heading north.

No worries. I pull everything out and keep the Guinness broth and onions bubbling happily.

Finally, they come in the door and after some long-awaited hugs and trips to the potty to freshen up, we serve drinks. Nitti is studying to be Sommelier and has brought a sparkling wine for a cocktail and a deeper Bordeaux for dinner. Neither Mylove nor I are drinking, but our guests are most welcome.

This gives me time to finish prep, so I place the brisket back into the slow cooker with the potatoes and cabbage. I chop more raw spring onions, fresh oregano leaves and then pull the hot potatoes and cabbage from the broth. I chop the cabbage into strips and smash the potatoes into the spring onions and oregano then toss it all with a quarter stick of butter.

I pull the Corned beef from the cooker and carve it into slices, and place two cups of the Guinness soup (the onions by now are so soft they make the broth thick) into my Ninja processor and add a half cup of heavy cream and three tablespoons of Dijon mustard and blend this into a sauce for the brisket.

Also new this year is a supporting dish, roasted root vegetables — white and purple carrots, rutabagas, and long radishes have been tossed in a garlic vinaigrette and roasting happily. All of this is set on the table for a night of celebrating our collective Irish pasts.

It is odd that this is the first time since I came out that Mena and I are able to share our first impressions of each other at that seminal nexus point for both of our lives. She has always been a member of the LGBTQ family, but I am the first member of the T tribe that she knew personally. I say "knew," because since my coming out, she has since found herself in not one but three photo-journalistic projects involving my T community. It's weird in that she didn't go looking for it, but it sought her, and the latest is a project where she has captured the relationship between blood sisters and brothers. The latest couple she had sit before her lens is the sister who identifies as "trans-masculine" and her thought to be "brother" who is actually a trans woman. I used quotes to acknowledge their names for each other. "Trans masculine" is a term used by some to acknowledge that they tho' they may still use the pronouns "she and hers" while presenting in more masculine manner, they are stating they do not choose to fully identify as male or a man. In this particular case, Mena documented their first coming out to each other — which is mind blowing when you realize they had lived as siblings for over forty years. The pictures are sweet, if a tad awkward, as each is getting to know not only their own skins but the person each has literally known their entire lives.

Nitti is, of course, not new to Mylove's and my journey and, as we devour this Irish American feast, lets on about how we have been talked about in a shared circle of friends. It's amazing how part of the world (as talked about in our current media) can seem like a place of transgender military bans, bathroom laws, and Transgender Day of Remembrance body counts, but to our actually large "cross-section of America" circle of friends, Mylove & I are seen as how we truly wish to be — a shining example of committed love, ecstatic marriage and joy.

So, there's that.

As I toast some of Gramma's sodie bread, and make Irish black tea for dessert, we bask in the luck of the Irish to be together, to be friends, and to be in love.

So how do you make all this happen at your table?

Well, sure and begorrah', you know the drill — turn the page.

GRAMMA MADDEN'S IRISH SODIEBREAD

This is one of those foods that appear out of nowhere in stores starting March 1ˢᵗ. But I cannot imagine eating it without the aroma of its baking still lingering in the air as you munch! It's also that for most of the year, caraway seed is content to be merely the guest star in rye bread, ... but for today of all days, it's the star of Sodiebread. It needs a better agent, is all I can say!

St. Paddy's is one of my high holy days... so I start the night b'fore, and I combine the dry ingredients while I'm gettin' the skillet "toastin' hot" — in go the caraway seeds. I shake it to keep 'em from igniting — then I drop the toastie lil buggers into the flour/dry ingredients to "perfume" them all night long whist I dream of the Emerald Isle... this simple yet effective technique will elevate your game over any comers... but it does require a passion for St. Paddy's day that only the most "green of us" usually muster...

5 cups all-purpose flour	2 cups raisins
1 cup sugar	3 tbsp. caraway seeds
1 tbsp. baking powder	2 ½ cups buttermilk
1 tsp. baking soda	1 large egg
1 ½ tsp. salt	
½ cup (1 stick) unsalted butter, cut into cubes, room temperature	

The night before (or a few hours before serving, if you are making it day of)
In a large mixing bowl
Combine the dry ingredients.

In a hot dry skillet
Toast the caraway seed, shaking to keep them from burning, and when they are fragrant, dump them into the dry ingredients — stir to distribute them in the flour mixture.

(The next morning) Preheat oven to 350 degrees.
Generously butter
A heavy oven-proof 10 to 12 inch skillet with 2 to 2 ½ inch-high sides.

Whisk first 5 ingredients in large bowl to blend.
Add butter. Using your fingers (get in there!) rub the butter into the flour mix to make coarse crumbs. Stir in the raisins.

Pour the wet ingredients into the dry ingredients
Using a wooden spoon, stir until just well incorporated (dough will be very sticky).

Transfer dough to your prepared skillet;
Smooth the top, mounding it slightly in the center. Using a small sharp knife dipped into flour, cut a 1-inch-deep cross in the dough. (Which divides the entire circle into quarters.)

Pop that baby into the oven
As it cooks, I keep cutting into the "cross" to maintain it (which fills in as the bread rises).

After the bread has baked for 30 minutes
brush the top with buttermilk and repeat this at the 45 minute mark. This gives a crispy outer layer to crunchy crust. If it's crisping up too fast — cover with foil to protect that crust.

Bake until bread is cooked through
Your tester comes out clean, about an hour.

Cool bread in skillet 10 minutes. Turn out onto a rack and tie or tape your hands to a chair or any other stationary object, until you just can't stand it anymore (my record is 15 minutes, waiting for Mylove, was the only thing that stopped me) — the aroma of the caraway will soon get the better of you and you will eat this before it cools.

At least put the tea water on and try to eat it sitting down… slathered in Irish butter… good luck of the Irish with ya on that!

CORNED BEEF & KOLKANNON
(CABBAGE & POTATOES)

I put these together to reflect the way I made it this year — But they are Irish twins, in that they are made at the same time, until they are separated... read on and you'll see what I mean.

A NOTE about Corned Beef — *IT WILL SHRINK DRAMATICALLY — it will lose easily a third to half its uncooked weight.*

1 brisket of corned beef	1 red rose potato for each person (quartered)
1 can Guinness Stout	2 large yellow onions (quartered)
1/2 pint of heavy cream	1 bunch spring onions (sliced thin)
1 tbsp. dijon mustard	1 bunch scallions (sliced thin)
1 tbsp. EVOO	1 head of garlic (peeled/smashed)
1/2 head red cabbage (quartered)	1 lb. of Irish butter
1/2 head green cabbage (quartered)	Fresh oregano leaves
1 Yukon gold potato for each person (quartered)	Dash of chipotle

In a slow cooker
Pour a splash of olive oil, the potatoes, cabbage, yellow onions and garlic and toss to coat. Place the brisket in and pour the Guinness over — you're going to cook on slow for 8–10 hours, but...

at the four-hour mark, remove the cabbage, onions and potatoes. Set aside to cool.

When cool —

Slice the Cabbage into strips. Chop half of the onions.
Hold on the potatoes for now.

30 minutes before serving
return the potatoes and cabbage to the slow cooker to warm, while you remove the brisket and carve and plate.

In your food processors or blender (I'm not judging — one served me well for years!)
Take the un-chopped onion (you removed from the slow cooker at the four-hour mark) and a cup of the Guinness from the slow cooker, a tbsp. of dijon mustard and the heavy cream, puree into a sauce. Set aside.

In large mixing bowl
Take the potatoes & cabbage from the slow cooker, add the chopped onion, fresh

oregano and a stick's worth of the Irish butter and smash the potatoes into bite-sized chunks, add the spring onions and continue to mash. Transfer to a serving bowl (if you're being all fancy and stuff) and garnish with the chopped scallions.

In small sauce pan
Melt the remaining butter to liquid.

To serve
Pass the Kolkannon and have everyone put a generous scoop in the center of their dinner plate. Follow behind with a small ladle and the melted butter — fill the ladle and push the filled ladle into each mound of Kolkannon and leave the butter in the crater you create. You may need to demonstrate that Kolkannon is eaten from inside the crater out — you drag forkfuls from the inside wall of the butter reservoir, to drench the bite on the way to one's mouth, trying to retain structural integrity for as long as one can…

DELISH!

ROASTED ROOT VEGETABLES

(WHITE & PURPLE CARROTS, RUTABAGAS, & LONG RADISHES IN A GARLIC VINAIGRETTE)

This simple side is a great addition to any winter to early spring meal when the air is still this side of crisp. It's a nice light counterpoint to the butter onslaught of Kolkannon, so it doesn't need much to flavor it -- the spicy bite of the garlic and radishes plays well with the natural sweetness of the carrots.

3 tbsp. EVOO	**1 bunch white or orange carrots** (matchstick)
1 tsp. balsamic vinegar	**1 bunch purple or red carrots** (matchstick)
3 cloves garlic (pressed)	**2 rutabagas** (quartered & sliced)
Dash of salt	**1 large turnip** (quartered & sliced)
Dash of chipotle	**1 bunch long radishes** (sliced thin)

Preheat your oven to 400 degrees

In a medium bowl

Whisk the EVOO, balsamic, garlic, salt and chipotle together. Toss the cut vegetables in the vinaigrette.

In a roasting pan, spread the veggies in a layer.

Roast for 30 minutes, stirring occasionally.

Serve with fresh ground black pepper.

CHAPTER 8

• EASTER SUNDAY! •

EASTER EGG SALAD
GRILLED SEA BASS WITH CHIVE BUTTER
QUINOA WITH ALMONDS, MANGO & ONION,
ENGLISH PEAS WITH TARRAGON & LEMON
EASTER EGG TRUFFLES

"THE BUNNY TRAIL"
EASTER SUNDAY LUNCH

Chocolate for breakfast? Of course! As per every holiday — I get my passion from my mom. She loved all holidays, but had a special place in her heart, good Catholic girl that she was, for the spring fling. It helped that it was at the end of what seemed to be the eternity of Lent. The breaking of the fast of chocolate alone was worth its weight in gold. We always had a basket filled with all of the classics including: the resurrection of a "peeps" (those incredibly in-edible marshmallow (?) thingies that it only just dawned on me were supposed to be chicks) that invariably would be stuck to the Easter grass in a basket leftover from last year and surprisingly, still… "fresh." Not even the ants would try them! The chocolate bunny that would be dismembered ears first, jelly beans (save the blacks for daddy), and my personal fav — the robin eggs (malted milk balls covered in a brightly colored candy coating).

This was a tradition that Mylove and I joyfully carried into our marriage. And our ritual of tearing into the basket of sweetness with the same gusto we reserved for the Christmas Stocking is always a time to surprise each other. I had a huge repertoire to draw from, making a giant sugar egg diorama like I had made back in Mrs. Mormon's 4th grade class. Once for Mylove, I needed something "more special-er" than the cross & lilies we used back in 4th grade from the back of a "Paas" box. I inserted a cut-out from one of our favorite photos — a pic of our beloved Aria & Zuzu snapped one day as we were hiking on "Dirt Mulholland" — they were staring down at what would soon become our beloved house!

I've also bedazzled gold and silver painted eggs with rhinestones. But one year, I actually followed through on a lifetime goal — to make my own chocolate bunny for her. I sculpted a handsome fellow out of clay, then made a mold from dental alginate (it's sterile-ish) and melted two pounds of Perugina imported Italian dark chocolate. He was quite the snappy chap, sporting a straw hat made of a waffle cookie and holding a sprig of bougainvillea clipped from the backyard. I was so proud that I had not only followed through on a life goal, but had pulled this one off nicely. Mylove was blown away — so much so, that she wouldn't try a bite until our guests could see it at our Easter lunch. I was preparing said lunch an hour later when she came up to me and said, "Tell me you put the Chocolate Bunny up so Zuzu wouldn't…" It wasn't until she said, "Zuzu" that I saw that she had in her hands the sprig of bougainvillea … which could only mean….

That our next move was to call the Emergency Vet clinic. They tried to reassure us that, while the dog and chocolate legend is fatally true, most times it's not really that bad because in most cases the chocolate has nuts or fruit, or most cases the chocolate is milk chocolate, or most cases the chocolate is American chocolate with very little cacao, and, the capper, in most cases, the chocolate is a bite of bar — less than an ounce.

But as I've said many times, Zuzu was not most cases. Even in this, she was special. Mylove's bunny was 1 pound of 72% imported pure dark chocolate.

The voice on the other side asked if we'd like to bring her in or induce vomiting ourselves.

We opted for the turkey baster and a cup of hydrogen peroxide.

As I tell this story, I realize that this may the first time a cookbook also has the mention of induced vomiting in it. Again, I'm sorry.

The moral to this story is ... if at first you don't succeed ... I tried again two years later with an even better rendition of Peter Cottontail reclining with his hand behind his head like a Playgirl Centerfold across a homemade Carrot cake. Mylove took no chances and dove into eating her bunny immediately, before our lovable Labrador could!

But this year, I was going to make good on another goal. Mylove and I were happy to be hosting our dear friend Audie and her husband, Bill. We have many friends and supporters, but one of the finest is the Audie. She sold us both of the houses we have been fortunate to own and our current palace is down the street from her. But Audie isn't just realtor extraordinaire, she knows everyone — plumber, electrician, lawyer, baker, Indian Chief. If you need anything, (as we did in the middle of the night two days before Christmas!) Audie knows who to get it from, and you won't just be getting a referral. When you call any of her contacts they drop what they're doing to help you out. And more dearly, she is a Guardian Angel that is constantly watching over us, checking in on us and, one of her favorite things — bringing us clothes.

I'm not joking, half my wardrobe came from her.

And Audie is the consummate host herself, she loves holidays as much as we do (great minds...) so, she's usually busy when we're hosting a holiday party, she's missed them all. So, we are overjoyed to finally be able to share it with her.

We're also lucky that our amazing friend Melissa will be driving down from the Bay Area to spend the holiday with us. M'liss is the infamous friend Marcy & I both wrote about in our previous books, who said, when Marcy nervously pulled her aside to "come out" about me, saying, "I have something difficult to tell you — Scott's a woman," M'liss replied without missing a beat, "Oh thank God! I thought you were going to tell me, you were getting a divorce." We loves us, our M'liss and are over the moon that she's coming down to visit. Rounding out our table will be Macky my BIL, and Duncan, our incredible gardener, foodie, and fellow video professional.

So, I better get started. And by "started," I mean, it's Saturday and I've already made Donny's truffle recipe into a mocha ganache, shaped them into egg shapes and chilled them in the freezer. I really want to make my own Robin egg candy coating (like an M&M or Jordan Almond), but all the better blogs say I need a sugar panning machine or dragee attachment, so that may happen next year. But right now, I'm going to settle for plan B.

I melt white chocolate. I use bamboo skewers (giant toothpicks) to dip each egg into the white chocolate and shake off the excess for a delicate coat. I then take a large grapefruit and spear it with the back end of the stick to hold it. It looks like a fifties deco chandelier or a 3rd grade science fair exhibit of satellites surrounding a sun.

Then, using colored sugar crystals from the cake decorating section at the supermarket, I use a blow dryer to re-melt the top layer of the white chocolate so the sugar will stick. The colors are amazing! Next time I do this, I'll figure a way to mask off stripes or other geometric variations, but for now I settle with jewel encrusted gorgeousness.

Next, I'm going to melt 72% Belgian chocolate and dip the other half of the frozen truffle egg ganaches in it and decorate those with silver pearlescent cake decorating pen. I can get better designs, but they're not as colorful. Nice variety with the colored eggs. Back into the freezer with everyone being reminded that the freezer is off limits until tomorrow.

M'liss arrives and we eat leftover baked Ziti (my mom's good Friday classic!) then run off to see the Fifth Dimension in concert. My brother, Ronnie, has been the musical director and keyboard player with them for over thirty years. Florence La Rue is the only original member still performing, but wow, the whole show is incredible and M'liss, (herself a singer with The Young Americans in her youth) Mylove and I sing along with every song with heart and tears.

Mylove sings "My Girl." at the top of her lungs with her eyes searing through mine into my soul. It takes my breath away — I can't hear anything but her voice... and then she kisses me. I'm not exactly sure when or even if I ever came to.

After the show, I'm able to introduce Mylove and M'liss to Florence. She's an amazing and inspiring woman with whom I've been coaching in the writing of her book. She was gracious and excited to meet Mylove. And we all celebrate creativity, love, and friendship in the hallway outside her greenroom. Ronny catches up with us and Florence excuses herself to greet the fans lining up outside.

M'liss hasn't met Ronny (who you may remember from my first book taught me to never assume your best friend's reaction to your gender transition, and with whom I produced my first feature film, "the kiss"). Next are the boys in the band, Miles Robinson the drummer, and JD Collier the bass player. Miles has been with the band longer than Ronny, and these amazing men are Ronny's "go to" guys that I usually see at his home studio. I have seen them a number of times over the years, but only Miles has seen me looking this good (feminine presentation). I am brought into their hugs with gusto once the recognition software kicks in. And we're able to revel in a night of great music and more love.

It was on this high that we returned to the house. M'liss and I have eggs to color, while Mylove shouts directions from the couch. This is by design. I love surprising her with the finished product the next morning.

Before anyone knows it, it *is* the next morning and this Easter Bunny hops up the stairs before the others wake to put the finishing touches on their baskets — adding the truffle eggs and deploying them surreptitiously on the mantle. As the Easter bunny sneaks her way back into bed for one last snuggle, she hears... "Mylove?"

"Yes, Mylove"

"Don't be sad, I never had a chance to get anything for you."

Now this is, I should know, part of her game. She sets me up every time. One year that she "didn't have time to get anything," I got a pink purse for an Easter basket. Amazing. Another year, it was Sephora lip gloss. So yeah.

Only this year, there's something in her voice that makes me think this year, she means it. But I don't care, I'm about to unveil mocha truffle crystal jewels on her, nothing else matters. So, we ascend the stairs, put the kettle on for Fawkey, and wake M'liss. The truffle jewels are a huge hit.

I run for the shower and get my hair and makeup done. We've got guests coming and this Easter Bunny has much work ahead. As I start the juggling routine in the kitchen, Macky arrives with fresh OJ and, as I'm kissing him hello, while simultaneously building lunch I...

... almost missed my own Easter surprise. Mylove has managed to sneak a basket with Cadbury mini-eggs, a solid chocolate bunny and bag of Peet's fawkey in between us. Once again, she wins the prize for best holiday ninja.

The good news is that, I've been juggling between outdoor grill and the kitchen and it's time to sit. And in this flurry, I didn't notice until I went out to set the table that M'liss has been busy in the surprise department herself, fashioning the cloth napkins into Easter bunnies by rolling them diagonally and folding them in half. She secures them about four inches from the centerfold, creating the bunny's head, and arranges the rolled ends away to create ears. The piece de resistance is how she finds dainty dandelion blossoms for eyes and ties grass shoots into a figure 8 for the mouth adding more grass for whiskers. Only M'liss could be so spontaneously ninja creative — It makes my heart smile!

It's time for the egg hunt. Now, here's something that always gives me a tickle. No matter how old anyone is, we all drop into the hunt with the same glee. As I announce that it's almost time for lunch, but first you have to find your own egg, I pass out tiny pastel Easter baskets, and yes, I get a few "are you sh*tting me?" eye rolls, as Mylove and M'liss immediately start hunting. And it never fails. The "first-in" inspires all stodginess to evaporate, and then it's *game on.* After the last eggs are in their miniature baskets we all head out to the pergola.

The table awaiting us looks like Holly Hobbie and Lewis Carroll have made us a tea party. Thanks to Audie, we have a wonderful Easter table cloth that matches perfectly the pastel miniature baskets we all carry. At each place, M'liss's Easter bunny napkins preside over a Mad Hatter stack of dishes. I instruct everyone to place their miniature basket, with their egg inside, on the top of each tower and invite everyone to sit. A delightful giggliness percolates under my instruction for *Easter Egg Salad.*

I had been pondering this idea for years (decades really) and only five years ago pulled the trigger to start this tradition. I thought it curiouser and curiouser that we put so much effort into making, hiding and finding Easter eggs only to relegate them to school lunches the next day, cuz most of us go straight from chocolate goodies to leg of lamb without stopping in between. After pondering this for some time (to stay with the Alice metaphor), I came up with a deconstructed egg salad sandwich, using a stack of dishes, cups & saucers as you now see before you.

It works like this:

Picture before you, a stack of dishes that is:

    1. large dinner plate — what's on it is hidden by:
    2. an upside-down shallow soup dish, on top of which rests:
    3. a teacup, with its contents hidden by:
    4. a saucer, on which rests:
    5. the miniature Easter basket with the brightly colored Easter egg inside.

Taking a large knife in hand, you remove the egg and set the basket on the table.

On the saucer (that is now at the top of the stack once you've set the basket to the table), you peel and chop the egg into the desired size for egg salad.

Then: You remove the saucer revealing the contents in the tea cup — curried egg salad, *minus the egg.* Then you sweep the egg from the saucer and stir the egg into the curried salad mix of yogurt/mayonnaise, dijon, minced onion, pickle, celery, & yellow curry powder.

Then: You lift the tea cup and remove the upside-down soup dish to reveal: toasted bread brushed with seasoned olive oil, on which is a bed of arugula and heirloom tomatoes tossed in a balsamic vinaigrette. Spoon the egg salad onto the greens and you've got...

Easter Egg Salad!

This is a show stopper! It's playful and happy and ... sooooo good. It also sets the stage for a happy spring celebration with bright vibrant flavors, and gives everyone a chance to relive Easter childhood memories.

It's also gives me a chance to get the next stage of lunch onto the table, grilled halibut with chive butter, quinoa with toasted almonds, dried mango and caramelized onion, and English peas with tarragon and lemon. The hardest and most time consuming is the quinoa which steams happily in the oven while you're hunting for Easter eggs. The peas are flash sautéed in the wok with lemon and fresh tarragon. Everything here is quick, fresh and peak flavored.

But it's the conversation that sparkles most. The magic of the "Easter egg, Mad Hatter's stack" salad has done its trick — that, and the spring breeze and sunshine. Audie regales us with tales of her having been a mural painter in her younger days for some of Hollywood's biggest celebs. M'liss shares her days on Art Linkletter's House Party when she was four years old. It's a grand day!

So... how to make all this? Well, let's hop to it!

Admit it, you saw that comin'... *down the bunny trail...*

EASTER EGG SALAD

I'm actually not sure this would work with a standard hardboiled egg... I mean, you might get arrested or something... I'm kidding of course — but there is something magical about this that might only work on Easter Sunday when everyone is little more open to playing with their food.

1 hard boiled egg per person (and dyed, yo! It's Easter)	**DRESSING** (mix in a tea cup for each guest)
1/2 lb. arugula	**1 tsp. mayonnaise**
Ripe heirloom tomato (sliced thin)	**1 tsp. dijon**
EVOO	**Dash of curry powder**
Balsamic vinegar	**Dash of cinnamon** (come on, you knew I'd sneak one or the other in...)
Favorite herbs	**1/2 tsp. capers**
Salt to taste	**1 tsp. of minced onion**
Killer crusty/coarse bread (toasted)	**1 tsp. of minced celery & leaves**

Serve it like this:
put the toasted (and buttered) bread on a salad plate.

Toss the arugula with the olive oil/balsamic/herb/salt dressing and spoon a few leaves over each toast. Place thinly sliced heirloom tomato on top... *and cover it with a larger soup bowl.*

On top of that:
stack the tea cup with the dressing.

On top of that:
stack the Easter egg (in a miniature basket with grass)

Then...

invite everyone to peel their own egg
mix it into the dressing
then spoon it on top of the arugula & toast — enjoy!

(PS if you'd like to see this in action, go our website *www.zuzubean.com* for a demo video.)

GRILLED FISH WITH CHIVE BUTTER

We have a chive plant in a pot on our back deck. Of all the things we've grown — this little beauty is indestructible. It's such a trooper, that I hate to let its great efforts go to waste — so I invented chive Butter. (I think... I mean, I can't be the first girl to say, Hey, what if I harvested all that great flavor before it shrivels in the sun? So my claim may be a bit... overstated, but everyone I tell about this seems to be hearing it for the first time, so there you go...) This amazing stuff could make anything taste amazing, (toasted bread, pasta, rocks, sticks, dried leaves) but it's especially good for fish. You make it ahead of time and keep it in the fridge for any occasion — it keeps as long as regular butter does refrigerated, but mine never lasts longer than the next fish I grill. You make it in your blender and wrap it in foil (or I use the wrapper the butter came in, or parchment paper) and slice it chilled to let it melt onto the fish... YUM!

CHIVE BUTTER
1 pound of really good butter (softened)
1 large bunch fresh chives
Juice of 1 lemon
1 tsp. dijon
Dash salt
Dash of ground chipotle powder (to set off the flavors)

The night before (or days ahead... at least)
Throw everything except the butter into a blender and puree.

Mix in the butter and continue to whip until thoroughly blended.

Scrape the contents onto a piece of parchment paper or foil or the butter wrapper.

Wrap the parchment or foil around the butter — twisting the ends like a tootsie roll to make a tight compact roll. *Refrigerate* for at least an hour. This is killer on warm bread or fresh grilled fish — but you've been warned — it's too good to put down, so use in controlled doses.

GRILLED CHILEAN SEA BASS
Fresh filets (one for each guest)
1 tsp. salt
1 tsp. fresh ground black pepper
1 tsp. sugar

(my fav) it's rich, so with this full menu use ¼ lb. fillets for each person. These are best if you can let them rest at room temp for 30 minutes prior to grilling.

Fire up your grill
in a glass bowl
Mix together the s&p with the sugar and sprinkle on both sides of the filets, let rest for 1/2 hour.

Rinse the sugar/salt rub from the filets grill on a medium heat.

Turn according to your preference (we love ours rare, rare — practically sashimi)

Add a generous pat of your chive butter on the grilled first side.
Cook until the butter melts. Careful of the flare up when the butter drips onto your fire.

Remove and plate...

Serve it up!

QUINOA WITH ALMONDS, MANGO & ONION

Quinoa is a mysterious grain with a bad rap — conjuring up hipster beards and militant food allergies... but really, it's a great choice, especially on special occasions like this one. It's nutty, and the perfect counterpoint to fish, especially when fabulized with toasted onion, almonds and mango — seriously, how could you go wrong? I use organic chicken broth (I always keep it on hand) but you can use any broth you like. It's best to stay light as we're serving it with fish — and i find the chicken broth tends to give the grains a firm foundation in flavor, that will balance the sweet surprise of the mango. We're gonna bake the grain in a ceramic baking pot. Mine was made by my beloved Gerhard, but any stoneware/porcelain or glass "dutch oven" or casserole dish with a lid will do.

1/4 cup (dry) quinoa per person
Chicken broth (I use the old skool, "up to the first knuckle" method of measuring liquid to grain that many people use for rice)
1 large ripe mango (cubed)
1/2 lb. toasted almonds (chopped)

1 large brown onion (minced)
1 clove garlic (pressed)
1/4 cup fresh basil leaves
1 tsp. fresh oregano leaves

Preheat your oven to 350 degrees

In hot, dry, cast iron skillet
Toast your onion until caramelized... remove from the pan and toss in the almonds, toast until crispy.

In a saucepan
Boil your chicken broth with the garlic clove. Then toss in the quinoa and stir for five minutes.

In an oven-proof, ceramic lidded "hot pot"
Add the mango, onion, almonds, basil. Pour the quinoa/chicken broth in over the other ingredients, put the lid on.

Bake in the oven for 35 minutes.

Serve right from your hot pot.

ENGLISH PEAS WITH TARRAGON AND LEMON

This one is as easy as it sounds. Because the simplicity is the freshness of beautiful spring vegetables. And tarragon's unique almost licorishy character loves to waltz with the bright sunshine of lemon. The trick is to get everything hot without overcooking them. I use a blazing dry wok that I'll toss the wet peas into — then close the lid, shut-off the heat ... count to 10, then dump into a waiting olive oil, tarragon and lemon "bath." Stir vigorously and faster than you can say VO-EEEEE-LA, you've got spring in a bowl.

1 lb. of English peas (shucked & washed)
1 lemon (zested & juiced)
1/2 cup fresh tarragon leaves (chopped)
1 tbsp. olive oil
Pinch of Kosher salt

Can you believe I actually started to type directions… if you need a refresher look at the above paragraph. VO-EEEEE-LA!

EASTER EGG TRUFFLES

You've heard me wax poetic about Donny's magical truffles — these aren't so much complicated as they are pure labors of love, and like all things worth it, you gets whats you put in or put out. Donny's recipe gets a Scottie sparkle here by happy accident. I wanted a candy coating shell (like an M&M or my Easter fav, Malted Robin's Eggs) but when that was a bust (there's a reason the dragee machines cost boo-koo bux — they work!) I had to improvise… luckily, I had a niggle that I might be biting off more than I could chew so I bought some colored sugared crystals — magick! I saved three days of work (and 3 lbs of imported Belgian chocolate!) and created incredible jewel encrusted Easter eggs that had the snap & crunch of a candy coating! So… if you really wanna blow minds, commit to this at least three days before showtime — a week is better — and read on!

THE GANACHE FILLING
2 cups heavy cream
1 1⁄2 cups dark chocolate (cut into small pieces or callets)
5 tbsp. salted butter (at room temp.)
1⁄4 cup liqueur or brandy of your choice (Donny likes Grand Marnier, I use brandy)

THE SHELL(S)
1 cup white chocolate (melted)
Various colors of cake decorating sugar crystals
Also, you will need
A large grapefruit
Several bamboo skewers (one step up from a toothpick in diameter)

Three days before, make your ganache.
In a saucepan:
Bring the cream to a boil. Put the dark chocolate pieces in glass bowl. Pour the boiling cream over the chocolate pieces and fold until the chocolate melts (resist drinking the concoction OR better still, have a back-up amount ready in case).

Fold in the soft butter.
Fold in the Liqueur. **Chill overnight in the freezer.**

Two days before:
Divide the ganache into individual eggs.
Line a baking tray that will fit in your freezer with parchment paper. Using a small spoon, scoop out the amount of chocolate you want to make your egg — the amount will determine the size of each egg — I went for the Malted Robin Egg size of my childhood. About a heaping teaspoon. Place each scoop on the tray and freeze overnight (see why we start three days early?)

One day before:
Shape the ganache into the shape you want.
Wet your hands and roll the scoops into the perfect egg for your truffles (which should tell us all how you see the world — HA! Are you a short and squat kind of

Easter Bunny or long and pear shaped?) Put them back on the parchment when you have the shapes you want and return to the freezer for another day.

The final day
Finish and decorate.

Get your materials ready — spread several squares of parchment paper in front of you (to catch the sugar crystals) take the bamboo skewers, the grapefruit and set them all in your work area. The name of the game here is chocolate's melting point (melts in your mouth not your hand refers to the candy coating which we ain't got yet). Chocolate melts at below 98.6 (our body temperature) so we have to work fast and in batches.

Make the shell — melt your white chocolate in small pan.

Take a few ganache eggs from the freezer and stick the bamboo skewer into one end and dip it into the white chocolate to coat — spin or tap the egg-cess off back into the pot and roll the egg into various sugars to decorate — be creative and experiment. I rolled some, sprinkled the sugar directly on some, poured it in stripes on some, variety is the key! Alternate colors etc. But truly some of the most spectacular were the ones I called the unicorns where the rainbow colors were mixed randomly — but you have to coat the entire egg before the white chocolate cools. IF they cool too quickly, you can have a blow dryer on standby to warm up the outer coating so the sugar crystals will stick.

Jab the empty side of the bamboo skewer into the grapefruit to hold your stick while the sugar sets.

When you are done with this batch, stick the whole bouquet into the freezer.

When you're ready to hide or serve these little jewels, gently roll the egg back and forth slightly to loosen the egg from the skewer and get ready to take a bow!

CHAPTER 9

YUCATAN CHICKEN

GRILLED POBLANO CHILE TAMALES

HEIRLOOM TOMATO SALAD WITH CILANTRO PESTO

ANNIVERSARY CAKE

(Glazed Passion Fruit pound cake with passionfruit curd)

"JUST PUSH"

There're usually two major holidays in April. Our anniversary and that other day ... oh, yeah, Easter. It was April 29ᵗʰ, 1989 that Mylove and I watched a friend smash a coconut as we stood before Rabbi Shelly Moss (tho' neither of us is Jewish) and our dearest family and friends, and pledged our love to each other forever.

This year, we're celebrating 29 years on a journey that neither of us could ever have predicted would take the turns it has! But we've gotten through every twist and turn, mountain and valley, with light, laughter & love.

But this is a year neither of us expected ... well, what was about to happen. On paper, it looks amazing — Our dear friends were coming up for the weekend, my Aunts were coming in from Europe, everything was lining up for a four-day celebration that would be three days of hoopla, then magically, the sacred fourth day (our actual anniversary) would be "just us" and we could celebrate it with the highest romance possible.

As I said, it looked great on paper....

First, we were going to get through our "new normal" of meeting an old and dear friend for the very first time.

And here's the dirty little secret about coming-out for those of us in the trans community ... it never stops. It can seem like "a thousand and one" coming-out parties in that, as much as it feels like we are always under scrutiny, always in the process of being "clocked" or "read" as women who were raised by wolves by the strangers we encounter, it seems that to those with whom we are close, we are forever explaining, or apologizing, or informing ... it can feel endless.

But in this "social-media age" coming-out has taken on a new twist. As most of our readers know, Mylove and I have been very visible between promoting our books, speaking at Universities and Corporations, and appearances on TV and Radio, it seems we've told everyone our story many times over. We post and blog and tweet (and whatever else is the lingo on the platform du jour) our comings and goings as a way to stay engaged with our audiences and readers — which includes most of our actual friends. So, it's odd and, I'll confess disorienting, at this stage of our journey to meet-up with a dear friend who "hasn't seen Scottie yet."

Yes, she's seen pictures, and she's quick to point out that she's been following our journey, but, she's yet to actually be with us in the flesh. And awkwardness ensues....

This was the case for our dear Sko. Sukoshi Rice is one of the most amazing women in our life and what's odd is that in the last ten years, though she's been a force of nature in our active daily conversations, emails and phone calls, we haven't seen her. Nor she, us. The real seen. Eye to eye, because you're in each other's embrace.

A couple of months ago, Sko asked if we would be available in April. She would be coming to town on her way to San Diego and would leave the day before our Anniversary. Our Aunts would be coming into town from Europe the day she was leaving so we could have an elegant hand off. We said, *sure*. We like to think our anniversary is a national holiday and here it was shaping up that we weren't alone in that belief.

And *that time* is finally here. Sko will be picked up by my B-I-L Macky (Brother-In-Law) who also drives for Uber, and we'll have the ever lovin' Sko in our house (finally) once again. And the bonus is that she's going on from here to visit our dear Cat in San Diego, so Cat will come up early and we'll all have that slumber party we've always joked about having, but that I have always dreamed would happen. Hey, I'm making up for lost time, and you may have had those teenage slumber parties before they became your alibi to really be with your boy or girl friends… but I did not.

Like I said, this all seemed great on paper — three months ago.

But I'm burying the lede here…

Mylove has been on a new chemo regimen since last October. The good news is that the side effects are very mild and she's responding well — so well, in fact, that life around the house doesn't really seem to revolve around her treatment and care. We have folded bi-monthly infusions and a slightly lesser energy level into our lives. Our diet was already very healthy, and her doctor visits "painless."

And the bad news? This ain't the lede.

We've been fighting the ghost of Christmas past — literally. We've still not been able to shake that week in the hospital and three weeks of self-injected intravenous antibiotics, thingy. You didn't really think I would go a whole chapter without breaking another cookbook rule, now did you? This whole shebang, we surmised, has taught her body that it can store fluid in Mylove's chest wall. This does two really messed-up things: decreases her lung capacity above while weighing down on her diaphragm — which seriously impedes her ability to breathe. And since February has required three drainings (thoracentesis, for those who like terminology) of two liters of fluid at a time.

But, that still ain't the lede.

No, the lede is this: My B-I-L Macky is having to play Uber driver for Sko because...

... we are at the hospital.

Mylove has just had a catheter inserted into her chest wall. I will play Nurse Nancy and drain it for her, every other day to give her relief, and hopefully get her back to her "normal" (whatever that was) routine.

I think we both are either completely delusional or overly optimistic, but neither of us felt the need to put a stop to the love train that is thundering down the tracks with our name on it. I have learned through our cancer experience to follow Mylove's lead and support her in whichever ways she turns. It's her body and she knows it better than anyone, amazing even her doctors, and if she says, "party on, Wayne," then, party on, we do.

So, luckily, I have been preparing for this.

Sko is a great cook who's spent time in a Belizean Commune (her sons Rasta & Pablo were born there), and she's a great improviser. But she's also from Georgia, and I'm sure spice is not something that she gets, unless she's in her own kitchen.

I should take a moment and redress something that I never did at the start of this book, and get to a single tool that has changed my cooking completely... *sous vide.* I should probably do a whole chapter on this amazing device, but let's, for the sake of brevity (HA!), boil it down (see what I did there?) to this: Sous vide, plain and simple, is a cooking technique in which ingredients in a plastic bag are immersed into a pot of water and heated at the perfect temperature for the perfect amount of time to achieve the perfect texture.

I use it for making the most amazing chicken thighs (Mylove won't even order chicken in a restaurant anymore — says I've spoiled her) to perfect ramen worthy soft-boiled eggs.

And with this magical device (which was a gift actually *for* Mylove from our dear Donny — he too, wants the best for Mylove), I've discovered the eighth wonder of the world...

Passionfruit curd.

Hear me out. Curd is the lamest name for this creamy, puckery spoonful of sunshine. It's like lemon curd, only a thousand times better. If our marriage had a flavor it would be passionfruit curd. Now, *you* can spread it on crumpets, toast, each other, but I had to invent a platform worthy of this glorious concoction (other than Mylove) and I'm making it for Sko and Cat, in honor of Mylove.

Oh, I tried a few things like shortbread, which made a lemon bar-like confection that was pretty amazing, but still didn't quite cut it.

And you are hearing it here *second* because I posted this on FB as soon as it was done. I am just about to invent *Anniversary Cake*. I say *about to* because, like everything else in our amazing dynamic, constantly evolving, marriage, I just haven't done it … yet.

But here's my thinking: I'm going to base it on the classic iced lemon pound cake but everywhere I'm supposed to use lemon, I'm going to insert passionfruit. I'll use a one-to-one substitution in both the pound cake and the icing (traditionally made with lemon juice and powdered sugar), and I will spread the glorious curd between two layers of cake. When it comes down to it, I just can't imagine anything that could possible compliment passionfruit, except for *more passionfruit!*

Even so, I will garnish it with fresh blackberries, just cuz. I need something to add contrast and finesse without taking away from the pucker of pure sunshine. And… have you seen a passionfruit? Not quite what we're looking for in the looks category. They have a face for radio.

Where was I? Yup. The curd I made last weekend, and the rest, I'm planning on making tomorrow morning. But that's just for dessert.

Sko arrives and we'll have a few hours to hug her and let her settle before Cat arrives. And this is where we start to realize … Sko hasn't seen "me."

It's odd because she knows "everything," knows what's been happening, knows about the process both Mylove and I have been going through, knows the ups and downs, and even the sidewayses, both through our writings and chatting with all of our mutual friends. She's read our books, even given them to a few friends and acquaintances in Georgia, so what's there to talk about?

She confesses that she has some questions, but doesn't want to impose, and I, being the shy wallflower who never has anything to say (right!) give her our standard line, "Ask me anything, you're family."

And she asks, "So, how is *it?*"

Now, in these situations, especially when its family and more importantly, someone I really respect and love, I try to give as thorough an answer as humanly possible, and I'm sure you can imagine it might be well more than anyone bargained for. Sko might, as Mylove often says, *"not want to know that much about it!"*

In this case, especially since I have a chance to help dispel fears and worries about us and do a solid for both my family and friends and the community, I can get off into the weeds pretty quickly.

Which happened.

And I'm sure even Sko forgot what she even asked as Cat arrived and we hugged and hugged and drank tea and caught-up. It's during these times that I remember that sometimes, I'm trying to forget that I was raised by wolves.

This is "girl talk." This is sisterhood. This is the time when I'm trying so hard to not pinch myself with immense gratitude that I transitioned, *while* at the same time, I'm also trying to not miss a second of any of this, *all while* being painfully aware that this is all going on in my head *as* I'm supposed to be 100 percent involved in being involved, and not self-aware that I'm self-aware... and... UGH!

This is where I have to confess that I'm still dumping files in the trash cans of my mind and setting them on fire — a daily clearing space from the socialization cache that was retrofit onto my operating system. But it's painful to admit to myself that it is even there in the first place, and the decades of ache and longing to be *here* to be accepted into the sisterhood, to be "just one of the girls," have worn grooves in my psyche and they make it far too easy for my thoughts and reactions to drop into those all too familiar neuropathways ... instead of just fucking being here.

Now, to be crystal clear, none of this is based on my reading any reactions from these three incredible women. They are gentle and caring "big sisters." Even Mylove knows when to guide and when to step aside and let me bump my own nose. And they all are doing great "just being here." No, sadly this is all me. All my own mind.

Because I am missing this. I am missing that which I have always dreamed about because I can't stop freakin' *realizing* I'm here, as I'm trying to *be* here!

I'm happy to say, I eventually calmed down, and we drank tea and Sko even played guitar and sang. We stayed up till the wee hours (which as we all get older, ain't nothing wee about 'em the next morning!). We solved our families' and friends' issues, digging in and sliding over years of never really being apart despite geography.

But the next morning, I felt like I had had a foxtail in my shoe — a little annoying poke that something isn't settled, wasn't right ... something's not ... done. I realized that I had skipped right over Sko's question. In an effort to give her a complete answer, I had not answered her question at all. She really wants to know *how* I *am*. She genuinely wants to make sure I'm doing better than okay, that Mylove is doing okay, that we are both okay. Like any big sister would.

I sit down next to her and ask if we can pick-up where we left off. I've got a day in the kitchen to get to, but making sure Sko's good, that her question got answered is my first priority (okay second, right after making sure our pre-anniversary dinner is on track). She hugs me. And I realize I've overshot my mark — I've put both of us on the spot before our first cup of fawkey. Nobody can, or should be expected to get that heavy without caffeination. My bad. So, I brew it up and we prepare to open up our hearts.

Sko tries to get in the spirit and rally-up her question, but before she can pull it together, we are both distracted by the need for more coffee and a little breakfast and, before I know it, it's time to make a cake.

This is, as I described, a bit of gamble, so I need to "go all in." I've been using white flour substitutes for sweets for Mylove and in this case, coconut and almond flours just seem to be a better move than white flour. I'm thinking the denser, moister flour will better complement the curd. But… will it be too heavy? I'm out on limb here.

I love being able to stay in the conversation while I serve-up nourishment and create tonight's extravaganza. Our kitchen is open to the living room and Mylove is holding court from the lounger as I mix and grind and spread and make … magic.

Sko comes from the south, and every time she comes, she brings us grits, which I love (tho' it's usually too bland for me when I order it on the road so I usually order a side of grilled onions and jalapeños to make it you know, *edible*). But today, I'm gonna serve up the Southern Cali version of grits, namely *tamales*.

Hang with me here. I'm very proud of our Latin roots in La Ciudad de Los Angeles, and to me if you're gonna take the time to grind corn into meal, why laze out and merely boil it with butter when, with just a touch more effort, you can have… manna. Or should I say *maña?* It doesn't even take a certain *knack.*(See what I did there?)

I like to boil the masa in a hearty vegetable broth and add fresh corn kernels, a lil chopped, caramelized onion, and a touch of sage before steaming these babies in traditional corn husks. In the past, I have stuffed them with almost everything, but tonight, I'm using roasted poblano chilies (roasted on my grill), and a creamy Havarti. Yes, it's straight-up Shi-shi blanquita gringa LA appropriation, so sue me. I'll finish these with a roasted tomatillo salsa, Olé!

As we sit down to dinner, the conversation naturally turns to our anniversary. Both of these amazing women have been stewards of our love — always supportive, always there when we need them. And to be able to celebrate this with them is incredibly special. You know how, with your best friends, time and space simply cease to exist? If you share past events with them, they can put themselves there without any effort at all and catching up with each other is like rolling down a grass-covered hill on a summer night — exciting, sometimes dizzying. And you can't imagine going through these experiences without each other. Absolutely delicious.

As we pass bowls and platters around, we are physically nourishing each other with pure sisterhood. And dessert time almost snuck up on me. But I got the anniversary cake out of the fridge before I took out the salad, so it will be the perfect temp. I want the cake moist and room temp. The tea kettle is whistling, so we adjourn to the living room for our sugar fix.

Both Cat and Sko are fans of both of our first books, and stay very connected to many of the themes and questions I posed in GBTM. For example: Mylove and I are still figuring things out, even after these years — like if we like sharing lipsticks (I do, she hates it until I get a color she wants), and which night cream is best. Oh, and what to call each other. We may have settled on "My Honey" as a reference, but we still aren't sure about the third person use of *spouse*. And both Cat and Sko wanna know if we are any closer to an answer.

Mylove starts to giggle — and I know why.

Last summer we attended a dear friend's very Indian wedding. After five formal events where a sari was required (I was in bliss and silk), the last event was a formal black-tie and evening gown reception. This was a place where friends who had known Mylove and me and our legendary marriage might in many cases be hearing or experiencing the transition I/we, and of course, our marriage, had enjoyed for the very first time. The short answer is there were very few hiccups, most, were, okay maybe *very* surprised (some might say *shocked*, in some cases), but they merely took a breath and steered into the skid, and all came out into the straightaway with us, celebrating our love and resiliency and brilliance…

But the bride's parents' experience was the most sitcom-esque of them all.

Now, Mylove and the Bride's father had been friends for years, while I am usually the one late to each conversation they're usually engaged in, and I get a smile and handshake but little more than that. I am, and have been, however, the high-profile side of Mylove's side of the conversation and usually she finds herself having to answer the question, *"and what crazy part of the world has your husband narrowly escaped from this time?"*

It wasn't different this time as we attended the first of the weeks' worth of esoteric Indian ceremonies (this one was a puja or offering to the Gods & Goddesses for their blessings on the whole shebang). I had stepped away to get Mylove a cup of chai and returned to find her with the bride's father engaged in the above dialogue. When Mylove answered his query by pointing to me and saying, "well, why don't you ask *her?*" he merely stared with a confused look at this (I'd like to think) beautiful redhead dressed in a fantastic sari with a polite smile as if to say, "why would this woman know more about where your husband had been, than you?"

Or at least that's what I hoped he thought. Rather than, "Shit man, why are you dressed like a woman?" But whatever he thought, he nodded and looked back to Mylove and smiled and was quickly pulled away by distant cousins who had arrived from India and needed tending. Mylove and I smiled to each other (as I said, you never stop coming out, ever) and went on enjoying the rest of the event.

As we were saying goodbye to the bride and getting directions to the next event in a few days, she apologized for her father's behavior, saying, *"I never got a chance to tell them about you. But they're conservative middle-aged Indians. They mean well, but some of this is a little ... much for them, I hope you don't feel uncomfortable and you are most welcome, and I'm sure the next time they see you, it will be different."*

I was... embarrassed. That we had caused any ripple in the bride's universe and celebration was to me, mortifying. We apologized profusely, which only made matters worse, because now she's apologizing again, and that makes us apologize again, and, and, and....

Geezus, Mary and Vishnu, what a ... buncha blech. By now, Mylove and I should be getting better at shaking stuff off, but we love the bride dearly and it's not our place to even be a sideshow at her event. Finally, we all laugh and reassure ourselves that all is well. Or will be.

And indeed, it was. The next time I see the bride's father, he gives me a fatherly kiss on the cheek and welcomes me. And, to cap it all off. Lest, I wonder if he really "gets *it* and me," when we come to the black-tie reception, there are table cards that let each guest know what table to sit at for a formal sit-down dinner. I saw one that reads, "Mrs. Scottie Madden." I burst into tears. It's an amazing night, and after a week of five saris, Mylove and I are finally driving home and as I wistfully repeat aloud the words that made my whole year, *"Mrs. Scottie Madden,"* I hear Mylove gently clear her throat.

"Well, *actually*..." she says, trying not to trample the newly blossoming flowers in my heart's garden, "technically, *I'm* Mrs. Scottie Madden."

Her words are like a thunderclap — the calm silence of bliss and exhaustion pierced by the lightning bolt of clarity ... of course, she's right. "Oh, my Gawd, that's so... true."

As I turn the implications over in my head I suddenly realize, "And that makes me, Mrs. *Marcy* Madden, that's... FREAKING AMAZING!"

Now, I have said before that Cat's cackle can shatter glass, but this time, she rocks the house, almost shooting anniversary cake out her nose. It takes us another few hours of girl chat and slumber party silliness to calm down.

But eventually, sometime after midnight, we all trundle off to bed which for Mylove means our double lounger chair which allows her to recline enough to sleep (sleeping in our bed irritates her lungs and her brand-new catheter). Sadly, I cannot sleep in the lounge with her (I've tried many nights). It's too cramped for my larger frame. Ah middle age, so much fun! And this temporary situation makes her trials all the more exhausting as we both use cuddles to recharge.

So, to get sleep, we forge ahead, but it really won't matter in the end, cuz in about an hour and a half... Mylove wakes me up. She's in incredible pain in her back which was tweaked during the procedure. She's also running a fever — 102.

Any of you out there who have danced with chemo know this is the ALLSTOP line. The warning track before you smash into the wall. So, I jump up. We're off to the emergency room.

Unfortunately, it takes three doctors and eight hours before we can get them to realize that the back pain is *the* priority symptom (we have had our share of know-it-all doctors) and finally, a handsome doctor tries listening to us. Yes, it took me spelling it out, "IT'S HER BACK!" which finally turned things around. They switched up their strategy giving her pain meds which made her relax, and they realized that it was her reactions to the "Twilight" drugs they used during her procedure that had slowed down her whole system. The pain was the best indicator that her body was still in shock from her catheter surgery and also that nothing was, well, "moving." Which only made her back hurt more.

She was admitted to the hospital and spent the next day with pain pills and laxatives and God knows what else. She would stay for another night. The following day would be our anniversary and we were really hoping not to celebrate it in a room with a view.

Sko and Cat came to visit and Sko brought Mylove's guitar. No one seemed to mind when we sang together into the night until we all needed to sleep, once again. My Aunts came in from their European cruise, each with a terrible flu. Apparently, the whole ship went down (okay, bad description, but you know what I mean). So, we had to settle for discretion and valor and the better part and all that... and phone hugs. We would see them when we were all healthy enough to be around each other.

That night, Mylove insisted that I not stay there with her at the hospital, but sleep in our own bed, so I went home to finally shower and sleep. Cat, Sko and I returned the next morning with guitar in tow. We sang love songs and massaged Mylove's feet and waited for her tests to be analyzed. This was the day of our anniversary and everyone had planned by now, to be out of our hair, so we could celebrate. Cat and Sko stood to leave and, as Sko and I hugged, I realized in all of the drama that I still hadn't answered her question about how I was doing — the real answer, the one a big sister wants for reals from her little sister, the one that will let everyone breathe and move on.

But as we both pondered this dilemma, we realized...

... we had the answer. She had just spent three days in our new normal and saw that, despite the chaos, Mylove and I were still us, Still a couple, still blissfully in love.

"*It*" was great. "*It*" was better than great. "*It*" was better than imagined. So, good in fact, that "*It*" wasn't even an issue anymore. "*It*" was academic. "*It*" was the center of our lives and yet, "*It*" wasn't a big deal, really. And that was good enough for Sko

As these amazing women left, they got a bonus. Mylove's tests came back (all good) and we could...

... get on with our anniversary!

We decided how to celebrate on the spur of the moment, just like we had done most everything in our life together. We could split a pasta and salad at the same restaurant we had talked our way into (well after closing) on a late Saturday night, 29 years ago. On that night, we went to the Il Fornaio in Del Mar, California, near the Inn where we spent our wedding night. So, this year we went to the Il Fornaio in our hometown of Woodland Hills. But this time around, it was Mylove who stepped up to the maître d' and asked him for a table for her and her wife to celebrate their 29th wedding anniversary. She went on to explain as we were led to our table why we chose his restaurant.

I just walked in shocked bliss. Her words seemed to echo off the walls and permeate the crisp white table linens. Her *wife... Her* wife.

I couldn't even tell you what we ate. Let's cook.

SLOW GRILLED YUCATAN CHICKEN

Brined overnight and then glazed with a reduction of the brine, this grilled chicken is best when using a very slow grilling time, so make sure you have enough time to let everything come together.

3 lbs. fresh chicken thighs	1 jalapeno
1/2 gallon fresh squeezed orange juice	2 pasilla chiles
1/4 cup kosher salt	1 large onion
6 cups water	1 head of garlic (peeled smashed with a flat edge of knife to release their juices)
1 half brick (2 and a half tsp.) achiote (this seasoning mixture is sold in bricks and can be found in Latinx grocery stores)	Fresh oregano
	Fresh marjoram

In a large mixing bowl
Whisk all of the above ingredients except the chicken.

Rinse the chicken well and submerge
in the brine for at least 12 hours but 24 is better.

Light your grill in the INDIRECT method
(ie. the heat is not directly under the meat — but rather creates a convection cooking environment. Add fragrant wood chips if using a gas grill, you'll want the wood smoke...

Cook the chicken for at least 2 hours (low and slow!)

Make your glaze
We made this brine lighter in its salt to liquid ratio so we can use the brine as a base for the glaze — Reduce the brine by cooking at very high heat until the liquid cooks down and the brine becomes a thick orangey glaze) — if it reduces in volume too much you can add water and an apple to thicken and sweeten.

During the first hour of the grilling time, (because of the brining process) the chicken's moisture is maintained. But during the second hour...

Generously baste the chicken with the glaze
I call this sending the skin to "the burn ward." Allow the skin to caramelize, and as it starts to crisp up, brush the skin with the glaze (sometimes I literally take the pieces off the grill and toss them in the glaze and return them to the fire - it's messy AF, but... it's effective) the goal here, is to to create a perfect crispy crust and moist meat. When they are done to your taste, plate 'em & serve 'em!
Enjoy!

GRILLED GREEN CHILE TAMALES

I'm a sucker for anything steamed in corn husks! These take some time to set before steaming — best made the night before, if you have the time, but if you're rushed they can go right into the steamer. After steaming, we set them on the grill for 10 minutes before serving — this last little embrace by the grill adds that perfect spark of flavor.

4 cups grits or Masa

1 cup of corn chips (pureed into meal — 'member that bag of crumbs I told you to stick in the freezer? Go get it!)

1 cup fresh corn kernels (2 ears — cut the kernels from the cob)

1 large red bell pepper

1 red onion (sliced)

2 cloves garlic

1/4 cup olive oil

1 quart chicken or vegetable broth

4 large poblano chiles roasted

1/4 lb. cotija cheese or other dry cheese

corn husks

Is your grill going for the Yucatan Chicken? Lucky you. Use it or you can preheat your oven to 400 degrees

Get a small (1 quart) sauce pan & a large pot (1 gallon) of water boiling

Rinse, dry, then brush the onion, garlic, red pepper, corn and poblano chiles with olive oil and place on your grill (or a baking sheet in the oven) cook until the skin of the chiles begin to 'separate" when you pinch the skin away from the flesh.

In the small sauce pan of boiling water
Pour the grits or masa in and stir — bring back to a bubbling boil for 5 minutes, cover and shut off the heat.

Get the chicken or vegetable broth boiling.

Get a tea kettle of filtered water boiling
Our tap water taste horrible — so we have filtered water. We'll use this to rinse and soften the corn husks.

Remove the vegetables from the grill or oven
Cover the chiles to let them sweat. Dice the onions, red pepper and the garlic and set aside. Peel the skin from the chiles and tear or cut into strips.

In a mixing bowl
Mix the roasted corn kernels, the corn chip meal and the cooked masa or grits. Stir in a 1/4 cup EVOO. Then pour the chicken broth in slowly to make the dough.

Rinse your corn husks in the boiling water

Make your Tamales

Spread a husk flat and put a spoonful of the masa mixture — flatten with your hand or the back of the spoon. Lay a few strips of the chiles on the masa, add the onion, red pepper & garlic and crumble some cotija cheese. Spoon more masa on top and seal the vegetables and cheese inside. Wrap the husk around to seal the tamale in good and tight. Wrap another rinsed husk around that and tear a thin strip from another husk to use to tie the tamale closed. Repeat this process until you've used up your masa.

Put these in your large pot
and steam on high for thirty minutes or more.

I like to put these on the grill for at least ten minutes prior to serving just to add that last bit of smokiness.

You can top them with salsa but they're so moist you don't need a sauce.

Serve & enjoy!

HEIRLOOM TOMATO SALAD WITH CILANTRO PESTO

And here's another thing about Mylove... (I love starting sentences that way!) As I've said a few times — She likes her things... dark meat is all there is (never eats white meat) fruit & ice cream don't really go together (except for black raspberry ice cream) — chocolate and fruit never goes together (except those dark chocolate oranges that you smash on a hard surface to break it into "sections") milk chocolate isn't really chocolate (unless it's in your cocoa), banana (anything) other'n bananas on cold cereal is a crime against humanity (including dark chocolate dipped frozen bananas?) — thems the rules. I don't make 'em — I just know that these are, in fact, written in stone. Like cilantro.

Aha, you knew I'd eventually get there, thank you. I love pesto — basil pesto and all other variations. I am a poly-pesto-amorous. But not Mylove — she's monogamously monogamous in the fresh herb sauce department. BUT — this dish represents a ray of daylight in her walls of exclusion. I started making cilantro pesto one day when I left the bunch of fresh new basil at the check-out stand one day and had to "improvise." (It's not really improvising but you get the drift.) Mylove fell head over heels for the bright fresh bold flavor and it knocked tradish basil pesto right out of the relationship!

3 large ripe heirloom tomatoes (diced)	**1 orange** (juiced)
1/4 red onion (slivered)	**1/4 cup toasted walnuts**
1 bunch cilantro (rinsed)	**1/4 cup parmesan cheese**
3 cloves garlic (peeled)	
1/4 cup EVOO	

In a blender or food processor
Put the cilantro (including the stems), garlic, EVOO & juice of an orange. Puree into a mad delicious smelling paste.

Add the walnuts
Add the cheese
Blend until smooth

In a medium glass mixing bowl

Toss the tomatoes and onion to release the juices and coat. Add the pesto and toss some more.

Refrigerate for at least 30 minutes — tossing once or twice to get everything to meld.

Enjoy!

ANNIVERSARY CAKE

This is my invention of the year... the sous vide makes the passionfruit curd waaaaay too easy, and I could eat it by the metric ton. But I don't eat a lot of bread, so I needed another vehicle (other than my finger) to get it to my mouth — so, I let me eat cake! It's a very simple thing really, but made elegant and otherworldly by combining with other simple ingredients, it's like lace on a wedding dress — separate it's just frilly, holey cloth, but over a satin sheath it's the stuff of which dreams are made...

I make this cake in two bundt pans to make a bottom and top layer with curd spread between the layers — this makes an elegant, festive "shape" of the cake. I divide the batter between the two pans.

THE CURD
½ cup passion fruit puree
1 stick of butter
¾ cup organic sugar
8 egg yolks
1 tsp. lemon zest
1 tsp. salt
2 lbs. fresh black berries

THE GLAZE
2 Tbspn passion fruit puree
3 Tbsn. owdered sugar

THE CAKE
1 cup Irish butter, softened, plus more for pan
1 ½ cup + 3 tbsp. sugar
1 cup passion fruit puree (get this delivered to your door from Amazon, what a country!)
½ cup milk
4 large eggs
1 cup coconut flour
1 cup almond flour
1 tsp. salt
1 tsp. baking soda
1 tsp. baking powder

Make your curd — at least 1 day before
Whisk all the ingredients together and pour into a high heat tolerant plastic bag in your sous vide

Cook at 167 degrees for one hour (if you don't have a sous vide you can cook this on your stove top — medium low heat for 30 minutes)

Pour the curd into a blender to emulsify
Run the blender on high for about thirty seconds.

Transfer to a jar and refrigerate overnight.

4 hours before you plan to serve the cake — Preheat the oven to 350 degrees
Butter 2–9 inch bundt pans.
Dust with sugar, and tap out excess; set aside.

In your standing mixer
Cream your sugar with the butter. Add the passion fruit puree, eggs and milk. Mix on medium.

In a separate bowl
Whisk together your dry ingredients. Add these to the standing mixer and mix on medium.

Pour batter into your prepared pans.

Bake until a cake tester comes out clean, about 35 minutes.
Cool on a rack for ten minutes. Then invert the pans and allow to cool for another 10 minutes of more.

Unmold the cake and cool some more.

When they are cool to the touch — Time to build us a cake!
spread the curd generously on the bottom layer — place the top layer on and prepare to glaze…

In a glass mixing bowl
Mix together the glaze: Stir 3 tablespoons sugar and 2 tablespoons passion fruit puree until smooth.

Pour the glaze onto the cake.

Garnish with fresh blackberries!

CHAPTER 10

· MOTHER'S DAY ·

PRESERVED MEYER LEMON APPETEASER

SUSHI SALAD WITH FRIED RICE BALLS & POKE

CURRIED COCONUT SOUP

VANILLA SWISS ALMOND BRÛLÉE

"... THEN WHAT DO MAYFLOWERS BRING?"

If I'm being honest with myself — I haven't exhaled since before Christmas. Mylove's health has got us both scrambling to stay buoyant — positive energy has always been our mightiest tool and our most powerful chemo. Keeping a positive outlook, for us is truly life or death.

So, when Mylove was finally able to come downstairs to sleep in our own bed — it meant so much more than a mere location change. Her breathing-thing (which is what we call it, because the doctors' explanation is even more vague, "Sympathetic, secondary response of the body with cancer") had, as I described last chapter, forced her to sleep in our lounger because lying flat in a bed was impossible. Until now. This giant leap for Mylove has us both breathing a little easier… We're still not ready to be running any marathons just yet, but we've got a reason to celebrate!

Usually during May, we have few days worthy of a party — May Day (I loved placing little baskets of flowers on my neighbor's porch in second grade… Dear Ms. Barton, she was such a cool teacher!) also, my sister KJ is a Taurean, (May 8th), and Mother's day (who doesn't love to throw down on a big brunch for those who give up their lives to have us?) — but this May, we're going to chillax a bit… circle the wagons, if you will and take things a day at a time.

The good news is that Mylove's appetite is starting to wake-up. So today, I'm going to make our own little dinner party. I do the cooking here, but you know how it goes — a "normal" supper is usually a one plate affair with the occasional side-salad. But rarely does Mylove want courses — she's perfectly happy with just some braised green beans, and out-and-out *ecstatic* with a bowl of "stupid pasta" (which is a pasta with olive oil garlic, avocado and cilantro). I'm not saying she would starve if she picked our menu — but I would go out of my mind. I usually compromise in the middle with something at least *interesting*, on a "normal night." Tonight, ain't our new normal…

… but we're both silently praying it is.

Cancer can be like that. When we first got the diagnosis, we both felt like we'd been pushed off a cliff and we had to learn how to fly before slamming into the ground. We had to quickly get over the idea of it being a death sentence — to confront the amorphous devil-beast that cancer is in our society, literature and "vox-populi." We had to dig in and understand that it wasn't this malignant Balrog outside or separate from Mylove, but rather her own cells, her own body. We couldn't hate it, because we weren't fighting an unknown supernatural menace (as our imaginations had trained us to see it) we were talking about *her* body. *Her* cells. *Her* life.

I say we, but I really mean she. Mylove is the one who is really dealing with this. She's the one who has to ride tall in the saddle when her very life is on the line. She's the one who has to confront her own mortality with every breath, *"what was that pain in my lower back? That wasn't there yesterday,"* *"Why is my vision blurry today, is this a side effect or a new symptom?"* She's also the one who has to administer her own treatments, from taking a shoe box full of pills and supplements every day, to self-injecting her antibiotics intravenously, to tending to "Junior," her name for her colostomy, to now having to attach the hose to her catheter that drains her lung cavity every other day. I have no freakin' idea how she does it. She is a real superhero — she's super*human*.

"Yes," she corrects me, "you do. You described the exact same superpower being transgender."

She has me there (and here and everywhere) — that is how I described the four decades of my life tamping down gender dysphoria with every breath — trying to contain a fire-breathing dragon of despair and destruction that threatened to devour me at any given moment. Maybe it's why I can see what she's going through? I never thought about it 'til now. Oddly, it's the other way around, vice reverse" as Mylove's mother would say — when family counselors try to describe what/how a transgender person is to their loved ones, they often say, *"it's like getting a cancer diagnosis — it's not their fault or choice — it just is."* I hated that from the moment I heard it. That's really messed-up to equate being transgender with a disease. I rejected it as a being a well-intentioned, yet freakin' misguided attempt to explain reality. Now, gender dysphoria? Well, not even that. Gender Dysporia is curable. It's a symptom not even a disease.

But we are, Mylove and I, realizing that we used the same superpower required to *deal* with our collective and now, after almost three decades of marriage, fused realties. So, in that, and that alone the example has a tiny bit of merit. But please, dear God, let's find another way to help our cis-gender family understand.

We take a moment to chew on that — helping the cis and straight world understand us has been the desired focus of our life in between doctor appointments and chemo. It's given Mylove a great sense of joy and purpose. Her book has been popular. We've given lectures and presentations, conducted workshops — she's been the driving force for our new found parallel-career.

I guess that's another reason why we're so "lit" tonight — last night we did a video interview/workshop with a classroom full of budding MFT's and LCSW's (marriage & family therapists, and licensed clinical social workers). We've done a few of these, where the students ask questions after reading our books and watching the videos of past presentations, and we're seeing that we can still do this even if Mylove isn't always up to travel.

Most of our friends have read our books, and they've heard us (Mylove and me) speak on our YouTube channel and website. But when we're here live and in the flesh, they seem to always ask the same questions we get everywhere, only expecting to hear a different answer, their answer. How'd we do it? How'd Mylove do it? She's always inspiring as she describes the "wasn't ever easy to lose your King," — which I personally love (not the King part — it still makes me a little queasy) but the "wasn't ever easy" part. I want people to see not so much how she did it, but that she did it. She confronted her deepest fears, and conquered them. She saw where she could be small, be less human. Be selfish. And went, "nuh uh, not on my watch." She listened to her heart and saw that love is... love.

Which I'm realizing is what she does with cancer. She confronts her deepest fears every day and will not allow them to run her life — despite all that she goes through every moment of every day, she remains upbeat, wise, happy, funny and... Mylove.

 And apparently hungry. I can hear both our stomachs, I realize I'm standing when I should be doing the poké. Which, BT-Dubs, should be on Mylove's eat every night list. She loves, loves, loves raw fish, but would never make it for herself. She says it's because I've spoiled her. She won't even order it when we're out — she says she doesn't love poke, she loves my poke. Just like she loves my chicken, and my pasta, and my... fill in the blank. Which I love. She is my greatest muse and my greatest joy — but seriously. I'm not home every night — somebody's gotta get that paycheck... as I've said, on those nights she'll probably eat a bowl of broccoli and be happy as a clam... or... sorry... back to fish.

My poké recipe is simple — soy sauce, rice wine vinegar, a dash of Asian fish sauce, a few drops of toasted sesame oil, scallions, grated fresh ginger and crushed garlic. I will toss in one avocado, cubed, and a quarter cup of fresh chopped cilantro. I toss a ½ pound of cubed sushi grade ahi into the sauce and put it into the reefer to chill.

Asian soups are rarely an all-day on the stove affair. It's one reason they are in my repertoire. Because its function here is to give a little bottom end to the dinner, I'm not going to add a buncha meat. Tonight, the star is the ahi, but if you wanted this soup as the main attraction, it's the perfect base for chicken (and/or shrimp). I take my trusty cast iron wok and get it slammin' hot, then toss in thinly sliced onion, more garlic, and matchstick cut zucchini, carrot and celery. I add some coconut oil to flash sauté, then de-glaze that with some sake. Once things mellow out, I stir in a can of coconut milk, 2 tablespoons of green curry powder, kaffir lime leaves, and the juice of a lime. I then add a cup of chicken broth. This will get served with fresh chopped basil leaves.

I plate the salad — arugula, daikon ribbons, sliced oranges, and classic seaweed salad tossed with ginger wasabi vinaigrette. A huge scoop of poké is placed in the center. Now, I fry the rice balls since they are way better hot and then hurry them onto the salad plates and send them to the table.

I bring the soup to… wait for it… the dining room!

Okay, I need to explain that — Sleeping in the lounger has also meant eating in the lounger — which meant eating in the living room — which meant eating in front of the TV. I… okay… *hate* that. Mylove, loves it. She uses the TV as her best tool to distract herself and recharge herself mentally to get through her day. And I get this. I don't say anything. But she knows how important the dining room is to me — I work hard to create a nice meal and I don't ever like adding in outrage or cheap laughs (She loves MSNBC and old sit-coms). And I'm just never comfortable leaning over my dish on the coffee table.

But we're here! In our dining room — which I painted myself when we first moved in. (The previous owner had had two huge white IKEA shelving units that she neglected to move when she painted the walls their current mint green — when I moved them out (they were hideous) she hadn't painted behind them! They left two, huge, janky off-white rectangles. It's now the pleasing mint green and decorated with Mylove's father's watercolors (he was a very good artist) and a vintage chandelier.

"You really went all in tonight," she says as she sees the full spread. "*appeteasers*, poké *and* soup?"

I just shrug. Can I help it, if I'm happy?

The candles are lit, the settings are out and we are sitting. Together. Celebrating light, laughter and our love.

Mylove and me.

And she still doesn't know I made her favorite dessert… *Crème Brule.*

Guess that's another one she'll stop ordering out…

Turn the page to see how all of this is done.

PRESERVED LEMON APPA-TEASER
(SUNSHINE ON A SLICE OF BREAD!)

One of the oft-overlooked aspects of marriage (or love for that matter) is the true "knowing" of another person — I'm not talking about the often celebrated "she really gets me" kinda stuff, but rather the everyday little things like this humble recipe. Mylove is the daytime TV watcher and she's forever saving up clips from her daily watching and she'll play a "greatest hits of the day" for me when I get home from wherever my travels took me that day... These clips will be everything from the cutest lab(rador) on the planet in a commercial for irritable bowel syndrome, "She's just like Zuzu!", a great zinger that someone gets in during a news report or this... or a recipe from talk show that she just knows I will truly dig. When I saw this one it blew me away and I studied it like a musician listening to a guitar riff on the radio to master it in her bedroom. The first time I made it we all agreed — it was "in the show." I have turned many friends on by bringing this as a hostess present and a cult is forming here in the San Fernando Valley...

1 tbsp. salt	Splash of white wine — or champagne vinegar
1⁄4 cup + 1 tbsp. EVOO	2 handfuls of baby arugula
5-6 meyers lemons (or any thin-skinned lemon) **make sure you capture the juice** (all is precious)	1⁄2 lb. provolone cheese
	1 loaf fresh good crusty bread (sliced or torn — I prefer torn if it's casual, but it if you're plating, then sliced — it looks prettier)
1 healthy sprig of fresh basil	
1 crushed clove of garlic	Fresh ground pepper

A few days before serving (I always keep a jar of these in the fridge)
In a glass 1 quart jar with a sealable lid (I use canning jars) thoroughly mix:
The salt, EVOO, wine, & garlic. Add the lemon slices. Add the basil sprig.

Cover the jar and set in a safe place for 2–3 days
(honestly, it's going to be amazing almost immediately BUT if you can wait, it's way better, if that's even possible.)

*Whenever you pass the jar, give it shake or roll to gently & thoroughly mix the magic that's inside.

When you can't stand it anymore, (or it's time for that party, finally):
In a medium non-stick skillet
warm a tablespoon of olive oil, then gently melt the provolone cheese until it's soft and gooey.

On a serving platter
Spread the arugula.
Drizzle the melted provolone (in strands) over the greens and then arrange the

lemons on top of the melted cheese.

Drizzle the reserved lemon oil and dust with fresh ground pepper

Serve with good crusty bread.
Stand back and don't let your fingers get too close — people tend to lose their minds around this stuff.

(ANOTHER COOL VARIATION IS BURRATA - JES' SAYIN...)

SUSHI SALAD
WITH FRIED RICE BALLS & POKE

This is a meal in itself — I first fell in love with Poke in Hawaii, where it's eaten as a staple — but with fresh raw sushi grade ahi tuna stirred with soy, garlic, rice vinegar and fresh ginger how could you possibly go wrong? It's usually served on a bowl of hot steaming rice — but for this salad version I've deconstructed it and we'll turn the rice into a garnish, rather than a foundation — with fried rice balls stuffed with wasabi and pickled ginger. We'll use fresh peppery greens to build on instead. I'm going to show you how to make the traditional pickled seaweed salad that no poke is complete without. (And a variation if you're inland, away from the fresh stuff) that adds the perfect textural counterpoint to the raw fish. The one thing that makes this perfect is a Japanese condiment called Gomasio, which you could make yourself (and many hard core macrobiotic peeps still do) but you've got enough on your plate and any healthy grocery store should have this sesame seed, dulce (ground dried seaweed) dry concoction that just seems to tie it all together.

1 lb. sushi grade raw & fresh ahi tuna (cubed)	1⁄4 red onion (sliced thin)
1 cup rice	2 garlic cloves (crushed)
Wasabi paste	Sesame seeds
Hiyashi Wakame (seaweed)	Pickled ginger
Fresh ginger	Rice vinegar
1⁄2 cup high smoking point oil (Peanut, Canola etc.)	Soy or tamari
	Ponzu
3 scallions	Fish sauce
1 avocado cubed	Toasted sesame oil
1 daikon radish (matchsticks)	Dijon mustard
3 tangerines (peeled and sectioned)	EVOO
1 cup of arugula leaves	

Make your rice — 1 cup.

I use my rice cooker, you can use your favorite method. While it's cooking, you can start the poke — the longer it marinates the better. But the fresh avocado has a short lifespan, so don't go more than a few hours.

Make the poke

In a glass bowl, whisk

The garlic, soy sauce, rice vinegar, ponzu, fish sauce, fresh ginger, and toasted sesame oil. Add the Ahi tuna (cubed), scallions and avocado.

Stir it all to coat and refrigerate until plating.

Now make your "pickled" seaweed salad. Hiyashi Wakame.

(I've also used fresh snow peas sliced thin if you can't find the seaweed.)

In a mixing bowl
Add 1 Tbsp. each of Rice vinegar, fresh ginger (are you seeing a trend here?) toasted sesame oil, toasted sesame seeds. Toss in the wakame and let marinate.

Make your bed of greens
In a mixing bowl
whisk a splash of olive oil, a splash of rice vinegar and a ¼ teaspoon of dijon mustard.

Add:
the daikon radish, tangerines, arugula & the red onion. Toss to coat.

Plate the greens on individual salad plates for each of your guests.
Spread a layer of seaweed salad, on each bed of greens.

Divide the poke into generous scoops onto each of the seaweed/greens beds.

In a cast iron skillet
pour enough of your favorite high smoking point oil — peanut, canola, etc. for deep frying. You will want the oil to be deep enough for the rice balls to be immersed halfway.

Wet your hands and...
form small (no bigger than 1 inch in diameter) balls of rice. Poke your finger into the center and stuff that hole with a slice of pickled ginger and a pinch of wasabi (the amount depends on how adventurous you and your guests are — some actually *enjoy* shooting wasabi out their nose, I'm not judging).

Fry these in the oil until they have a golden crust.

Dry them on a paper towel and let them cool.

Divide the rice balls among the plates.

Pass the Gomasio and serve with chopsticks!

CURRIED COCONUT SOUP

This is my homage to glorious Thai "Tom Kha___ (you could put whatever in this magic broth and it would be amazing.) We already have an intense menu, so here, simpler is better. (Did you ever imagine me saying that? Me neither!)

The key here is to have everything prepped — you're gonna work fast at high heat to preserve the crunch of the veggies.

---

1 can of coconut milk
½ cup chicken or vegetable broth
½ lb. crimini mushrooms (sliced)
¼ lb. snow peas
1 zucchini (sliced into matchsticks)
1 carrot (sliced into matchsticks)
1 stalk of celery (sliced thin)
½ large onion (sliced thin)
4 kaffir lime leaves
1 lime (juice)

¼ cup sake
2-4 tbsp. green curry powder
Fresh ginger (crush it with a tenderizing hammer so it will release the juice — but is a big enough chunk that you can find and discard before serving)
1 stalk of lemongrass (or 1 teaspoon if you don't have fresh) **chopped into chunks**
1 serrano or jalapeño chile
¼ cup fresh basil leaves

Get your wok hot. The key here is to have everything prepped — you're gonna work fast at high heat to preserve the crunch of the veggies.

Toss in generous Tbsp. of coconut oil. Toss in the vegetables to coat and stir fast — deglaze them with the sake.

Add the kaffir leaves, the ginger, chiles & lemon grass.
Add the chicken broth — keep it hot.
Add the lime juice.

In a mixing bowl
whisk the coconut milk with 2 tablespoons green curry powder. It's important to get it all dissolved here before it goes into the broth.

Stir the coconut milk/curry mixture into the hot broth.

Taste.
What does it need? More this? More that? This is where the dish becomes *you*. Are your guest fire breathers or soft mouths? Adjust accordingly.

If you're plating now — make sure you remove that ginger chunk. If your serving from the pot at the table, no biggie — just make sure you know where it is… (or went!)

Garnish with fresh basil.

VANILLA SWISS ALMOND BRÛLÉE

This is a bit of history in a ramekin — When we first started dating our favorite flavor of Ice Cream was Häagen Daz VSA (Vanilla Swiss Almond) But even more importantly…

Mylove loves, loves, LOVES Creme Brûlée. One year for her birthday, (despite her fondness for carrot cake) I made her Crème Brûlée for her "cake," which required the purchase of a chef's torch. And really, who could resist the cracking of the delicate "glass ceiling" hiding the goodness below? (Hmmm… an apt metaphor for today? Me? I would never?) I have also tried, with some success, the old skool method of using the broiler — with both of these methods, you have to be on your toes or you will torch the custard below. Most restaurant custards are ho-hum. But not this one — vanilla sugar, and dark chocolate covered almonds to the rescue!

NOTE: This one requires significant cooling time (at least 4 hours for the custard to set) so plan accordingly, maybe even the night before, so there's no "traffic jam" for your attention.

> 1 quart heavy cream
> 1 vanilla bean, split and scraped
> 1 cup vanilla sugar
> 6 large egg yolks
> 1 lb. dark-chocolate covered almonds
> (cut in halves)
> 2 quarts hot water

Preheat your oven to 325 degrees

In a saucepan
pour the cream, vanilla bean and its pulp and cook over medium-high heat to a boil. Remove from the heat, cover and allow to sit for 15 minutes. Remove the vanilla bean (toss it into your vanilla sugar jar.)

In a medium bowl
whisk together ½ cup vanilla sugar and the egg yolks until well blended and it just starts to lighten in color.

Add the boiled cream a little at a time, stirring continually.

Pour the liquid into 6 (7 to 8-ounce) ramekins.
Divide the chopped chocolate covered almonds among the ramekins.

Put the ramekins into a large cake pan or roasting pan.

Pour enough hot water into the pan to come halfway up the sides of the ramekins. Bake just until the crème brûlée is set, but still trembling in the center, approximately 40 to 45 minutes.

Take the ramekins out of the oven and let them cool.

Refrigerate for at least 3 hours and up to 3 days.

Remove the crème brûlée from the refrigerator at least 30 minutes prior to showtime.

Divide the remaining 1/2 cup vanilla sugar equally among the 6 dishes.

Spread it evenly on top. Using a torch, melt the sugar to form a crispy glass crust.

Allow the crème brûlée to sit for at least 5 minutes before serving.

CHAPTER 11

· BEGINNING OF SUMMER BACKYARD BBQ ·

PRA-SA-QUE CHICKEN

GRILLED FIGS WITH BLUE CHEESE, BASIL & JALAPEÑO

SWEET POTATO PIE

CUKES & UNS

BANANA PUDDING WITH 'NILLA WAFERS

"TIME HEALS ALL WOUNDS"

I haven't spoken to my baby sister, Shane in three years... My first call to come out to her went better than even Lib's legendary, "I'm always here," call. So, I was blindsided to hear from my Godmother who has regular visits with the elusive Shane that the reason she had been dodging my phone calls for over five months was that she "didn't buy that I had wrestled with being transgender my whole life."

We'll get into just how rejection by one's baby sister, can be a very special kind of suck, but... she *"didn't buy"* that I had wrestled with this my whole life?"

I couldn't figure out if she was having an issue accepting the time frame or me. Was she holding onto a technicality? Was she trying to say that in her experience I was "her happy big brother" all her life and if this was true it hadn't happened on her watch? The truth is, I have never known... I never let things like this go on unaddressed. I tried calling her for months at different times and days of the week — and the times I did get a human on the other line stopped after her hubby Bobby (who was never a good poker player) couldn't cover for her — we both knew she was standing right next to him, making him say she was "out" and could he take a message. When I said as such, I got, "ARE YOU CALLING ME A LIAR?" I replied as calmly as I could, having just been roared at, that, no, I was not calling him anything, but that we both knew the truth. The click of his hanging up on me, still rings in my ears...

The truth is, Shane and I are the most insane of the four of us when it comes to cooking. She even wrote her own cookbook — "Mommy Can I Have That?" which is actually a genius idea, taking classic recipes and modifying them for her son, who had had epilepsy through his childhood and needed to be on a Ketogenic Diet to support the powerful anti-seizure drugs that victims of this brain shocker need to get through a critical childhood phase. Those who do can live healthy normal adult lives. And Shane was amazing — helping her son navigate childhood classroom birthday parties and all the holidays when kids get to eat the things that we all associate with "normal childhood." Her son got his versions of these treats *and* he knew how much his mother loved him.

And really, of the four Madden girls, if Lib and I are the most alike as chill, laid-back, open-minded, free spirits, Shane and I are the most alike as the hardcore, hard-driving, disciplined strivers. Shane and I are the "S's" of the family (Our parents are the J's,

Lib (aka Kimm), and KJ are the K's) also in a further testament to my mother's sense of humor, she also made me Shane's Godparent.

So, yes. A dinner is needed to hash all of this out. She is going to see that whether or not it was my whole life, (srsly?) it most certainly is my present life. I am her big sister. I am a woman despite any of her beliefs. And like most of the things in our early life, once again, it's my role to introduce her to that which will open her mind, broaden her horizons and show her that she doesn't know everything.

But first, I'm going to show her that despite her initial reluctance, I have never stopped or even waned for a second in my love for her. I have been waiting patiently for today to hug her, love her, help her understand and of course, feed her.

To recognize her new Southern lifestyle — she's in Chapel, South Carolina... couldn't be further from her SoCali roots — I'm making a southern backyard picnic, with new traditions and our mother's famous cukes & uns.

First-up is grilled figs with flatbread & dippin' oil. This is one of my "go to" crowd pleasers, and since I've got a lot on the line, I'm going with the sure-fires. Cuz, heck yes, it's my baby sister, but for pete's sake, I haven't spoken to her in a year now, and from what my Godmother says, she's... hurt.

But Shane does this, she "does hurt," very well, and I have to remember that. When she's hurt, she lashes out. I must confess, I have taken this personally — not that she's rejected me, but that she even could. You see, I feel responsible. After our mother passed away, my father... well, he sorta lost his mind — certainly for a long time, his way. Okay, if I'm being real, he never really recovered from the loss.

But he was sooooo... I think, *terrified* of messing up "his girls" (now with my mother gone) that he panicked, and married the first woman he could find to help raise his daughters... and, well, frankly, he chuffed this one.

His second wife was a straight-up train wreck of a human, incapable of having an adult relationship with my father, let alone his teenage daughters, and my sisters ate her for breakfast, lunch, and dinner; taking out their grief and anger of losing their mother on her — and she was too emotionally immature to deal with it, playing right into their childish traps, weighed-down by her own insecurities.

It was a mess that I would deal with on weekends home from college, where I tried to pick-up the pieces, trying to be some kind of stable for both my sisters and my dad, while myself dealing with "dad's second wife's" outbursts.

Finally, after three years of chaos, Lib, (who was herself out of the house) and I moved KJ and Shane down to San Diego and we all four lived together — quite happily, I might add, and we healed, grew-up and... did it all in our Madden way. Which is why I am saying I'm responsible. I did bring her up better than that — I raised Shane to believe in herself, in being a woman, in being a Madden. She could do anything. She could, with hard work and sacrifice, be anything. Love was the answer. Family was the answer.

So, what the fuck happened? Where did I go wrong? How could she allow herself to foster hate and intolerance substituting these adopted southern "ways" for the tolerance, love and family-first values that she had been raised with?

I hoped to find out — and BBQ chicken can heal all wounds...

Actually Prasa-Que to be exact — this is my secret potion — a bbq sauce that I'd been perfecting for over five years of intense experimentation — I'm serious, I kept copious notes and tried different ratios of sugars to savory to spice to get the perfect lip-smackin' finger lickin' potion that would transform base lead into gold.

I call it Prasa-Que, because when Mylove and I first bought this house on Prasa Rd. it was the first time we really felt like we were going to live where we wanted to — not where we *had* to... It was the first time we were going to be "big kids" and have a real home, and we celebrated by getting a real bbq grill. I cooked almost every meal for a year on it, celebrating our good fortune. And I embarked on the quest to come up with my own bbq sauce that would belie the warmth, spiciness and sweetness of our life.

If this doesn't soften Shane's heart, nothing will.

I'm going to recognize and honor her adopted Southern life by making a sweet potato pie to serve with the chicken, and to freshen it up, I'm "going home" and making my mom's famous summertime staple — "Cukes & Uns." This is a seemingly bottomless barrel of pickled cucumber slices and red onion rings that was served at every meal from June first until Labor Day — my mom just kept replenishing the supply with fresh cucumber and onion rings to a brine that got better and better the more it aged. This should seal the deal.

Shane's hubby Bob (who is my same age) and I have never seen eye to eye. As a former Navy Sailor who took his training with nuclear arms into a civilian career, working first for San Onofre, then moved my sister, niece & nephews to the South to get a new nuclear facility on line. Bobby has always been defensive around me. I'm not sure if he was worried about doing right by my sister — in which case, good for him, or if he was feeling judged for being a conservative republican.

The fact is, I'm torn about Nuclear power. But I am disgusted that it can be thought of as a "conservative thing." We have to solve our power issues in this country — with global warming as our first consideration — but responsible use of our resources doesn't mean making decisions like we're not going to be around for their consequences.

And truly speaking, I'm a feminist, and a realist who knows my sister only too well: Bobby didn't "take her" anywhere. Shane is her own woman — tho' she's a bit skewed in some of her observations, she is nobody's property. So, as long as he's a good man and she is happy and treated right, I'm good.

As we sit down, we all sense that we're trying. Shane is still guarded, but she lives my Dad's axiom — the best defense is a hell of a good offense. And for Shane, this means that she's talking like we haven't skipped a beat — she starts with the subjects anyone would use — all safe subjects, weather, food, the kids and their studies.

We catch-up on all things. Shane is a truly amazing woman: when no one would step-up to coach my niece Judy's lacrosse team, Shane took the reins and taught herself the game at night. When Bobby's company had to go dark for some months — Shane got her real estate license and brought in the supplemental income until Bobby got back online. She's actually been keeping tabs on me through my Godmother and has been sending me prayers.

She's not sticky with her pronouns, but she's also not fully accepting either. I can feel her reservation, but I also feel that's she's trying. It's a start — baby (sister) steps as they say. Her "coolness" is offset by the warmth I get from my niece Judy — she's all in being with her Aunt Scottie Jeanette — when she says it, it has southern twang that is actually charming.

All of our grievances seem… to be a little less important. Family is more important. And food prepared with love has done its magic.

If I'm realistic — this is a great start — and as I serve the traditional "after BBQ' Southen' dessert: banana puddin' with 'nilla wafers, I'll take the "W"— because after all these years, and all that time of railing at the moon that I "brought her up better than that" I can see, that yes… maybe we did.

Yes. It would be good if all of the above was true.

Sadly, it's not. In the latest transgender survey, of the over 15,000 respondents — 40 percent report out and out rejection by their family, and an additional 20 percent report no support. Like Nuclear Power, being transgender for many in the world can be thought of as something that many "don't subscribe to," refusing to even accept our mere existence. I never, in my wildest dreams, thought anyone in my own family could ever "not accept me." This isn't merely disagreeing with me, this is erasing me. This isn't disagreeing with my opinion or philosophy or even beliefs, this is refusing to see me as me. It's an attempt to make me as I am, invisible. To forget the me that I am while I still live. To look past me or through me like I'm a ghost. Either a memory of the past or a fantasy of the present.

By someone in my own family.

I honestly have no words. The good news is that this dinner may happen one day. I pray for it every day. I could write Shane off as she has tried to do, me. But… I was brought up better than that.

AUTHORS NOTE:

The above chapter was the way this book was going to go to print. HOWEVER! My Godmother, my Aunt Phyll, passed away quite unexpectedly. Nobody saw it coming. It caught us all off guard. She was in the hospital complaining that her back hurt and the next thing we know she's got only days to live. Shane drove the 12 or so hours from South Carolina to Florida and stood beside my Godmother's life-long companion, my Aunt Mish, through the maelstrom of fear and chaos, and stood in for me, Lib and KJ. She did a magnificent job and Aunt Mish was grateful to have someone beside her to support and love her as she said goodbye to my Godmother (they were very close). At first, Aunt Mish, who was very aware of the riff between Shane and the rest of us, found herself trying to keep "two separate camps" up-to-date on the last days of my Godmother's life (with two of us on the west coast, one in the UK and Shane). This was embarrassingly painful to know that we were becoming a burden. Before this "riff" we were a united front — tell one of us, you've told all of us. We spoke to each other multiple times a day.

I was losing my mind — I was trying to figure out how to be in two places at once, to relieve my Aunt Mish of any of the burden that I could. As the next in line of this side of the family (behind my Godmother) I had duties and responsibilities. And really? What's important? My Aunt Mish couldn't (and let's be real shouldn't) have had to navigate the riff between Shane and the rest of us — ever, but especially at a time like this.

And my phone rang.

The caller ID blew my mind.

Shane.

She spoke non-stop for ten minutes — filling me in all the details about my Godmother and Aunt Mish. No time to book a plane ticket. My Godmother wasn't going to make it through the night. I would have to instead wait for details about… funeral services. My Godmother is catholic — very catholic (but don't worry — she loves her niece and Goddaughter (me) completely and totally) and they don't like to wait long to bury their deceased.

I let Shane finish. I was still stunned by the news of my Godmother and it wasn't lost on me that her predicament was the instrument of healing — she hated that we had the riff in the first place (having had one herself with her brother that was never resolved) my Godmother would always admonish me to "solve it" and would do anything she could've to get us back together — even this. I knew to go easy on Shane, here. I said to her how grateful and proud of her I was that she had stepped up and stepped in for all of us.

There was a pause... then Shane talked again for another ten minutes straight, telling me all the things I so longed to hear — how sorry she was for what we were going through with Mylove — how she was so sorry she wasn't there for us. How she missed me. How she was keeping tabs on us through FB and was proud of the work we were doing.

And just like that it was gone — the riff. The stupidity. The hurt. All gone.

At the funeral, it was like the four of us had never been apart. We fell back together as quickly as we had fallen apart. My Aunt Mish was so pleased that we were on our best behavior, that we had "put aside our differences for our Aunt Phyll." But the truth was bigger than that. The differences dissolved. The questions were of detail not acceptance. Shane wanted to know how I was, not why or if I was.

Lib said it best, "It" (the misunderstanding) went away because "it's" always do. "It" had never been based on anything. "It" wasn't real in the first place, so how could "it" survive?

That's why she's the wisest of the four of us.

So... Now, I can't wait to have that BBQ. This time for real.

Stay tuned for that — but in the meantime, turn the page...

PRA-SA-QUE CHICKEN

Okay, yes, I don't really do beef enough to coach anyone else — but I have a theory with BBQ restaurants. Their chicken is the true test of who and what they are. If an Oklahoma Roadhouse grill chuffs the chicken — they ain't worth anyone's time. It's like the "veggie plate" on menus that are there as a "compromise" that there are "those people" that come in with their "normal customers" — which shows they don't think thru the ball as cooks. And if they skimp here, where else are they skimping? So, if they smoke their chicken with care and give it every bit as much attention as it should be, you can bet their brisket is the best in town. So, use the Prasa Sauce on beef, pork or anything you want to satisfy that "nothing else will do" craving for bbq.

And while we're at it — there's so much said on what the difference is between BBQ & grilling that I'm not going to fight — suffice to say, I agree that BBQ is "low & slow" (whereas grillin' is high and mighty) in that, low temperatures, + slow cooking time = tender & moist & smoky is worth the wait. — Whatever side you're on, they just have different attentions spans and outcomes — This one is low and slow...

MARINATE:
2 chickens cut into traditional pieces (I cut the breasts into three pieces)
2 cups Pra-sa-Que Sauce (recipe on the following page)

Fire up that grill!
I have a four-burner gas grill — I can go "indirect" by lighting all burners just to heat the grill then turning off all *but one* burner and putting the chicken on the unlit side of the grill. I put some green tree twigs (An oak hangs over my grill) to create smoke. Close the lid and let the first marinade dry out a little.

Periodically sop the pieces with more sauce and keep them in the low heat for at least two hours sopping the pieces and turning them to expose them to the heat & smoke.

One half hour before serving time,
check the heat with a thermometer, we're looking for 160 – 165 (I like the meat moist and tender) if you're freaked by pink meat then go for 170 — but stay on it (anything past here will kill your hard work!) If you're close, but not quite, light the other burners and baste the heck out the chicken pieces to caramelize (I stand over them and dip the pieces into a bowl of the sauce each time I turn them).

Let them rest off the grill for 5 minutes before serving!

PRA-SA-QUE SAUCE

I love, love, love, that there's a cuisine that inspires as much "fandom" as the NFL or NASCAR. BBQ — with each region sportin' its own take on the slather, sop, baste or brush that can only be called "que" … People who don't know each other are instantly bonded by the "sauce," or equally dismissed as ones to be pitied, as sadly misguided…

I will pit Cali (and by Cali, I mean "So Cali," the NorCals are… all right, I guess) against anyone — KC, Carolina, Texas, Louisiana, we got you all beat, so y'all better just stick to your cornbread and banana puddin,' and leave the alchemy to us.

Why is ours better? We're everything you are plus Chipotle & Jack. We're the freshness of California's agricultural bounty, where y'all are using ketchup. We're the sweet bite and sting of our cultural backbone (some are right when they say heart) of Mexico with the Chipotlé — smoked jalapeños in adobo sauce. We're the additions of our immigrant parts — we're pomegranate molasses from our Armenian cousins. Jack Daniels from our Kentucky immigrants (we're visa sisters).

One summer I decided to nail this and after three batches I hit the sweet spot — this has a grow-up bite of fire — if you have softer mouths to feed — you can back off on the chipotle — and if you're really not a fire breather, you can use just the adobo sauce they're packed in — it's the flavor we want most.

Okay, so I'm ready to put my money where your mouth is and you be the judge!

PRA-SA-QUE SAUCE RECIPE — MAKES ABOUT 1.5 TO 2 QUARTS — WILL LAST ABOUT 3–4 WEEKS IN THE FRIDGE.

Good 'que sauce has three parts:
"The Caramel"
"The Chili"
"The Herbs & Spices"

I find it best to make this days or a week before you wanna use it — to let the flavors age together — but it's tough to make it and forget — it will call to you from inside your reefer… so I do allow myself a taste of it to give me the "strength" to resist… and like the best "que sops" it's designed to caramelize as it dances with smoke and fire. That is, it's best sampled on a hot piece of meat!
You'll need a large cast iron, pot. (I use the South African Potje Pot which looks like witches' cauldron — you can use a 5-quart Dutch oven)

Okay — enough talk girl, get to it!

The Carmel:
Get your cast iron pot blazin'

THE CARAMEL

1 1⁄2 maui (large sweet) **onion**

1 1⁄2 heads of garlic

EVOO (you're pouring as needed, at least a 1⁄4 cup)

1 cup Jack Daniels
(try another Bourbon if you dare.)

3 – 4 chipotles (in adobo sauce — you'll find this in the Latinx section of the market) **use a healthy spoonful of the adobo sauce!**

1⁄4 cup balsamic vinegar

1⁄2 cup brown sugar (packed)

2 tbsp. dijon mustard

1⁄2 cup apple cider vinegar

1⁄2 cup pomegranate molasses (available at Middle Eastern Markets)

A few large pinches of salt

THE CHILI: (VEGGIES)

3 large heirloom tomatoes (chopped)

3 large red bell peppers (chopped)

3 large sweet (not hot) **Anaheim chilies** (chopped)

HERBS & SPICES

Tarragon bunch (your call — I love the licorice bite so I use about 1⁄4 cup)

Basil bunch (again your call — but I could bathe in basil so go for it)

1 tbsp. of ground cumin

1⁄2 tsp. smoked paprika

1⁄2 tsp. finely ground Lapsang Sou Chou (yes, this is smoked tea) this is a secret you can either share or not — BUT as a tea it was too intense for me — BUT I ground it into a fine powder in my spice grinder and it's perfect secret weapon — all the smokiness you want without artificial ingredients.

Dry caramelize the onions & garlic. Get them brown and stir to keep from burning, then turn down the heat, get the Jack ready and hit the mixture with EVOO (you're pouring as needed, at least a 1⁄4 cup) and before it can smoke, pour in 1 cup of the Jack Daniels. Stir and let sauté.

In a small bowl
mix the chipotles, a healthy spoonful of the adobo sauce, the balsamic vinegar, brown sugar, dijon, cider vinegar, & pomegranate molasses. Next add a few large pinches of salt. Add the mixture to the pot and stir.

Let it blend to a thick honey-like consistency.

Chop and add to pot

The "Chili" (Veggies)
heirloom tomatoes, Bell Peppers and Anaheim Chilies.

Stir them into the pot — reduce heat, add:

The Herbs:
Tarragon. Basil. Cumin. Smoked paprika, and the ground Lapsang Sou Chou (smoked tea).

Cover the pot and turn the heat down.

Let it simmer for as long as you can stand it, the longer the better, BUT the longer — the slower, so turn the heat down — don't hurt your new baby!

I've let mine go for eight hours before I couldn't stand it any longer, but I keep checking and stirring all along the was — a cast iron is not a slow cooker — so don't be afraid to give 'er a stir and keep it from burning.

When you can't take it anymore —
pour the mixture into a blender

Add 1 cup of filtered water
This may take multiple batches — depending on how big your tomatoes were. My batches are usually two blender loads. So, I require 2 cups of filtered water. The color will lighten — but don't worry, it will caramelize again when you baste it on your favorite meat. You want it a smooth pourable consistency — it will thicken under refrigeration.

While it's still hot, go ahead and dip in whatever is dippable at your fingertips — you deserve it!

Now... see what I mean about SoCali Sauce? Wait'll you taste it on your favorite "griller!"

GRILLED FIGS STUFFED WITH BLUE CHEESE, BASIL & JALAPEÑO

A combo of flavors that will tease their taste buds and tickle their fancy! I take this to potluck parties and such — and the legend grows!

2 fresh ripe figs per person
Crumbled blue cheese
1 roasted & skinned jalapeño minced per every 4 people

2 fresh basil leaves for every person
1/4 cup EVOO
1 tbsp. balsamic vinegar for brushing
Pinch of salt

Heat your grill

Rinse the figs and the basil leaves
Set in bowls. Take a basil leaf, put a small chunk of blue cheese and chunk of jalapeño on it and roll it into a tube.

Using a chop stick
Poke a small hole in the figs. Stuff the basil tube into the hole and push it all the way in — the cheese will begin to soften and will seal the hole closed.

In small mixing bowl
Whisk the EVOO and balsamic together, add the pinch of salt

On your hot grill
Brush the figs with the EVOO mix and grill — turning & basting until they are done — the cheese will melt and the grill marks are pronounced (about 2:00 minutes per side — figure at least 3 sides...).

Arrange on a serving plate
Take a bow!

SWEET POTATO "PIE"
(FANCY-SCHMANCY ROASTED SWEET POTATOES)

Since this is a savory side dish, I'm riffing on the southern belle's personality traits rather than her actual DNA. You can roast sweet potatoes in the oven the day or night before to save time and keep the skins on -- they will make our crust for the pie!

5 large sweet potatoes, roasted	3 stalks celery
1⁄4 cup EVOO plus one splash	Gumbo spices to taste (smoked paprika, filé, sassafras, etc.)
1 tbsp. red wine	5 radishes (thinly sliced)
6 medium shallots	2 tbsp. fresh cilantro leaves (thin ribbons)
3 cloves garlic	
1 large red pepper	

Make the "Crust" for your pie
Scrape the pulp from the sweet potatoes into a bowl and set aside.

In a glass pie plate
Pour a splash of EVOO into a pie plate and arrange the skins like a flower blossom, (or pinwheel — whatevs floats thy boats) with the ends meeting in the center and the other ends radiating out to the edge. Overlap them to cover the entire bottom of the plate.

In a hot dry cast skillet
Add sliced shallots, garlic and red pepper, when they're just starting to caramelize, turn off the heat and add the EVOO and shake to make sure it doesn't burn, then de-glaze with the red wine, add the celery and gumbo spices.

Add the above to the mixing bowl with your sweet potato flesh/pulp
Mix together and spoon it all onto your crust. Spread it evenly to cover, then swirl "peaks" on top — they will brown & crisp-up for a nice, yummy texture and look.

Bake for 30 minutes in a 350 degree oven

Let it rest for 15 minutes before serving.

Garnish with thinly sliced radishes and cilantro.

CUKES & UNS

This is what summer tasted like to my mom. She used to get a lot of recipes while listening to the daytime talk shows that blared over her vacuuming. We would constantly be surprised by these things, but the really good ones, like "Cukes & Uns" made it into her repertoire. She used to start this when the last spring breezes took on that summer "snap," filling a classic Tupperware bucket with a brine and cucumber slices and onion rings, that she would restock, creating a seemingly bottomless supply that we would eat every supper until Labor day. I can't believe I still love pickles as much as I do today! I've updated this slightly (are you surprised?) but I do so in her honor!

This is best if it has at least three days before eating. My mom would serve us at supper and "Restock" more cukes & uns as she was returning it to the refrigerator for the next day. The differences of the varying times each individual slice gets in its briny bath made each bite slightly different from the previous one — which was also surprising about my mom, who's cooking "signature" was astounding consistency, more precise than any Swiss watch, and so for her to have this little bit of "unknown" in one of her dishes?.. well, it was the beginning for me as a woman, of understanding that I didn't really know my mother... but I was capable of learning who she was for real, if I merely paid attention...

7–10 Persian cucumbers (sliced in thin rounds)	**½ cup salt**
2 large red onions (sliced and separated into rings)	**¼ cup granulated garlic**
	¼ cup whole coriander seeds
2 quarts water	**¼ cup fresh dill**
2 cups white vinegar	

Create your brine

In large container with a lid

Add the salt, water and vinegar and whisk to mix. Once the salt is thoroughly dissolved, add the garlic, coriander, and dill.

Slice your "cukes & uns"

Add them to the brine.

Refrigerate until serving.

Restock as necessary — Mom would be proud.

BANANA PUDDING
WITH HOMEMADE 'NILLA WAFERS

Throughout my travels in the adventure called TV, I spent many a month in the south and loved the tradition of BBQ joints. Each town and hamlet had their own take on bbq, and all of them riffed on the classics — one of those, surprisingly (for this So Cali girl) is banana pudding. Go figure. But I stopped trying to find out why it's in every bbq joint (and how it got to be a classic) and dove in.

With both feet. I've resisted the temptation to make this into a pie because it would shift the ratio of pudding to cookie away from perfect parity. Which is essential.

THE COOKIES (Makes 5 1/2 dozen):	THE PUDDING
1 large egg	4 tbsp. all-purpose flour
1 tbsp. whole milk	1 1/2 cups sugar
4 oz. unsalted butter, room temperature	Pinch salt
1/2 cup vanilla sugar	3 large eggs separated
1/2 tbsp. bourbon	3 cups milk
1 cup all-purpose flour	1 tsp. vanilla extract
1 tsp. baking powder	5–6 bananas (plus one for garnish)
1/2 tsp. kosher salt	Parchment paper

Preheat your oven to 350 degrees

Make your 'nillas
In a standing mixer
Cream the butter and vanilla sugar (see I told you, you'd need heaps of this magical crystal!) add the bourbon.

In a mixing bowl
Sift together the dry ingredients Set aside.

In another mixing bowl
Whisk together the egg and milk

Add to the standing mixer on low
mix for a minute, then increase speed to whip it.

Slow the speed back down
add the dry ingredients. Mix together for 30 seconds.

Line baking sheets with parchment paper
Roll a golf-ball scoop of the dough between your hands then place in rows on the baking sheet.

Bake for 4 minutes
"Smoosh" the balls into flat cookies.

Bake for another 5–6 minutes until golden brown (about 10 minutes total in the oven). Cool on racks.

Make your Pudding
in a large, heavy saucepan.
Stir together flour, sugar and salt.

in a large bowl
Lightly beat egg yolks and combine with milk.

Pour the egg and milk mixture into dry ingredients in heavy saucepan.
Cook over low to medium heat, stirring constantly, until ingredients are thickened and smooth. Remove saucepan from heat and stir in vanilla.

In a separate mixing bowl
Mash all but one of the bananas until smooth. Fold them into the custard. Allow to cool for one hour.

Line a covered baking dish with your vanilla wafers.
Spoon a layer of custard onto the wafers, add another layer of wafers, and layer of custard until it's all used up. Refrigerate until serving time.

At serving time, add more wafers to each serving dish — scoop the pudding into each serving dish and garnish with sliced banana and a wafer. Use the wafers as edible spoons! *(Like Banana dip & chips? Great idea!)*

CHAPTER 12

(GRIYAPUHLUZA)

TURKEY MOLE WITH TORTILLAS

MOLCAJETE GUACAMOLE

TOMATILLO SALSA

MEXICAN SLAW

BLACK BEANS & RICE

CARROT CAKE ROLL

BLUEBERRY PIE

"BIRTHDAY BASH"

Mylove and I are moon children — born the 5th and the 9th of July, and this is our month. But you can come. Oh, and do bring presents. This is, and always has been, a sacred time for us. We have celebrated this time in the most amazing ways — like the time I had invited our circle of friends for Marcy's surprise party — only to discover four days later that they had already been invited to my surprise party! (I'm sure this was just "par for the course" for our friends — something they chalked up to "life with the Maddens.")

But seriously, Mylove's brother Morgan's birthday is the 4th, Mylove and her late cousin Nancy shared the fifth, our niece Kaylee's birthday is the sixth, Mylove's parents' anniversary is the 7th, I share my birthday with my Gramma Madden on the 9th... and it just goes on! My nephew Dane's birthday is just on the other side of the cusp on the 23rd... (along with Aria).

There's just nothing else to do but surrender to the party and go with it. Can you tell that I love a big bash? It's a chance to really lay it all out there in a grand fashion and get my grill on.

My grill on... ah yes... that magical word — few things in our house are emblematic of just sooooo much. It means, well, you could almost sum up our adult life with it. You see, homeownership is one of those milestones that can never look good on that much paper (anyone who has confronted that ream of paper called your "mortgage papers" knows what I'm talking about.) Your realtor and loan officer just seem to keep turning pages for about three hours as you dutifully sign your names over and over and over and over. This one says x, that one says y... one of the ones that bumped me when we were selling our "first" house to the new buyer was the disclosure that a nuclear incident had occurred "in close proximity." We had only owned this house for three years. Where, I asked, was this disclosure when we bought this house?

But I'm getting ahead of myself (again — or is it still?) anyhoo, we were selling our "first house" and moving to our current dream "treehouse" — Mylove and I had thought we hit the lottery early — no way were we ever going be to be able to get this much house on only our second try — it was perfect in every way — "housing bubble?" What's that you say?

Now, we were *selling* our house at the absolute tippy top of the market — we would make enough from the sale of our first house to not only put a substantial down payment on our dream house but we would be able to remodel the kitchen (it was smaller than a hobie cat's galley — which if you sail, you know there ain't one!) AND buy a real honest-to-goodness gas grill. I would be in "fat city" as cooking goes with a showcase kitchen and outdoor grill — I would kill!

But, you know how I know it was the absolute tippy-tippy top? There's only one way to know that: as we were in escrow, the market went over the apex and started its downhill slide…

Which meant that our buyer no longer qualified for their loan — and since we still had the house we had "equity" and therefore were on the hook for the price of our dream house, despite its rapid descent down/off the value cliff. (In simple math — we would be underwater before even moving in). In fact, as we sought a new buyer — we carried two mortgages for 2 and half months, until a new buyer finally stepped in and we were able to "arrest our descent" (if you're a mountain climber this is fancy term for digging your ice axe into the glacier as you are sliding headfirst toward the crevasse and pray you stop just shy of disaster).

The good news was that we made it into our new treehouse and tho' my dream kitchen would have to wait for, well, we're still waiting. My "big-kid" grill would be a lovely consolation prize. Which I described nicely in the last chapter — but what I didn't tell you was that since the galley is still small (it hasn't changed since last chapter LOL) I can expand my kitchen's capacity by walking the 12 steps through the living room and with the sliding glass doors open, remain in the living room convos with our guests without missing a word (I have to hurry through the back door and round the only blindspot past the jasmine bush — I might miss a word but that's all.)

So yes, the grill is storied indeed!

For backyard parties, there are convos both indoors and out, as I grill under the shade of an oak tree (from which I will occasionally grab a few leaves to toss in for a little extra flavor) and the mood is festive and fun.

All of the moon children and those what loves us will be coming to celebrate us all. And I'm ready — I've been using my classic brining technique with a Mexican twist on a turkey that I will bathe in Mole Sauce, cook on the 'que, and serve with all the fixins. July is the quintessential summer party time — it always has been. As far back as I can remember, the fireworks, watermelon swimming in a galvanized tub of ice, hand-cranked ice cream and red, white and blue have *always* been symbols of my birthday, July 9th — and tho' we didn't plan it (cancers are said to care 'bout this thing — but seriously, Mylove and I fell in love *before* we even knew each's zodiac sign) it just plain makes sense that July is the month of the greatest day in the history of the earth… Mylove's birthday.

Now, her experience is slightly different in that her brother *Morgly*, actually thought the fireworks of Independence Day were for him (and if you knew Morgan, you would know that there could be no other day) — so, how do you follow that act, when your birthday is *July 5th*? I'm sure just being the woman (and therefore *girl*) that Mylove is, helped a little — and being the only girl, I'm sure her parents took pains to make sure her day was as special as Morgan's was the day before. (It also didn't help that her cousin/sister-in-law shared the same day. Don't ask, it's a long story — but yes, they are the same person — Mylove's baby brother's late wife, Nancy).

In the long run — Mylove says she's lucky I understood, and we have always celebrated her day with passion — and tho' we are four days (and 14 years) apart, we treat the entire week (who am I kidding, month!) as a *festival of us*. And she's cool with dat.

Like this year — we've got the usual players here — it's a big turkey and we need lots of hands to turn to and help us eat it! Our dear friend Audie is here. Macky too. And Donny & Vanita.

But the new kid here is my new BFF — Laura Faye. Laura started as a "Friend of a friend" (thank you Josh!) who "had an idea for a TV show." Here in LA LA Land, that's a thing, and it's a wonderful way to meet people you might never ever know otherwise. My friend Josh texted me and when the message thread introduced Laura as "Badass Science Geek." How could I refuse? And this moniker became her caller ID on my phone.

Laura it turns out, is the former editor and spokesperson for NASA/JPL's climate science website. And like many "former" anyones in this disaster of an Administration, she left when outright censorship created a hostile abomination of what had been. In this case, this toxic smog of fear and adversity turned one of the foremost groups helping to arrest the destruction of our planet, into an impotent propaganda machine for special interests. Laura's 10-year run done, she was now a very dangerous woman indeed, becoming a whistleblower on the strong-arm tactics that none of us ever thought we would face in this land of the free. And for Laura it was now time to stand up for the home of the Brave.

Needless to say, we hit it off and stay tuned for something dangerous to come from us both. Laura is a new thing for me to have in my life — a friend who never knew my past. Oh, she knows that I had been raised by wolves, but she has only known Scottie Jeanette. And when we're not talking about ways to save the earth (favorite subject) we're talking about the best colored bathing suit for me (she thinks my conservative blue one-piece looks like a 1970's East German Olympic leotard). It's as fun as I had imagined it to be — there's no asterisk about anything I say or think in her mind, for her, the context is just another "badass woman," working to change the planet for the better. I have to ignore my own impulse to make these innocent innocuous moments benchmarks in my transition and take them for what they are. What I always prayed for, dreamed of and worked at...

... being just a normal girl.

And not quashing that thought with the drive to be different, to dare to be unique, to rise above normal, away from the binary, to step up and out into real.

But for now, it's time to put my money where her mouth is — she's read my book and knows to expect big things from my kitchen and now it's time for Scottie Jeanette to put up or shut-up. Which is just how I like it, right?

All-in all, there's about 20 of us here to dance and laugh in the sun as the aroma of Holy Mole wafts across the backyard.

Mole is to me, what cannelloni was to my mom — the test of a restaurant's chef. She always said if she went into an Italian restaurant and there wasn't Frank Sinatra music playing and/or their cannelloni sucked, that chef was off her list. I agree. And the same goes for me and Mexican restaurants and their Mole — if you skimp or go bottle in your house, I'm out. This strict rule has served me well round the world.

Now, the history of Mole, especially the Mole Negro, and Mole Rojo (the two most gringos have heard of) supposedly dates back to the coming of a Bishop to visit the mission in Mexico. Legend has it — (as reported by Sunset magazine — so you know it's true) The local women who cooked for "the padres" were asked to prepare something special for the "big padre." And they turned to their Aztec roots for inspiration. Chocolate had been the sole privilege of the Aztec Priests (men only) and therefore was a natural choice for the big padre's rank and honor.

The feminist in me doesn't know whether to protest it by appropriating the sacred chocolate, or boycotting — but the alchemical magic that happens when you put in effort (which the mamacitas really did) makes this an easy choice.

Now, about their effort — I'm not sure if they put forth so much effort that only the most dedicated (mostly women) would ever make it again. They supposedly cooked for days, roasting vegetables and fruits, toasting nuts and seeds and stirring and stewing it into a nectar of sauce that would be worthy of the turkey that would bathe in it.

I can make a qwik mole in a few hours, but like all things, you get out what you put in. And with a sop that is actually chocolate and a myriad of amazing ingredients on a BBQ turkey wrapped in tortilla... how could you possibly mess that up?

You can't. This recipe makes you a star! What better way to celebrate our birthday? We'll cook this bird on the rotisserie of my grill, slathered in as much Mole as possible (and pass more for serving.) I'll grill handmade tortillas (bought locally this time — I'm cray, but not that cray). But, I will throw down with handmade guac (in my Molcajete) from scratch — there's nothing better. Also, there's fresh tomatillo salsa that is my BIL Mikey's recipe — so flippin' good. I'll round out the plate with black beans and rice and my sister Shane's recipe for Mexican slaw.

The magic of this array is that it involves several trips to the buffet table which switches up the conversation combos — when I'm cooking like this, I can spend a long time with my back to the party if I'm not careful — and these folks (as much as I'd like to think) are not here for my cooking — they too, are here to celebrate us — so I need to show-up. This menu is made way ahead of time and with the exception of carving the turkey into burrito-able bites and grilling tortillas — there's nothing that should get between me and the ones we love (and what loves us!) except a plate fulla Mole.

After too many trips for more salsa, it's time for cake and pie.

Mylove is easy — her very best favorite cake ever is carrot cake. I, on the other hand am the outlier — big surprise, I know. I used to always request German chocolate cake — until one year I asked my mom for blueberry pie. And that did it. It became my birthday "cake" ever since.

As we blow out our candles and sing (both in and out of key) the smiles light up the twilight.

And our birthday month is just beginning...

Let's cook!

QWICK MOLE

Okay, okay, why should you listen to this "Blanca" about this most sacred of Oaxacan Magical Spells? You're right. You probably shouldn't. And I wish I could tell you that I learned this as I was tied to the apron strings of mi mamacita (Tino's mama, Mrs. Romero taught me tortillas, which I'm still trying to spend this lifetime perfecting to honor her legacy — but sadly, I didn't even know there WAS a "cult of Mole" to join until college) but... here in La La Land, a, great Mole is available without even a hike — still... I had to try my hand at it.

And like the mamacitas who broke tradition when they prepared this for the Spanish Bishop, I too, must give-in to my subversive streak by daring to make this sacred dish... In their spirit and memory, I hope I do them proud.

I call this Qwick Mole (and I confess until just now writing this, when I thought for a moment, I'd get even more clever by dropping the "C," I didn't get that this could imply the powdered chocolate milk drink of my childhood) because the traditional way of making this Mole is a two to three-day process. Which everyone should do at least once in their life!

But this version is made over several hours. Again, this is one where time must be respected. Mole has its cult following because it IS a religious experience — prayer and meditation are just as important as chiles and chocolate because you will find that you'll never be able to make it the same way twice. And, though I've laid out the foundation here, it's up to you to stay on top of it and constantly adjust the flavors to get that "perfection" that your tongue is looking for. This is a very complex potion — you're using fresh ingredients for a reason — they are alive and true Mole afficianistas have all endured too many attempts that come to the table lifeless. The difference comes from subtle (or not so subtle) course corrections right up to serving time. And this is okay. I consider it part of the ritual. Cuz when you get it right, this is truly something that no one has ever had in their life (even if they had Mole for breakfast — they didn't have YOUR Mole). So don't be afraid to "futz," to adjust, to tweak, and add... for Mole, more than probably any other dish, is one where the end does really justify the means.

1 large chopped onion

1 head of garlic (peeled and chopped)

A splash of EVOO

3 whole chipotles (canned in adobo sauce)

3 large heirloom tomatoes (chopped)

1/4 cup strong black coffee

1 bottle dark ale

3 roasted pasilla chilis

3 roasted red bell peppers

1 large banana (mashed)

1/4 cup good chunky organic peanut butter

1/2 cup roasted pepitas (pumpkin) seeds

6 large ripe plums

1/4 cup pomegranate molasses (you can find this any Middle Eastern grocery)

1/2 cup shaved dark chocolate bar

1 tbsp. fresh oregano leaves

1 tsp. cinnamon

1 tsp. toasted cumin seed

1 tsp. ground anise seed

TO ADJUST — HAVE ON HAND:

1 cup raspberry jam

1 cup shaved chocolate (additional)

3 fresh corn tortillas

1 cup cream

NOTE: The brining process for the turkey is just like I explained in the November chapter

Now, where was I? Oh yeah — HOLY MO-LAY! (insert crowd cheering here)

In a very hot dutch oven (cast iron pot with a lid)
Add chopped onion, garlic to caramelize. When brown and sugary, add a splash of EVOO, 3 whole chipotles (you can add a dribble of the adobo for extra heat and flavor) the large heirloom tomatoes and the dark ale.

Let it simmer, then add the black coffee.
Simmer until it's a nice "stewie" sauce. Add the roasted pasilla chiles, roasted red bell peppers, and the spices. Stew some more on an exuberant flame (stay on it with the spoon — the cast iron is your friend — but help it out!)

In a medium mixing bowl
Mash the banana into the peanut butter. Chop & pit the plums and stir to mix.

Add the above to the dutch oven.
Add the pepitas and reduce the flame — simmer for another hour or so. Lastly add the chocolate. Let it simmer for another hour or so.

Using an immersion blender
Blend the mole until it's smooth and silky in texture.

Now taste. How is it? What does it need?

Good Mole is like a Carlos Santana song, Complex, layered, catchy, familiar and surprising at the same time, yet completely suddenly unexpected; a blazing solo on top of a 5-piece percussion section, (not to mention the bass, keys and brass. Spiritually high, intense and oh, so sweet.

So the question is... *How's yours?*

This is where your tongue makes the big bucks — you have to remember that your mole will be the cuddly blanket for your grilled turkey (this recipe also kicks butt for chicken). And with that in mind...

Who's not pulling their weight? Is it the flavor, the spice, or the overall character?

Remember those items I told you to have on hand?

Now's the time...
If your mole is too bitter (which could be depending on the ripeness of your plums, tomatoes and chipotle, and/or the sharpness of your ale) you can...

Try the raspberry preserves.

Too "malty" too "ale-y"?

Try the cream, or the tortillas.

If it starts to lose its overall character...

Add more chocolate — a little at a time — good Mole is not a "Chocolate sauce," but a "trip to the Yucatan."

Shut it all off and let it sit for a few hours or even overnight.

Just like our marinara, time melds all flavors, let it rest and see what happens. This is the true test — what do the flavors do when they get to rest from the flame?

When your sauce matches your dreams...

YOU'RE READY FOR THE STAR OF THE SHOW — THE TURKEY!

Cook your turkey your favorite way (which is now brining, right? Right? Okay, I thought so..) Fire-up your bbq, grill or rotisserie
Slather this all over your brined turkey and roast, adding sauce generously throughout the cooking.

Let your turkey rest at least a half hour before carving
put all of the carved pieces immediately into a covered serving pan with more Mole.

Oh, and I probably shouldn't have to say this, but... don't forget to also pass the Mole at serving time.

Oh-lay!

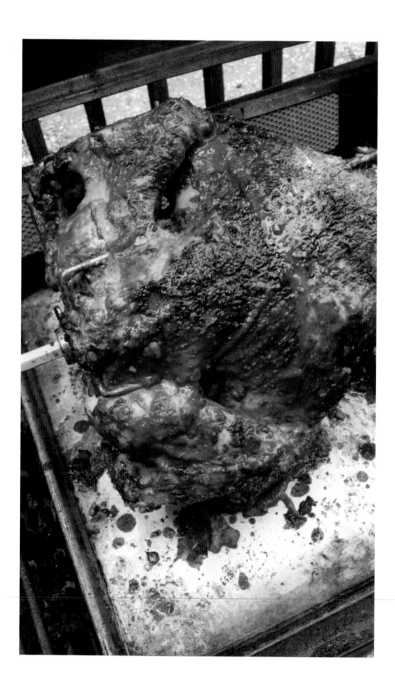

MOLCAJETE GUACAMOLE

Guac is guac you say? To that, I would reply Como no! Claro que si? Guac is our middle name here in So Cali (or is it our maiden name? I forget) and yes, I hear you, how could you go wrong with avocado, garlic, onion, salt & lime? The truth is you can't, but oh you can go soooo right — when you put just a little bit of elbow grease into the mix. A dear friend gave me a gift card to a cooking store and I finally had an excuse to buy a rock. And not just any rock, but the traditional volcanic mortar & pestle with three legs that is the ancient crucible for which to grind one's own. It really is worth it, and it makes for the traditional serving dish that adds a certain "no soy" (or "je ne sais quoi" — tomato, potatoe) to your favorite spread. The cool thing is you can make this right before serving, and everyone will love it being part of the show, so you don't have to do anything but grind and serve...

3 ripe avocados	1 jalapeño (seeded)
1/2 onion (chopped)	2 tbsp. fresh cilantro leaves
1/2 ripe tomato	1 lime (juiced)
1 clove garlic	1 tsp. cumin seed
	salt

In a hot dry skillet
Toast your cumin seed

In your Molcajete...
Grind the cumin seeds with the pestle. Add the garlic and grind that into the cumin seed.

Grind
the cilantro leaves next. You should now have a delicious smelling paste.

Grind
the onion, jalapeño, tomato and add the lime juice and salt.

Now for the guest of honor, cube the avocado (like described in the February Cupid Salad. Add to the Molcajete and grind gently to the consistency you like, from chunky to velvety smooth, it's your magick spell, so cast away, Gandalf!

Garnish with some cilantro leaves.

Serve with chips. (And slather on your Turkey Mole burrito — but I didn't have to tell you that did I — always one step ahead of me!)

TOMATILLO SALSA

Like I said, I need to give credit where it be due. And this is special thanks to my dear Brother-in-Law Mikey, my beloved Lib's hubby. It's insanely simple (something that is perfect in a labor-intensive meal) and yet, it's so packed with flavor it tastes like you slaved for weeks. The secret is the charring of the skins and transferring that smoky, caramelized goodness to the flavor profile. And don't be a-sceered to have several dishes that are all hitting the same ingredients — we're building a burrito bar and the more choices people have the better chance you have something for everyone.

---

7 ripe whole tomatillos
(outer "papery" husks removed)
1 onion (sliced into rounds)
3 cloves garlic
1 jalapeño

I tbsp. cumin seed
1 lime (juiced)
½ cup fresh cilantro leaves
Salt to taste

In a hot dry skillet
Toast your cumin seed and dump into a waiting bowl.

Add all of the vegetables (whole) into the skillet
Cook until the skins on the tomatillos are charred. Now, don't overcook these — char them to a dark brown — careful not to burn the actual flesh of the fruit.

Transfer everything to a blender or food processor
and blend till smooth — add the cilantro and pulse to chop.

Transfer to a serving bowl and stir in the lime juice.

Taste.

How much salt to add?

It's up to you — you're the one getting Recklass!

GRILLED MEXICAN SLAW

Mexican Coleslaw is found all over SoCal and I must confess, I learned this from my little sister Shane. It's the leaner, meaner version of its blanquita cousin — coleslaw (which I also love) but this one is bursting with flavor with toasted cumin, fresh cilantro, fresh jalapeño (try the fiery red sister, the Anaheim for color if you can get 'em) and lime. We're gonna step all that up one notch to showstopper (like this meal needs it!) by grilling the cabbage and onion. It's the perfect complement to tamales and grilled chicken — I use this whole technique all summer, riffin' on the basic theme with different veggie combos.

½ **green cabbage** (sliced into three rounds)
½ **red cabbage** (sliced into three rounds)
1 **large red onion** (sliced into four rounds)
½ **lb. cherry tomatoes**
1 **jalapeño** (or Anaheim) **chile, whole**
3 **cloves garlic**
½ **cup fresh cilantro leaves**
1 **lime**
2 **tbsp. EVOO**

1 **tbsp. rice vinegar**
1 **tbsp. toasted cumin seeds** (whole)
¼ **kosher salt**

ADDITIONAL "BASTE"
¼ **cup EVOO**
Splash of rice vinegar
Pinch of salt

Your grill is already hot if you're making this with the Turkey Mole (if not fire it up!)

In a large mixing bowl
Whisk together the EVOO, squeeze the garlic and add the rice vinegar, lime juice (add some of the zest if you like).

Prepare your baste in a small bowl
whisk the EVOO, splash of rice wine vinegar and salt. Grab a basting brush and set it aside.

In your super hot skillet
Turn off the flame, then add the cumin seed and shake vigorously to prevent burning and toast (it'll be less than 20 seconds in a hot skillet, and when they are fragrant, dump them into your large mixing bowl (you'll hear them crackle and sizzle when they hit the oil and acids.

Take your prepared cabbage, onion and chile along with the baste to your hot grill throw them all on the grill and brush the baste on (careful of flare-ups!) and immediately turn them baste side down, and brush them again. Cook them until they get good grill marks — turning them once more to cook evenly (about 4 minutes per side) generously basting the grill marks to caramelize. Remove them from the grill and...

chop the cabbage into bite sized pieces
mince the onion and chile, toss all into the dressing. Chop your cherry tomatoes, toss with the slaw and add a pinch of salt to taste.

Serve.

BLACK "BEANS & RICE"
(AND A WHOLE HOST OF SUPPORTING CAST!)

Beans, beans, the musical fruit… My mother sang this lil ditty to us as children and as a girl growing up in So Cali, I have to admit, that the song used to be true — until I discovered the Indian secret spice — asafoetida. Leave it to the Indians who wouldn't dream of a meal without their beloved dal to have (like most everything else) already figured this out. I confess, I do keep a few cans of beans in the Larder, BUT THOSE ARE ONLY FOR EMERGENCIES! That's why god invented the pressure cooker. I soak the beans the night before in a few shakes of asafoetida and cook them in the pressure cooker the next day. The rice is cooked your favorite way — I love our rice cooker but you can go whatever way you are most comfortable with.

BEANS	RICE
2 cups dry black beans	1 cup rice (dry)
5 cups of chicken or vegetable broth	6 cups broth
1 tbsp. asafetida	1 dash granulated garlic
3 tbsp. EVOO	1 tsp. fresh grated ginger root
3 cloves fresh garlic (peeled)	3 tsp. lemon zest
4 ears of corn (steamed, roasted and cut off the cob)	Juice of 3 lemons
4 carrots (split & roasted then diced)	1 tsp. smoked chipotle powder
3 large pasilla chiles (roasted and skinned — deseeded)	
3 roasted yellow & red bell peppers	

Cook the beans until tender
Use the broth (chicken or vegetable) instead of water. In the pressure cooker, this usually takes four times up to pressure and sustained for 5 minutes before I turn off the heat and let it drop to no pressure. Repeat this four times.

In a hot, dry skillet
Roast the carrots, chiles, onion, & bell peppers. Add the corn. Add the EVOO. Add the chipotle and lemon juice. When the beans are done add them and simmer for an additional 30 minutes.

Cook your rice until tender.
Fluff it with a fork. It will have plenty of flavor.

Stir the rice & beans together in your serving dish

Garnish with the lemon zest.

INSIDE OUT CARROT CAKE ROLL
(MARCY'S FAV IN THE NEW "EASY TO MAIL" CAN!)

One summer, Mylove was away on the east coast directing a big project during the entire month of July — and I was heartbroken to be missing her birthday... I took my heartbreak out in the usual way — figuring out a way to blow her away remotely! Carrot cake is her very best fav and she's (spoiler alert) incredibly persnickety about how it's done. It has to be very moist, and it has to have a real cream cheese frosting.... Making it wasn't the issue, so much as delivery was not going to be easy, she was on location at a summer resort in the Catskills, where an all-volunteer workforce would be not only receiving all shipments, but in charge of finding her among a thousand other people...

How many cream cheese frostings do you think could make that trip and still be as delicious as Mylove would deserve (demand) on her birthday? Well, FedEx would get it there before it had a chance to dry out, and if I made it so the frosting was on the inside of the cake, it should survive the 3500 miles journey... I made it into a roll and modified a FedEx tube so not only could I get it in, but Mylove could get it out to enjoy it.

Needless to say — that was a birthday that went down in history! Sliced into servings, like a yule log, she had a birthday party with homemade love!

A quick note — I hate, hat,e hate, the whatever that bulsh*t is they mix in with powder sugar — grind sugar in a spice grinder to get the same effect without the cornstarch crap. You're welcome!

CAKE
3/4 cup coconut flour
1 tsp. baking soda
2 tsp. corn-free baking powder
(I use Hain baking powder)
1/2 tsp. salt
8 eggs
1/2 cup coconut oil
1 cup locally sourced honey
1/2 cup fresh pineapple (pureed)
1 tbsp. vanilla
1 tbsp. apple cider vinegar
2 cups shredded carrots
1 cup raisins

2 cups toasted pecans (chopped)
1 tsp. cinnamon
1 tsp. nutmeg
1 tsp. cardamom
1 tsp. ground ginger
1 tsp. orange zest

FROSTING
1 cup sugar (grind this in your spice grinder to resemble powdered sugar)
1/2 block (4 oz) cream cheese
1 1/2 tbsp. milk
1 tsp. vanilla
1 tsp. orange zest
pinch of salt

Preheat the over to 350 degrees

Make the Cake
grease a shallow flat baking pan (12x18x1 inch high sides)
line it with parchment paper.

In a stand mixer
combine eggs, oil, honey, pineapple puree, orange zest, vanilla, and apple cider vinegar. Mix until smooth.

In a small bowl
mix coconut flour, spices, baking soda, baking powder, and salt. Stir until totally mixed together.

Add the dry ingredients to the wet ingredients
Mix until completely combined. Fold in carrot, toasted pecans and raisins.

Pour batter into a sheet pan
Bake for 12 minutes — you want this to be a touch underdone so it can be rolled.

Dust a clean cloth towel with your powdered sugar and turn the cake out onto it.
Peel off the parchment paper and using a wooden rolling pin, roll the cake in the towel completely into a log around the rolling pin and let cool for 15 minutes **on the pin.** While it's cooling make your frosting.

Make the frosting
In your stand mixer
Whip the cream cheese and milk into a smooth, fluffy paste. Add the sugar in scoops as you continue to whip. Add the vanilla and orange zest until it's super smooth.

On a clean, dry surface — time to roll your cake (black magick warning!)
Carefully unroll the cake (keeping it on the towel) — spread the frosting evenly on the top. You're going to roll it back tighter into the finished roll.

If you too want to ship it away
Slip a piece of parchment paper between the bottom of the cake and the towel — make sure it's wide enough that when you roll it back tighter, you have paper on the side that you can fold over the edges to protect the ends. This is also a good way to store it until serving time.

If your masterpiece is merely going on a journey from the kitchen to the table,
then you can just roll it up tight (the towel is useful to help you roll it, but don't let the towel get tucked back into the roll) and transfer to your serving plate.

You can also frost the outside, and decorate it with more chopped pecans and candied carrot ribbons. Enjoy! — Happy Birthday Mylove!!!

BLUEBERRY PIE WITH FRESH SUMMER PEACH & GINGER I'SCREAM AH-LA MODE

As I said, my mom finally hit on what would become my favorite birthday cake — blueberry pie! I love the old skool goodness of double crust crispy, flaky, yummy on top of chilled blueberry goodness! Yes, ala mode with vanilla bean ice cream... duh! A word about homemade ice cream — this is easily three of my four food groups (do people still get that joke? Food Pyramid, anyone? Anyone? Never mind.) With my table top ice cream maker which has its own built in refrigeration unit, I can make ice cream in 90 minutes from the time I get a hankerin' to my second bowl. (It's the one place where my discipline completely can take a freakin' hike!) And I highly recommend it!

PIE-YI-YIE: Filling first...	"DOUBLE CRUST"
3 pints fresh blueberries	3 cups flour
1 cup sugar	1 tsp. salt
1 tbsp. balsamic vinegar	1 tbsp. sugar
2 tbsp. cornstarch	2 sticks butter (frozen)
2 tsp. flour	1 cup ice water
Juice of a lemon (hold onto the zest!)	1 egg
1/4 stick of butter (for "dotting")	2 tbsp. "sparkling" sugar (I discovered this magical stuff one Christmas and now I always have some on hand — it's larger crystals make everything sparkle!)

(Note: this filling "spell" works for most fruit — I've done fresh peaches and strawberries with this ratio of fruit to sugar and cornstarch/flour)

In a saucepan
Mash half of the berries the vinegar and sugar. Stir to cook on a medium high heat.

In a separate mixing bowl
Take a few spoonsfull of the juice. Sift in the flour & cornstarch and whisk until smooth. Add this to the saucepan to make a thick syrup. This will happen fairly quickly, so watch it closely. When it starts to thicken, slowly crush the remainder of the berries with your hands, into the saucepan. Turn off the heat and let cool completely — oh, and wash your hands, silly, THEY'RE BLUE!

Meanwhile...
Make your Crust
This makes a "double crust" as I said, the trick is to **not overwork the crust!**

In a large mixing bowl
Whisk the flour, salt & sugar thoroughly. With a cheese grater, grate the frozen butter into the flour, until it's "pebbly." (Again - take off your wedding rings.)

Add water a tablespoon at a time
Gather into a ball — careful not to "overwork" your dough. Wrap it in plastic and let it chill another hour. When you're ready, roll out the dough, and line your pie plate Then divide it into two portions — wrap them in plastic and let them chill another hour. Trust me, this was a hard lesson for an impatient filly like myself to learn. BUT one of the most important ingredients besides love in any dish is TIME. And nothing teaches you like that better than a simple flour, salt, butter and water. It can either be divine or you could resurface your patio with it.

When your filling has cooled, your dough has chilled and you are ready...

Preheat the oven to 450 degrees
Roll out one of your balls onto a floured surface.

Line a pie plate with it.
Stir the lemon zest into the filling

Spoon your filling into the lined pie pan.
Dot with the reserved butter.

Roll out the second ball of dough

Here's where you have to decide just how fancy you want to get. I love the old school lattice top. But some like the solid top that will crack in just the right places to tease you with the filling peeking out — either makes my mouth water and the choice is yours. If you are feeling geometrical, then cut the dough into strips to make your lattice. This is a game of thinking in 3-dimensional space and the good news is even if you mess up the pattern of "over and under" which you accomplish by laying the longest dough strips down, then laying a strip across the first one, bend the second back so you can get under it, then across the next — this will make sense when you've done it wrong and then the bending technique will free you up to fix it.

Once it's covered,
pinch the edges of the crusts together by using your thumb and index finger on the inside hand, to pinch the "seal" closed with the index finger of your outside (the edge) hand.

Whisk the egg into a froth and brush the top crust.
Then sprinkle the sparkling sugar on the top.

Bake for 15 minutes then reduce the heat to 325 degrees and continue baking for 45 minutes.

Let cool completely.

Serve ah la mode!

AND FOR YOU TRULY RECKLASSES —

I'SCREAM: FRESH SUMMER PEACH & GINGER

I learned something this summer — I love fruit ice creams — that's not what I learned, I knew that — but I've been trying to "crack this nut" for a while. Most of the fruits I love are better in the freezing process when they get a splash of balsamic vinegar — except that they can curdle in the cream. SO what I learned is: coconut milk. If I mix the sugar and the fruit(s) with balsamic and coconut milk and let that all "melt" into an incredible syrup, I then make up the difference (to make three cups) with heavy cream. I get the "mouth feel" of creamy goodness with the tart punch of fruit.

1 cup fresh peaches (chopped)	**1 cup coconut milk**
2 tbsp. fresh ginger juice	**¼ cup coconut cream**
1 cup of sugar	**1 cup** (ish) **heavy cream**
1 tbsp. balsamic vinegar	

In a bowl on medium low heat
Stir the balsamic vinegar into the chopped peaches, add the ginger juice, toss to coat. Add the sugar and stir to dissolve — don't worry if it's not dissolved yet — it will. Pour in the coconut milk and coconut cream, and let it sit for at least an hour. (longer is better.)

Blend to a smooth custard in your blender
I used to think I liked chunks of fruit in my ice cream. BUT — turns out I was wrong. I want the punch of the flavor rather than a solid chunk of frozen fruit which seems to tone down its flavor. But, if you prefer yours inferior (no judgment — I ain't hurt) then, by all means reserve some of the fruit as chunks before putting everything into your blender.

Pour the mixture into a large (four cup) measuring cup

Add enough heavy cream to make three cups of liquid.
Add to your ice cream machine. And freeze into magick.

CHAPTER 13

· SUMMERTIME SACRILEGE LOBSTERFEST ·

LOBSTER BURRITOS

MEXICAN STREET CORN RELISH

CHIPOTLE SWEET POTATO TART

SALAD NARANJÁ
(Orange, Onion, Olive & Chili Salad)

"I'N BEIN' A PIG..."

I wrote lovingly about Mylove's Applewild Posse — Mitzi, Bunny, Christie and Marcy in GBTM, and now we've come full circle. Every two years the Girls (and their husbands) meet at one of their homes for a long weekend. With two gals on each of the coasts, it's a great excuse to visit places we might not normally go. And each location has a unique flavor that seems to paint in a section of each one's personality for us interlopers-by-marriage...

This time, we're scheduled to go to my favorite place of the four possibilities — Mitzi's family summer estate in Woods Hole, on the cape. This 19-room mansion is right on the freakin' water! A point of lawn and tree covered land that juts proudly into the Cape's waters! But...

And here's where I am starting to resort to one of the oldest arrows in my quiver for getting through life — denial. Denial's not a "fooling of one's self" — that's for amateurs — rather it's a Jedi mindtrick that cloaks debilitating thoughts and fear with "reasons" — but...

... Mylove has just sent an email to the other gals — She's not physically "strong enough" to make the journey.

I'm... blindsided. We didn't even talk about it. I feel... well selfish, and silly... and down-right stupid. I should've seen this coming — Mylove has been having to sleep sitting-up again. She's back to sleeping in the lounger again, and barely able to get outside and take her short walks to the end of the street — the drainings of her lungs are twice a week now, and they barely get her a few hours of relief. But I've been hoping that maybe a trip would break this cycle — I even researched how to get vacuum bottles in New England (since taking them on the plane would be illegal) but this is really just an example of how silly I am being. I'm holding onto... hope. I've always been her champion — I shouldn't be pushing here, even suggesting it is reminding her of her predicament. She's sending me a message by sending a brutally painful message to the women who know her better than almost anyone (save for me).

This is freakin' scary and huge...

So huge, in fact, that I wish to beg your indulgence — I have to take a moment to "get right" with this. So, if you wouldn't mind — I'm going to restart this chapter with an

August that happened two Augusts ago — the cast of characters is all the same — the Applewild Girls. I will return to real time as soon as I can...

We join this chapter currently in progress...

We're on the other side of my transition — in this case, I really should say our transition — we went from four seemingly cisgender/heterosexual middle-aged married couples to three seemingly cisgender/heterosexual middle-aged married couples + one same-sex married couple with Mylove's child bride (Moi) still going through puberty.

Last time out, (at Bunny & Gary's Carmel Chateau) was the first time it was five girls and three boys — and I must say that we got through most of the awkward silence during the welcome hugs. I learned that these amazing women were following their beloved Marcy's lead, and if Mylove was cool with it, then who were they to question?

That didn't mean there wasn't the occasional misgendered pronoun. But the intention was there, as was immense love and an epic big sister Bunny, giving her new lil sister, Scottie Jeanette, expert "woman in the workplace" advice and my most favorite-est earrings. (I wrote this whole account in detail in my blog, "Raised By Wolves.")

Which brings us to here. Wood's Hole, on the Cape in Massachusetts. The ancestral home of Mitzi. This is a special place for the Applewild Girls, and I absolutely fall in love with the 19-room mansion on "Woody point," where, out the front windows is a small harbor, and out the back, the open cape. It's a breathtaking hunk of property that Mitzi and her brother have struggled to hold onto since they inherited it. Neither is wealthy and even though all they have to do is pay the estate taxes, (which are more than the average mortgage) it's enough to be a heartbreaking burden on them both.

Of all the places, we could meet, this is the one place that ties the girls together the best. Each has memories of spending time here as children and watching their eyes light up as each walks through the door is worth the price of admission.

This will be three days of sun, swimming and eating — the crowning jewel is always a good ol' fashioned "Lobsterbake."

Now, LOBstah (yes with a capital Lob) here on the cape — or anywhere in New England, is a sacred thing. Everyone is the best at doing it, and everyone knows what happens if you get a bad one... it's your last time serving it. There is zero tolerance for incompetence.

As a SoCal girl, I knew the legendary LOBstah snobbery of New England, second only to New York's claim on Pizza (please). No matter how amazing a chef you might be, some local LOBstah shack in anywhere Cape Cod is better than you — and don't even try. With this in mind, I never understood Lobster rolls. (What? A lobster mixed with mayo and pickle and served on some jankie hotdog bun? Seriously?)

With the Applewild girls, it might be the only time in two years that any of them have actually gotten the chance to eat the sacred bug (As my divemaster used to call the cranky crustacean) — so the pressures and anticipation are on.

Christie's husband Jeff got us all to agree to have it the way his family craves the crustacean — boiled as always, but then served with cucumber and butter sandwiches (there's that jankie white bread again) and wait for it... potato chips. Now, Jeff, honey, I think I went along with this, just to watch your eyes light up — and the truth is, the potato chips are probably nessa for the cucumber & butter "sandwiches" — now, I'm not a good judge here, I put habanero on my ice cream, but, seriously, I need a lil sumpin' sumpin' even if it's just grease & salt.

Maybe I need to back-up so you'll understand that I'm not as cray as I sound... FLASHBACK to late spring, 1988... Mylove and I have been engaged for a year, we're a year from getting married. As (then) San Diegans, Baja (Mexico) is practically our backyard and as an alumna of San Diego State University, I know my way around south of the border, and ever since mentioning lobster, I've been hearing my bride-to-be wag on and on about how there's nothing better than Maine LOBstah, bla, bla, bla... But, see, I grew-up on the Puerto Nuevo Lobster shacks, where "twomediumismorethanonelarge." And I knew there was nothing that could *ever* compete with a hand-made tortilla the size of a manhole cover, hot off the grill, slathered in butter, with giant chunks of lobster and salsa so hot, it's a wonder it doesn't melt the vessel it's in, in where else? Good ol' Meh-he-co.

So far on this day, sunny day, it couldn't be going better — after enduring the two-hour drive hearing how the Maine LOBstah has a bigger claw, colder waters, yada, yada, yada — we 're here — not a big crowd, we're under a thatched roof, sun is setting and the whole beach is bathed in a golden orange glow, I'm here with the woman I'm going to spend the rest of my life with, I have an ice cold Corona in my hand, and I'm starting to feel *weightless* — you know that feeling you get when you're on the verge of a life-changing moment for the better? I look to Mylove, eyes filling with tears and whisper, "I love you..."

She is clutching a burrito that looks like a burst firecracker with shredded ends of tortilla fluttering in the breeze, contents spilling onto her hands, she has flecks of lobster meat at both corners of her mouth, two trails from her lips glistening with melted butter, pooling at her chin — cheeks stuffed deliriously with joy and says, half apologetically, half victoriously, "I'm bein' a pig..."

This. This, is the woman I would be spending my life with.

FLASHFORWARD back to Cape Cod, and I say... *"Mylove and I will make the LOBstah fest."*

Mitzi is only too happy to have someone else take over the chores, and before anyone else can protest, Mylove looks to me with her patented, "Have you lost your mind?" look and I smile. We're goin' Baja style — as my sainted father would say, "Faint heart never won fair maiden, nor made LOBstah burritos…" which is the old school variation of go big or go home.

So, that's what we're gonna do. I of course would never deprive Jeff of his beloved cucumber & butter sammichs, so I have double duty, but… I'm not gonna phone this one in — I'm bringing it with Mexican street corn, and a sweet potato tart all balanced with Salad Naranja… oh and his requisite potato chips.

We're an eclectic mix here — Mark, Mitzi's Hubby, grew up in LA and Berkeley back when Berkeley was first becoming Berzerkely, Mitzi, who shook off all the Yankee conservatism but kept the intelligence and grace, tempered that with a deep meditation practice and dipped it all in her adopted Virginia southern sweetness. Then there's Bunny, a self-made successful business woman and her Hubby, Gary who has the same Nebraska-charm of a David Letterman, dry, easy wit, and loves his Bun. And then there's Christie, the now retired family therapist who gave me the most loving and strong compass to navigate our way through gender transition, namely the concept of "Dignity," and her hubby Jeff who shares his beloved wife's dedication to social work.

What's missing in the above descriptions is the unbreakable bond of Mylove's "chums" that they taught to each of their spouses — we are all not only fortunate to be loved by these incredible women, but we know it, celebrate it, and are grateful for it — to the man, oh, and me.

As "one of the husbands," I had a special place, I was *the adventurer, the creative,* the *one from Hollywood.* I was their "answer man" for all the dish they had ever heard about La La Land, and the tales of my adventures would captivate them for hours.

Last time however, I ceased to be one of the boys. And I wasn't really paying attention because I was happy to be accepted as one of the girls. As I fill the lobster pot with water, I realize, I don't remember any issues, but I also don't recall any of our chats… not a one. And that's not like me.

But… luckily, not the me that's shredding cabbage and toasting cumin seed. As I make the dinner, playing the tapes back in my head is putting me back in touch with these cherished friendships that have developed in the past 12 years alongside Mylove's and her Applewild Girls' sixty-year bond. Which is good, cuz it's taking my attention away from the pressure of completely shanghaiing (yes, it's a word, look it up) everyone's taste buds and expectations for New England LOBstah…

It's only then when I notice that Mylove is also nervous about my oh-so-bold move… And I might be breaking one of cooking for others most basic rules, namely — meet or exceed expectations… and to exceed these expectations I have to head for the meeting point and then blow through it on the same road, whereas I have suddenly taken us south of their expectations, down "nine miles of bad Mexican highway…"

Oops…

As we sit down, the bibs and nut crackers come out. I've got bowls of drawn butter at every place, right next to individual bowls of salsa and guac.

The tortillas are warm, the chipotle sweet potato tart is steaming and the salad Naranja — the classic Spanish concoction of sliced oranges, olives, fresh oregano, Bermuda onion and chili powder — tips the scales in my favor.

Now, I forgot to tell you (as I forgot to remember myself) that there's this thing called "island corn." Island corn is almost as sacred to the Codders as their precious Maine LOBstah. Apparently certain strains of corn were grown on the islands around Martha's Vineyard and now they are gold standard of corn on cob in these here parts.

Mexican street corn is… well, not that. Grilled on the streets of the city, it's usually then slathered in mayonnaise, lime, chili powder and cotija cheese. It's *so not* island corn, (which is usually served with the barest butter and salt to savor its "island corn-ness.") that, this may be even bolder than servin' up LOBstah burritos.

Am I high?

… well, yes, but I'm also *right*. Judging from the flecks of tortilla on everyone's chins, butter glistening…

We're all bein' pigs.

LOBSTAH BURRITOS

Deceptively simple and oh sooooo good. The secret is actually in the tortilla. (Seriously how one could improve on LobstAH? Whether you go homemade, or snag these from your local mamacitas, the world is waking up to what we, who grew up in Cali have always known — life is better wrapped in a burrito. I won't pretend to do them better than I can get at virtually any taco shop in my neck of the woods, but since Tino's mom Margie showed me how to make the real deal, I do it once a year in her honor.

And while we're on the subject, it's not ever and never has been a "wrap." This is just what white people call it so other white people won't get all weird about that fererner food. Check your hipster beard and PBR at the door and call a spade a burrito or something like that.

---

1 lobster per person

1 lb. butter

4 cloves garlic (peeled and smashed)

2 cups flour

1 tsp. sea salt

4 tbsp. melted coconut or vegetable oil

OR (seriously, if it's good enough for the mamacitas) **lard**

3⁄4 cup hot water

Tortillas — makes 1 & ½ dozen.
Make the dough three to four hours before and cook them seconds before plopping them on the plates — you can even flip from skillet to plate while your guests are cracking their bad boys from their shells.

in a large bowl
Mix the flour and salt. Mix in your oil or lard until the mixture is crumbly Add the water and mix until the dough comes together.

Knead for 2 minutes, then cover the dough and rest for 20 minutes.

When you are ready to serve
Divide the dough into 18 balls. Roll each ball out as thin as you can.

Heat a cast-iron skillet to medium hot — it should be hot, but not smoking.

Cook each beauty for 30 seconds on each side, until golden brown spots show you it's ready to flip.

Tino's mom used two dinner plates to keep them warm. She would put a damp paper towel on the bottom plate and add each tortilla to the stack covering them with the top plate in between.

Now for the LobstAHs...
Get a large pot of water boiling vigorously.

In a smaller saucepan
Melt the butter and press the garlic into the melted butter

Add the lobstahs to the boiling water
It doesn't take long — most folks use the color of the shell to decide when it's done (going from deep red to just this side of orange) — I hate rubber, so I err toward underdone — and let them go no longer than two minutes under a vigorous boil.

Now here's where you have a choice
with the Applewild girls who grew up on the crustacean, cracking their bugs open at the table is actually most of the fun. But if timing is a factor, I crack the lobstah meat from the shells and immerse into the melted butter to keep warm. The meat is so dense it won't soak up too much butter and stays hot until serving time and moist! When it comes time, I fish out the serving and plate them myself. (And really who's gonna argue with butter on their lobstah, I ask you?)

Whatever way you go, serve the *lobstah* with individual bowls of the melted ("drawn" for those of you with a pinkie in the air) butter.

Then wrap the lobstah in the warm blankets of the tortillas, dip in more butter and enjoy!

MEXICAN STREET CORN RELISH

I make this a whole lot lighter than my Mexican friends who grew up on this "fair food," turning it from a street snack to a side dish. When you get it at the vendor's cart, the corn husks from a fresh ear of corn are folded back like the halberd of a mighty sword to hack your hunger into submission — but as a side dish, I prefer the sweet and tangy goodness of this ubiquitous salad to accentuate this meal.

In this recipe, I call for chipotle in adobo — which is one of the canned foods I actually can't live without, found in most markets in the Latinx Foods isle (or shelf if you live in a police state) "chipotle" are smoked jalapenos that are reconstituted in a traditional magical concoction of cumin, garlic, sugar and tomato paste called adobo. Spicy, smoky and sweet, it could make an old dish rag delicious!

6 ears fresh corn on the cob	1 lime
1 medium onion (sliced into rounds)	1 chipotle in adobo sauce
3 cloves of garlic	1/4 cup fresh cilantro leaves
1 jalapeño	1/2 cup unflavored, unsweetened coconut yogurt
1/4 cup EVOO for brushing on the veggies on the grill	1 cup crumbled cotija cheese
1 tbsp. rice wine vinegar	Salt to taste

Par - Steam the corn for five minutes while you heat the grill.

In mixing bowl
Whisk the EVOO & rice vinegar together

Take the bowl and a brush to the grill
brush the corn, onion rounds and garlic and grill to your taste — I like them to have fresh crunch. The corn is already almost cooked so what we care about here is the dark smoky caramelization.

In another mixing bowl
Mix together the yogurt, (which is coconut and thus will not curdle when mixed with the lime. Genius, right?) Add a chopped chipotle and a drop or drizzle of the adobo sauce (your call — are you a firebreather like me or a soft mouth like Mylove — no judgement)

Shave the corn from the cobs
Into the yogurt mix. Mince the grilled onion and garlic, chop the jalapeño into thin ribbons and stir it all together.

Add the crumbled cotija cheese & cilantro — stir and serve!

CHIPOTLE SWEET POTATO TART

This one has been my go-to recipe and the reason I bought a mandoline — it's an amazingly simple, surprising and yummy way to eat sweet potatoes or yams. I'm using coconut yogurt again because it plays so well with others. I've also served this at Thanksgiving and it brings a smile every time!

5 large sweet potatoes or yams. (sliced into wide strips — lengthwise with a mandoline)
1 cup coconut yogurt
1 tsp. dijon mustard
1 chipotle minced + a drop of adobo
3 scallions
1/4 bunch cilantro

Preheat your oven to 350 degrees

In a mixing bowl
Mix the yogurt, mustard and chipotle and adobo together

With the mandoline
Slice the potatoes into thin sheets (like a lasagna noodle).

In a 9 x 9 square baking dish
Spread a thin layer of the coconut mustard mixture, then lay the potato thins across the bottom. Brush with the coconut mustard mixture and continuing to layer the potato to make a square casserole. During the baking, the cream mixture blends with the thin layers of potato to cook into a wonderful tart that will be cut into squares like a tall brownie.

Bake for 30 minutes
Be careful that the top doesn't get dried out — if you start to brown too fast cover with foil.

Remove from the oven
Allow to cool for 10 minutes and cut into squares.

Garnish with the cilantro and sliced scallions.

SALAD NARANJÁ
(ORANGE, ONION, OLIVE & OREGANO SALAD)

I didn't realize (until I started typing) that this was the big O salad...

I first discovered this salad at a little hole in the wall called Bertas in Old Towne, San Diego. When most of the party hounds were trying to get into Rock Lobster, my friends and I saw this little pink house that was quietly standing like a wallflower while it's brashy older sibling was screaming for all the dinner patrons' business. It was a killer joint that I took Mylove to many times after that.

2 large oranges (peeled and sectioned)	**¼ cup EVOO**
½ red onion (slivered)	**1 tsp. ground chili powder**
1 cup large green Spanish olives (sliced)	**Salt to taste**
¼ fresh oregano leaves	

Slice the orange sections in half to allow the juice to be available.

In a "pretty" mixing/serving bowl
Whisk the EVOO & the chili powder. Toss all of the ingredients together, thoroughly — you want all of them to dance as one!

Chill in the reefer for 1 hour.
Give 'em a stir every now and again.

Serve.

CHAPTER 14

· ROBYN'S WEDDING SHOWER DECADENCE ·

PEACH COBBLER

RASPBERRY LEMON POUND CAKE

S'MORES PIE

NEVER THE BRIDESMAID...

I was promised to finally, finally be a bridesmaid... Yes, Yes, YES! I'm a feminist. Yes! YES! I know! I know! I KNOW!!! I'm just supporting/buying into patriarchal-binary clichés of womanhood and femininity etc. etc. etc. bla-bla-BLAH! I still want it. And my cis-ters can wag on til they're blue in the face about how the dress that gets picked by the bride will never be worn again, looks bad on every body type and it's a royal pain in the derriere to be asked, etc...

But... say what you all will (and do) it's still a rite of passage that women get to have — the women I know who share the above feelings are speaking from experience.

And that's what I'm talking about — they got to experience it, whereas I'm... (she says leaning further into the cliché...) making up for lost time.

So, when my dear friend Robyn, who's engagement, Mylove and I both have "mother-henned" called to say..."Sweetie, I've got good news & bad news..." Well, I held my breath and braced for impact...

I put her on speaker phone, so Mylove could hear. The good news? Tim, the reluctant groom-to-be, had finally agreed to a date and they were finally, finally, FINALLY going to tie the knot...

... and the bad news...?

Robyn cleared her throat, "I... Now, Scottie-dear, don't be mad... I know, I promised you... but... we are...

...*going to elope.*"

I was stunned. Yes. No one was going to be a bridesmaid. Yes, I was happy for her. She let me exhale. "So... we're going to have a party before we leave for Italy, and I'm hoping you'll come and would you like to make some of your fabulous desserts?"

Seriously. How could I refuse?

I loves me my Robyn. She's always been so generous and loving. I quickly got over the part about this being all about me and got back to it being all about her.

This entire year, as I started to get within striking distance of publishing this book you now hold in your hot little mitts, I've been testing recipes and posting the results on

Facebook. Robyn had been using this as a wish list and we settled on three potentials since there would be a variety of tastes and wants among her friends.

It was still going to be an elegant affair... and besides — I could take this opportunity to get a dress that I would wear after all was said and done.

The truth is, if I'm really honest with myself, I really wouldn't have had the emotional bandwidth to give to a real wedding if she had made good on her promise. And baking some killer desserts is probably all I can really handle right now.

Because now, Mylove... is not able to even leave our living room without my help.

We just can't seem to get in front of her fatigue. We got our second of two catheters last month which I must drain every other day (wait, that makes it seem like I'm doing all the work — Mylove is the one doing the work, I'm just the one handing her everything, holding her hand and stroking her forehead while a vacuum bottle fills.) It was taking everything she had just to lift herself out of our lounger (which had become her bed — making her way down the stairs to our bedroom had stopped last spring) and use a walker to make her way to the bathroom. So, we rigged her wheelchair in the living room to be her new private WC. Everyone knew to leave the upstairs and give her some privacy — she merely had to stand and pirouette and sit to do her business.

And just yesterday... even that became too much.

Last month, Mylove had a very... well, I guess the polite word is "matter-of-fact" chat with her very best favorite "Gyn-Onc"(Gynecological Oncologist) Dr. Axtell... and I can only remember one phrase — because it seared itself into my brain — a smoking white-hot scar that will never heal:

"At what point do people just... stop...?"

Dr. Axtell is an amazing woman — taking excellent care of Mylove for nine years now. She knows Mylove as well as I do. (almost) and certainly she knew what Mylove meant without — filling in the blanks herself. She paused and the world froze...

"Well, most people stop when they value quality over quantity."

We had been on the cusp in Mylove's cancer career for a while now. She had exhausted "the good chemo" options — these are the newer generation of drugs that have the same efficacy as the older class — but are "nicer" on the body — no hair loss, less visible side effects. What remained were only the old class of "cocktails," the ones that really roughed up the body. Which... well... we thought had been in our rearview mirror forever.

She had been through the classic scenes. Our dear friend, Tammy, who's a hairdresser came and cut Mylove's hair so it could be donated to "locks of love" — giving Mylove agency over her own hair, she was the one removing it instead of some disease or it's treatment taking it against her will. Then when it did start to fall out, Tammy came back and shaved Mylove's head so it would again be her decision, her doing.

Mylove really did have an amazingly beautiful head. She never did like the idea of wigs and instead rocked a variety of hats and caps and when it was warm enough she let her head shine forth.

But that was 2010... Now here in 2019, we left Dr. Axtell's office that day with the agreement that Mylove would finish out her current chemo regimen which would end in October. And that would be the end of treating cancer with chemo. We hoped that Mylove would regain her strength and then we could pursue building up her body's immune system rather than battering it with chemicals. We also left that day with a prescription from Dr. Axtell for Mylove to enter "palliative care."

Yes. It took both of our breaths away.

Pushing Mylove's wheelchair into the Palliative office was... surreal. Answering the intake questions here means saying the hardest things out loud that you've ever said in your life. Now, this could be merely the gateway drug into Hospice — but it's not necessarily the only outcome. But, that doesn't stop them from asking all of the really hard questions — do you have an advanced directive — if your heart stops how hard should we work to revive you?

Mylove was quite cavalier — I, was not. She didn't want to experience any further pain — if her heart stops and reviving her would require any more technology, she didn't want to wake up.

I couldn't stop the tears.

Thank God, that's not why we were really here, tho'. The Palliative doctor has massive pull in the hospital — when they speak, even EF Hutton listens. (anyone, anyone?) So, when Mylove mentioned that she was having trouble breathing, the next thing we knew, the Lung specialist was personally meeting us and inserting Mylove's second catheter to drain the other lung, which gave her some relief. But...

Our life has changed dramatically — now, a palliative nurse shows up at our house three times a week, a handsome physical therapist come once a week to relieve some of Mylove's discomfort and she's finally getting some care for her symptoms (which, to this point have been monitored and recorded but never given attention — much to my frustration).

Last week, we were supposed to go in for our very last CT scan — this would've told us what we already knew. That the chemo has "waned in its efficacy" or rather had stopped fighting her cancer and now was just weakening everything, including filling her chest cavity with the above mentioned fluid. But...

... Mylove was dreading making this trip to the hospital. The prior week, she sat on her bedpan as she rode in the car for the hour-long slog through morning rush hour traffic. She was not a happy camper.

It was at this time that I could finally see despite all my fears, a little clearer. Throughout the nine years we've been dancing with cancer, it was my job to talk to the doctors and hear the bad stuff (side effects) etc. so I could watch for warning signs while Mylove focused on using her super power of positive thoughts to heal herself. I would advise and give my opinion on things (which meant some full-blown fights with her doctors) but I was trying to always keep a bubble of calm and peace around her to promote her healing. And really, as two women fighting for our own agency in a world that seems to want to make all decisions for us, we fought for each other and especially here, would always be a united front with her in the lead. I was at my best for her when I was cheerleader, not coach. Teammate and not manager.

Which is hard as fuck when you're talking about the love of your life's... life.

But this year, something's changed. Mylove is the one digging in with her doctors, she's hearing it all — my role as filter and monitor, is not needed or wanted — And... like her deciding to end her chemo, I have to be okay with it — not just okay, I have to be all in.

Just like she's always been for me.

"Mylove," I say, mustering everything to turn up my "all-in" filter to eleven, so I will sound casual and confident, "why do you have to go through all this effort just to adhere to their protocols — if you know that you are definitely going to finish chemo, then this CT does nothing but confirm what we already know *and* stress you out." Mylove was instantly relieved. Yes. She was firm. She was confident with her decision... She was finished with chemo. I picked up the phone and called Dr. Axtell. We weren't coming in. Dr. Axtell agreed with our reasoning. There would be no reason for Mylove to stress out any more.

We, to use the vernacular... stood down. There will be no more trips to the hospital.

So... am I... looking for something, anything to hold back the tidal wave of fear that has been threatening to crush us ever since we heard those fateful words, "ovarian cancer" just nine years ago?

HELL YES!

I realize that I've been actually scared that any job I might've landed during this time would take me away from Mylove. Since my trip to NYC last July, (teaching a Showrunner's workshop for the WGA) and as desperate for money as we've been —

(and trust me — wanna blow up your career as an adventure-survival showrunner? Come out as transgender... and comedy ensues) it was Mylove who said even an eight hour day at an office is too much. Which... let's be real, is another sign that... well, that I've got something very real, very scary... very.. very...

... very not talk about-able to deal with.

So, Robyn's call is just the ticket. It's times like these, that I remember that I'm writing a cook book and realize I need to once again, apologize to you, my dear reader for giving you much more than you signed-up for. But I promise to make it worth your while — just like I promised Robyn three desserts to celebrate the love that she herself proclaimed was inspired by the one Mylove & I had.

I threw myself into planning these desserts. I knew I wanted to make the S'mores pie. I had been creating it in my mind for weeks prior to her call. Mylove has always loved Marshmallow fluff. Now, for those of you not from the east coast, I'm required (by Mylove) to make sure you understand that there is only one fluff. There is no substitute. Not the "crap" that others call spoonable marshmallow fluff (her words, not mine — I wouldn't even dream of head-to-head testing, I'm a "company girl" when it comes to those very few things that Mylove draws lines on — and this is one of them) nope nuh uh. This is the red capped jar with the blue text that simply reads "Fluff." It's the main character in fluffer-nutters — fluff & peanut butter sandwiches.

So, of course I knew I had to nail making it myself. A fool's errand, you say? And you could be right, especially after my above description of the high bar against failure. But as you no doubt might be able to guess by now...

It's just the sort of challenge this recklass wonder regularly loves to slam her head against.

So a'slammin' we go. But... marshmallows and marshmallow fluff are not that mysterious — and in fact, it seems, if we base anything on the amount of internet squawking there is on the subject, this is one guilty pleasure that a buncha people share. So... I have many mentors to draw wisdom from in the alchemy required.

But it's the chocolate that's had me stumped. I knew of course that I would be making a graham cracker crust (D'uh) so I'm 2/3 there, but when you make campfire S'mores, the beauty is that the toasted marshmallow goes onto chocolate and melts it. And if you're like me, I place my graham cracker with the bar chocolate on the hot stones that circle the campfire which toasts the cracker and sets up a subtle "layering" of different textures of chocolate that range from hard to liquid in a mere ¼ of inch of heavenly goodness — no matter how much you're able to melt your chocolate, since you're outdoors, this cooling/layering variety happens naturally between lifting the cracker from the stone, placing your perfectly toasted heavenly fluff ball (sometimes still flaming?) onto the whole affair, and taking a bite. Sometimes the second bite is even better.

So how to recreate that experience with a pie?

Well… I'm no expert. And I didn't even know that this existed before I read about it, but it seems that there's this thing called a chess pie. Now, legend has many reasons for this amazing thing being called a chess pie (all are fun — everything from pies being stored in pie chests, with the T being left off for sumsuch reason, to the original cook who created it being asked if her wonderful creation had a name and her reply — in a heavy southern accent — being, "oh, it's 'chess (just) pie."

But what intrigued me when I was drilling down, was that people described this as having "micro layers" of texture — everything from the crunchy crumbly goodness of a brownie to liquid magma of a lava cake. The truth is, there is no flour in this puppy, the binding agent is… wait for it… cocoa powder. Seriously. Eggs. Cocoa. Dark Chocolate. Butter. Love. Time.

As my dear friend Donny would say, "What's not to love?"

One down. Two to go. Robyn's been reading my FB postings from the get-go and the one that really started it all was the anniversary cake. Which I told you all about in the April Chapter. (funny… I never really put it together before but that chapter was all about Mylove getting her first catheter… sigh). Um… oh yes, cake. Sorry. I had done passionfruit, and I've done guava (ever since my dear friend Laura gave me a bagfull from her backyard tree) but what about… raspberry curd?

If I made a traditional lemon pound cake and spread homemade raspberry curd between the layers, poured a raspberry glaze, and decorated it with fresh raspberries wouldn't that look wedding-festive? Robyn squealed with delight.

Okay, so we only need one more…

Robyn was musing aloud (take notes girls, when the bride whispers her prayers aloud it's our job to listen!)

"I was wondering, if abundance had a color what would it be? — and a peach jumped into my mind! And I realized that, yes! It's the very symbol of beauty and sweetness. I had the most amazing peach this morning, and I thought…what about fresh peach cobbler…?"

I'm with her thoughts instantly — basking in golden sunshiny rays of peach colored warmth, "with warm vanilla-bean infused heavy cream." I say aloud dreamily.

Another squeal. My work here is done. Or rather just starting. Now, all I have to do it is pull three rabbits out of my hat.

This is the real art of catering that almost nobody ever understands — transporting amazing goodness to location. It's one thing to make these works d'arte in your own kitchen — but we weren't even going to Robyn's house for the affair — she was given an amazing house on the sand in Venice and parking was a block away.

But that's only the second half. The first half of my dilemma is that these are really only going to be best if fresh... in other words, I'll need to make them "day of" — I won't be able to get a jump on anything ahead of time, so it's going to be a full court press from the moment I wake up...

And... it's a wedding party — and Robyn and her posse all hail from Cornell — no pressure on how I look for said affair... it's only now when my vanity and my cooking ego agree to arm wrestle.

Which is probably good, because as we've been saying all along — the most important ingredient of any of the dishes in this book is love. So, I'm so "out of mi'head" worrying about all of the above, I'm just... Okay. Baking over my head.

The good news is that my Father said it's where I do my best work. The better news is that this one of the places where he was right.

Robyn was disappointed that Mylove would not be able to come and suggested that we could "facetime" her once things got rolling — like a wedding shower, there would be some "formal festivities" of which her participation would be greatly appreciated, and Mylove would no doubt enjoy (remember she too had worked hard to get this betrothal to actually happen!).

But the truth was... Mylove was really starting to see for herself just how... little there was of her. She had lost most of her upper body mass — and tho' she was coming in at "a buck and a quarter" as my father would say, the weight she carried came from edema in her lower extremities. She could see this and was just now starting to become "self-conscious" of it. She's seen a few pictures that friends have taken in the last weeks and has... seen what I've been telling myself is not what's happening.

I first started really noticing this at the start of the summer — but I realized I was seeing her sickness, rather than the sheer beauty that was Mylove. Beauty in this sense is the word I use to describe the brilliance, intelligence, kindness, beautiful, funny amazing being-ness that is Mylove that had flat-out captivated, inspired, cheered me, loved me, blown me away for the last three decades... I made a vow that day to never, ever see her as sick. I wasn't going to deny reality, I'm not stupid or naïve. But I could choose what to focus on. So, I chose to see the amazing woman that had rocked my world every day for the last thirty-two years...

I told Mylove, that I would make the appropriate apologies (guarding her dignity) and hurry home as soon as was polite.

Not sure of how my make-up is, but I'm on time... as long as you count making the peach cobbler there as "on time." Okay… I wanted it to be served hot and yes, if you're keeping score, I ran out of time, okay… the S'mores pie is amazing. The raspberry pound cake just needs to be plated and the cobbler… well, yes, I admit I'm rolling the dice — Part of it is by design: I've saute'd the peaches ahead of time in brandy butter and cardimom to make sure that all I have to do it pour the dry ingredients into the pan, top it with the saute'd peaches and pat with butter… oh, and warm the "secret sauce" — heavy cream that's been nurturing vanilla *habanero* sugar for two days…

… but nobody knows how to run this oven… And that was definitely not by design…

Luckily, Robyn has several things working in my favor — a fabulous spread of food for dinner — a cappuccino bar and… a bestie, who is a pro caterer, and together we get the oven on our side… finally.

Which gave me the courage to actually peek into the box I used to transport the raspberry pound cake — oh, didn't I mention that a sudden stop had given me pause that maybe things weren't all lemons and raspberries…

Before I look, I need to say… never *ever* go anywhere without your katana — your Excalibur — your Olivander's wand — this is your own go-to extension of you. For some it's a chopstick, others a chef's spoon, and still others a favored buck knife. For me, it's a blade-spatula. The thin rounded edge, flat blade knife spatula. This is my hand, finger and tongue — it stands in as my first lieutenant, when I'm off on other duties…

And I needed it now. Many years ago, I bought my father a set of chef's knives as a Christmas present, and the "roll-up" canvas carrier to carry them (like a pro chef) — when he passed, I inherited the whole kit and kaboodle. Thank Gawd, I rolled up my quiver before I rolled.

I may not have gotten my eyeliner straight, but when I have enough courage to look into the box that Macky had so lovingly helped with (and posted on FB) I see that SHIT! I need to straighten the top layer of the pound cake which has slid off the bottom layer… and I'm starting to hyperventilate.

I'm a hands-on kinda girl. Things happen. Accidents occur. It doesn't have to be the end of the world or your dessert! So, I re-sculpt the whole cake into an appealing shape — you can too.

Breathe. Get out your wand. Go to work.

Which I did. I was, of course helped by two things — the cake was soooo moist that it never really broke apart, I was able to get it back into position well enough. I had made the top layer in a traditional bundt cake with its distinctive decorative fluting, but the bottom I made in an angel food pan (with the bottom that lifts out) — I had already been through the harrowing process of using two spatulas to carefully lift the cake high enough to get it off the tall cylinder that creates an angel food's classic "hole," so I knew it was moist enough (thank god and yes, I'm sorta braggin') to withstand being re-built.

The second thing that helped? Extra berries. I had brought three boxes of fresh raspberries — and these I could use to "decorate" the cake, which was delicious camouflage. In fact, I was almost too good with the cascading raspberries... it was too pretty (almost) to eat.

I toasted the marshmallow of the S'mores pie with my chef's torch, mere seconds before the locusts descended. The soft peaks of the white marshmallow became smoky brown, a tantalizing contrast to the shiny white waves. I cut the first piece to reveal the dark chocolate heart and graham cracker foundation. That was the only incentive most needed. The raspberry curd/lemon cake was a bit intimidating, with everyone marveling at its color and elegance, but not sure they wanted to be the first to mar it's beauty, until I began to start offering pieces to the guests...

... but the cobbler.

... yes, I did need to offer the vanilla-infused cream as a topper, despite the fact that it was in a warm pouring vessel right next to steaming cobbler. But nobody needed any invitation to grab a spoon of the still oven-warm cardomom-perfumed, peaches. Those that allowed me to bath this cozy bowl of childhood, with the warm blanket of vanilla bean caressed (and habanero heated) cream, were grateful beyond measure. And came back for seconds. And thirds.

But the S'mores pie? Gone.

I didn't even see it go. I barely got a piece out to take home for Mylove and turned back to an empty plate that looked like someone had licked it clean.

So... you can draw your own conclusions, but I'd say... hat trick.

The night ended with everyone sitting in a circle and toasting Robyn as her beau, Tim and his posse of groomsmen joined us for the festivities. We showered them with rose petals and blessings for their marriage. It was beautiful night missing only one person. Mylove. I made my rounds for final hugs, collecting love and blessings for Mylove as I did.

The best compliment I received that whole night was the look of shock and surprise on Mylove's face as she tasted the homemade version of her childhood staple. *"I thought you were going to make the fluff from scratch."*

Now, *she* knows how to treat her lady.

So... how'd we make these?

"There was a pearl of light that danced on my lips for hours after every one of her kisses..."

PEACH COBBLER
WITH WARM VANILLA CREAM

This recipe has a zillion versions on the web but what they all have in common is faith in alchemy. By that I'm refering of course to the magic that happens that despite pouring the batter into the bottom of the pan and adding sliced peaches on top the batter rises over and enrobes the peaches in baked goodness. So, if you've never made it before, have faith in the process and watch the magic happen.

I like using a bit of brandy when I precook the fresh peaches — the alcohol burns off leaving behind a nice "bottom end" like a thumping bass track for the peaches to solo over the top. One other note — I don't like peeling fruit when cooking them — I feel the peel of most fruits is part of the overall flavor we expect and I want that. You can do what you wish... you're making it, right?

PEACH COBBLER

5 peaches sliced (about 4 cups)

3/4 cup sugar

Generous splash of brandy

1 cup all-purpose flour

1/2 cup granulated sugar

2 tsp. baking powder

1/4 tsp. salt

1/4 tsp. ground cinnamon

1/4 tsp. ground cardomom

3/4 cup buttermilk

VANILLA CREAM

1 cup heavy cream

1 tbsp. sugar

1 whole vanilla bean (split)

Preheat your oven to 400 degrees

Generously grease a glass 9x13 baking dish with butter.

In a sauce pan on med-high heat
Add the peaches, sugar and brandy, Allow the sugar to melt and the peaches to release their juice. When the peach flesh is soft remove from the heat.

Make your batter
In a mixing bowl
whisk together the dry ingredients (flour, sugar, baking powder, salt, cinnamon, and cardamom). Stir in the buttermilk.

In your greased baking dish
Pour the batter. Lay the peach slices right onto the batter. Drizzle the remaining peach syrup across the entire dish.

Cut the butter into cubes
and dot the baking dish every 2 inches.

Bake for 45 minutes.

While that's going — Make your cream
In a sauce pan on a very low heat:
Pour in the ingredients. Stir to dissolve the sugar and allow the vanilla bean to "wallow" in the cream for at least ten minutes.

Remove the bean
using a dull knife or blade spatula, scrape the vanilla pulp from the inside of the bean into the cream, then return the split bean to the cream while the cobbler bakes — you're really just warming the cream and nurturing it's embrace of the vanilla.

When you're ready to serve
remove the vanilla bean
and add it to your vanilla sugar jar, and transfer the cream to a pouring vessel (gravy boat).

Remove the cobbler from the oven
allow it a minute for the top to crisp up a bit, then spoon it into individual serving dishes and pass the cream.

Enjoy!

RASPBERRY LEMON CAKE

This will look very familiar if you're reading this cover to cover — like it's big sister, the anniversary cake, I make this cake in two bundt pans to make a bottom and top layer with raspberry curd spread between the layers — again, this makes an elegant, festive "shape" for the cake, (with the batter divided between the two pans.)

The lesson here (for me) was that variations on a theme can keep your game fresh and techniques (like making curd with the sous vide) can be applied to non-traditional flavors to delightfully surprise your guests. Have you ever heard of raspberry curd? I hadn't. It's amazin

THE CURD	1/4 cup fresh lemon juice
1/2 cup fresh raspberry puree	Zest of 1 whole lemon
1 stick of butter	4 large eggs
3/4 cup organic sugar	1/2 cup flour
8 egg yolks	1/2 tsp. salt
I tsp. lemon zest	1/2 tsp. baking soda
1 tsp. salt	1/2 tsp. baking powder
THE CAKE	**THE GLAZE**
1 cup Irish butter, softened, plus more for pan	2 Tbsps. fresh raspberry juice
3/4 cup plus 3 tbsp. sugar	3 Tbsps. powdered sugar

Make the curd at least the day before

Whisk all the ingredients together and pour into a high heat tolerant plastic bag in your sous vide — cook at 167 degrees for one hour (if you don't have a sous vide you can cook this on your stove top — medium low heat for 30 minutes)

Pour the curd into a blender to emulsify
Run the blender on high for about thirty seconds. transfer to a jar and refrigerate overnight.

At least 4 hours before you plan to serve the cake — **Preheat the oven to 350 degrees.**

Butter 2–9 inch bundt pans
Dust with sugar and tap out excess. Set aside.

In your standing mixer
Add the butter & sugar and whip into a fluffy cream.

Add to the mixer
the eggs, lemon juice and zest.

In a separate bowl
whisk together the dry ingredients — flour, salt, baking soda and baking powder.
Add this to standing mixer mix on medium.

Pour the batter into your prepared pans
Bake until a cake tester comes out clean, about 35 minutes.

Cool on a rack.
After 10 minutes, invert the pans but don't remove them yet. Let them cool another 10 minutes.

Unmold the cake and cool some more.

When they are cool to the touch — Time to build us a cake!

Spread the curd generously on the bottom layer
place the top layer on the curded bottom (not sure if that's a word, but it makes sense, right?) and prepare to glaze...

Make the glaze

Using a fork, crush enough fresh raspberries to get 2 tablespoons of juice.
Strain the juice into a bowl and add 3 tablespoons sugar — mix thoroughly, pour the glaze onto the cake

Garnish with fresh raspberries!

S'MORES PIE

Okay, Okay, I can hear your eyes rolling now... If you're going to all this trouble, why make it into a pie? And you know what — I got nothing... except this pie! Hear me out, or rather reserve your judgement until you try this.

Now, I'm not the first one to throw marshmallow fluff on a chocolate pie and call it S'mores... but there are two major flaws to that approach. First — the thang what makes it a S'mores, don't choo know, is the TOASTED marshmallow — hello? And second — as I painstakingly described in this chapter (and thereby revealed my... psychosis) I always try to get my bar chocolate all melty when making campfire S'mores BUT I realized that having it totally melt to liquid is not the point — it's the counterpoint — differing textures of the heavenly stuff from gooey goo to solid makes it a true S'more... so, merely making a mousse or a pudding is... well, a bless-your-heart try.

I've mixed it up with the traditional southern "Chess Pie" which by its nature has differing textures not unlike the ways a brownie gets crunchier the closer to the surface it gets from its soft middle. Call me crazy. But if you try this you will call me. Crazy?

Also — tho' Mylove believes there's no better substance on earth than original Marshmallow fluff — I just can't do that — but you can. You will need a chef's torch (Others have tried this in the broiler but I'm not that brave).

Oh, and one last thing (when you've completely lost your mind...) I like to decorate this masterpiece with homemade marshmallows (now, you see what I mean? About losing your mind, silly) I've included the directions and ingredients for these at the end of the recipe — please, do these the day (or week) before — they need to be completely set so they can withstand the toasting process if you choose to go "all in" — but they are definitely over-the-top... (and therefore not really nessa, but you'll make them won't you? I thought so.) Despite my tirade in an earlier chapter about cornstarch in powdered sugar, here you do need them both so... forget what I said when you make marshmallows?

CRUST

2 cup graham cracker crumbs

1/2 cup butter (melted)

1 cup brown sugar

FILLING

1/4 cup unsalted butter

1 1/2 cup granulated sugar

1/4 tbsp. salt

4 large eggs

1/4 cup Dutch-process cocoa

2 tbsp. coffee liqueur* (e.g., Kahlua), or substitute strong brewed coffee

1 tbsp. cold milk or cream

1 tsp. vanilla extract

1 tsp. espresso powder

2 tbsp. yellow or white cornmeal

1 cup dark chocolate chips

(MARSHMALLOW FLUFF) TOPPING
3 large egg whites
1/2 tsp. cream of tartar
2 tbsp. granulated sugar

3/4 cup golden corn syrup
1 cup granulated sugar
1/2 tsp. vanilla extract

Preheat the oven to 300 degrees
Make your crust

In a mixing bowl
Stir the cracker crumbs and brown sugar into the melted butter.

In a glass pie pan
Press onto bottom and up sides of pan until desired size.

Bake at 300 for 8–10 minutes,

Make your filling.
In a mixing bowl
Beat together the butter, sugar, and salt until smooth. Add the eggs one at a time, beating slowly but thoroughly after each addition; you want to combine them with the butter and sugar, but not beat in a lot of air.

Stir in the cocoa, liqueur, milk, and vanilla.

Use a food processor (mini, if you have one)
grind together the espresso powder, cornmeal, and chocolate chips.
Add the chocolate chip mixture to the batter.

Pour the batter into the crust.

Bake the pie for 45 minutes, adding a crust shield after 20 minutes.

The middle may look pretty soft; so long as the temperature has reached 165°F right in the center, the pie is done. Remove the pie from the oven, cool to room temperature.

Make the topping:
In your standing mixer
With a whisk attachment, beat the egg whites and cream of tartar until foamy. Add 2 tablespoons of sugar and beat until soft peaks form, set aside.

Meanwhile, in a saucepan,
add water, corn syrup, and a cup of sugar. Cook over medium heat while stirring until the mixture reaches **firm ball stage 248 degrees** on a candy thermometer. This step will take about 15 minutes.

Once the corn syrup mixture has reached firm ball stage
turn the mixer onto medium and in a slow steady stream, pour the corn syrup mixture into the beaten egg whites. Once all of the corn syrup mixture has been added, beat on high for 5 minutes. Add vanilla extract and beat on high 1 minute.

Spread the fluff on the cooled pie
Create peaks. With your chef's torch toast the peaks. Serve... or...

(ONLY IF YOU ARE TRULY CRAZY, AND BY NOW, COMPLETELY RECKLASS... THEN, AS PROMISED...)

MARSHMALLOWS

MARSHMALLOWS	
3 packages unflavored gelatin	¼ tsp. kosher salt
1 cup ice cold water	1 tsp. vanilla extract
12 oz. granulated sugar, approximately 1 1/2 cups	¼ cup confectioners' sugar
1 cup light corn syrup	¼ cup cornstarch
	Nonstick spray

In a standing mixer
Place the gelatin into the bowl along with 1/2 cup of the water. Have the whisk attachment standing by.

In a small saucepan combine
the remaining ½ cup water, granulated sugar, corn syrup and salt. Cook over medium high heat, cover and allow to cook for 3 to 4 minutes. Uncover, clip a candy thermometer onto the side of the pan and continue to cook until the mixture reaches **240 degrees F,** approximately 7 to 8 minutes. Once the mixture reaches this temperature, immediately remove from the heat.

Turn the mixer on low speed
slowly pour the sugar syrup down the side of the bowl into the gelatin mixture. When all of the syrup is in, increase speed to high. Continue to whip until the mixture becomes very thick, approximately 12 to 15 minutes. Add the vanilla during the last minute of whipping.

Combine the confectioners' sugar and cornstarch in a small bowl.
Lightly spray a 13 by 9-inch metal baking pan with nonstick cooking spray. Add the sugar and cornstarch mixture and move around to completely coat the

bottom and sides of the pan.

Pour the mixture into the prepared pan
using a lightly-oiled spatula, spread evenly into the pan.

Dust the top with sugar and cornstarch mixture to lightly cover.
Allow the marshmallow to sit uncovered for at least 4 hours and up to overnight.

Turn the marshmallow out onto a cutting board
and cut into 1-inch squares using a pizza wheel dusted with the confectioners' sugar mixture. Once cut, lightly dust all sides of each marshmallow with the remaining mixture, using additional if necessary. Store in an airtight container for up to 3 weeks.
I find that this added "flair" creates a nice dimensionality to the surface of the pie that elevates it even higher — it admittedly adds to your workload, so it can be skipped... no judgement here!)

CHAPTER 15

· THE LAST OCTOBER ·

THE PERFECT POACHED EGG
"I NEED COCOA" HOT CHOCOLATE
FRESH PEACH-STUFFED FRENCH "TOAFFLES"

"COULD BE HOURS — COULD BE DAYS"

It's been four months since I sent the above text — first to my sister Lib, then my brother's in Law... the second part went something like this... "but Ruthie would be surprised if it was more than three days."

The truth is, I was actually finished with this book and it was at the proofreader's when Mylove decided to rewrite the last chapter. And now, I'm struggling to see the keyboard through my tears.

But Mylove must've known. Last October, we were still in a clinical trial, for a drug called a PARP inhibitor, which was just starting to wane in its efficacy for Mylove. Her strength never really returned and that cold at Christmas left her vulnerable to a viral pneumonia which landed her in the hospital for the first ten days of the new year. (As you knew by reading to this point).

It was only a few days after Robyn's party that we were in full blown Hospice. Emphasis on the blown. It seemed so innocent at first — it wasn't a diagnosis, so much as a suggestion — maybe that's why I heard myself, calmly agree when Mylove said, "the care will be better, and we'll have access to more services...and when I get stronger we can always leave hospice."

The good news was that after a trainwreck of a palliative nurse, we got Ruthie — Mylove adored this Israeli fireball who had raised her children in India and was quite comfortable with our spiritual path and philosophy. And when we "entered" hospice, Ruthie "came" with us. I'm using quotes because "entering" hospice was not going anywhere — Mylove hasn't gone anywhere in these last months — the living room was her world. We were getting more services as she said — and more attention — trucks arrive the day we call them, bringing everything from a respirator (which looks like it escaped from an old Frankenstein movie) to a real hospital bed.

In these last weeks, I am Mylove's nurse, sponge nurse, & massage therapist when the real ones aren't here. (Which is every other day for Ruthie, and the sponge nurse and physical therapist come once a week.) I'm in a really surreal place between trying to cherish every moment with Mylove and trying to keep from falling from the cliff into the ocean of fear that...

... this is happening.

Oddly, I have perfected the perfect poached egg (double postive intended — I need all the positive I can get long about now) which is a blessing, because I'm trying to get as many calories into Mylove as humanly possible — it's not that she's not eating, she's just really particular about what "sounds good" to her. And not much is passing muster.

Okay, I'm fighting off hysteria and delirium. I'm not sleeping. I have tried sleeping on the couch (again) but since she's not sleeping much either. and using MSNBC as her distraction of choice (or reruns of the Golden Girls) I am at least trying to get some rest in our bed downstairs. Alone. (Well, as alone as one can be with two snoring dogs). I sleep with my cellphone on my nightstand as a $250.00 per month intercom system, that Mylove can use to summon me when she does get a craving. These usually come about 3:00 am, but she's worried that I'm not sleeping, (I'm not) so she tries to hold out as long as she can — usually about 4:00 am. I am elated to come when she calls to get her fresh squeezed orange juice and/or a poached egg.

As you know by now, she's a tough customer — and the perfect poached egg was elusive for the longest time — oh, I could do it and did throughout our three decades of marital bliss, but I'd also occasionally *miss...* and that would suck — I sought consistent perfection — and finally nailed it.

It would really warm me to my core to see her smile as I handed the crystal bowl with two perfectly completely runny yolks beneath the perfectly cooked white veils.

Since we went into hospice, I've set up a schedule with dear friends to come for a few hours every day to sit with Mylove and be with her while I get errands done — house business, and chasing her elusive cravings — trust me, I'm only too happy to find anything, no matter what, to get her to eat.

These friends are really brightening her days — and she's connecting with them on such deep levels. We have always known that we have the dearest friends — but to actually see them all step up and step in with such love and care is truly humbling. Mylove's spirit is radiant and so blindingly strong — everyone leaves reassuring me that she's going to be better than okay and out of that bed soon.

But one day, we start increasing the dose of pain medications — and again, it seems so innocent at first. A liquid Ibuprofen — I mean aspirin, right? Nothing to worry about. Then another day…

… the pharmacy delivers the liquid morphine. And the liquid Adavan.

And that's when you stop counting up and start *counting down…*

It was about this time that Ruthie pulled me aside and said, *"She will always be able to hear you right up until the very end, but if there's anything you need to hear from her…*

I wouldn't put that conversation off."

There are few things I've learned over the years, from having my mom lapse into a coma after a cerebral hemorrhage, and my dad after a massive heart attack, and my father-in-law after a stroke... Hospice nurses know their shit. They will never give you false hope and when they speak — you listen. Each time they have "pulled me aside" they have called the moment of transition to the very minute.

I pushed the couch next to Mylove's hospital bed and we created a giant playpen. And we had two of the greatest nights of our marriage — we stayed up all night and when we could no longer keep our eyes open I could lay on the couch but with my head on her bed and we could cuddle as we had done for 32 years.

In between talking about all the things we should've been talking about and anything else our hearts wanted to say, I made her cocoa with the recipe I had perfected over decades of erasing a bad day or celebrating a good one with a steaming mug of chocolaty goodness.

It's Thursday about 3:00 am (hmm... go figure) when Mylove asks if she could have French toast. Heck yeah, you can have anything you want!

Now, something you should know about our marriage is that Mylove was always the purist. She is of the less is more side, whereas I am definitely from the more is more camp. Throughout our years together, I have forever been riffing with just about everything — constantly creating, constantly experimenting, constantly searching for new better or different things.

But as I said earlier, Mylove has her "things." For those keeping score:

*dark meat of both the chicken & turkey — has to be on the bone (hates boneless, won't even try).

*Her fish must be moist, practically sashimi and no sauce. No matter how amazing it could be.

*She likes chocolate ice cream, considered anything else a waste of time and forget fruit ice creams (except Black Raspberry — go figger, it's an east coast thing).

*Mylove just wants French toast — not *banana* French toast, not *chocolate chip* French toast — she doesn't want them dusted with powdered sugar, slathered in whipped cream, if she says she wants French toast she's picturing a big pat of melting butter swimming in pure maple syrup.

And I know this.

But something makes me instantly see something more amazing. We still have some fresh peaches from the case I bought for Robyn's wedding shower... and I couldn't help myself.

I make the classic French toast batter with just a dash of ground cardomom — sliding two thick slices of brioche bread into the whipped egg, but instead of plopping them onto a hot skillet — I… lay one into the bottom half of our waffle iron, drop a layer of the fresh peach slices on top, put the other slice of the battered brioche bread on top and close the lid of the iron — the sizzle and aroma of peach, toasted bread and cardomom fill the air, and almost make me forget that I'm breaking the cardinal rule of this book (again, oops maybe still?) — cooking for the ones you love, means listening to them and fulfilling their desires not yours…

And despite knowing that I was on shaky ground, I was keenly aware that this was a metaphor for our love and marriage — I wanted so much more for her always. I wanted to shower her with everything I had and even tho' she was always happy with the simplest things — my hug. My touch. My kiss. She never needed more than that.

She gave me a teasing smile as she took her first bite, maple syrup mingling with melted butter cascading down the crevasses of crunchy toasted brioche enrobing the sweet golden peach… I was already calculating how fast I could make a plain replacement. Her smile broke into a second bite. "Boy, your cooking lately is… otherworldly, Mylove — I mean it, you are on fire!"

Whew.

We finished out that night with more giggling and some deeper talks. We have always gone deep -- we've been lovers, partners, and buddies (her words) enthusiastically grabbing this thing called life with all four hands. But tonight, the depth is mindblowing — we're talking about even what to do when she's… you know… gone. Like what to do with her body — where to scatter the ashes.

And you'd be proud of me — maybe it's her smile but something deep inside of me is soaking up every molecule of this present without spending a single second straying into the future.

The next night however is not as magical — she's incredibly restless in her body. Ruthie has instructed me to increase her morphine and Adavan to try make her comfortable, but we're just not getting it right. In between doses, Mylove keeps asking me to "raise her up," lying back is uncomfortable — but immediately after raising the electric bed so she's sitting up, her head falls forward and her chin gets buried in her chest making it hard for her to breathe. I lower her only to have tell me to raise her up again, and the cycle starts anew… this goes on for three hours, each time I try to lie down, once again, crawling back into our playpen after having vaulted out of it to keep her from choking, and it is taking it's toll. In a moment of frayed exhaustion, I finally lose my cool in brief moment of exhausted frustration and shout, "Damn it Mylove, you're going into the light, and I'll be left behind!" I burst into tears, mad at myself for being exhausted, for shouting at her, for FUCKING LOSING HER...!

And through the fog of morphine and Adavan and cancer and pain and looming death, she hears my soul's anguish and holds her arms out to me and whispers, "Oh Mylove, come here..."

And I melted into her hug, my body lit up with an electricity that was the one thing I knew better than even my own body — her love, I also knew to the very depth of my soul that...

... it was our last hug.

Even as her strength began to recede from her arms, still, she tried to keep her gaze on me. But the morphine was doing its job and she couldn't fight it anymore... I lowered her bed, and she finally slept.

The next day was a Saturday. And it wasn't like I called a bunch of people to let them know that Mylove might be leaving. Some who were here, were just showing up as they had been scheduled to, like our dear Auntieji, Linda who came in from Seattle and who, with our Granny Shyamala had planned over two weeks ago to be here on this day. Others, like Dana and Lisa who had come from Oakland had driven down to be with Mylove yesterday, and were going to leave today.

When Ruthie had said to me the fateful words — "Could be hours, could be days, but if it went three days I would be surprised." I did pass it along to Mylove's brothers as a matter of protocol but I sent it my sister Lib as a cry for help. She dropped everything to come from San Diego.

In the end — Mylove took her last breaths surrounded by about 25 dear, close friends. Her brother Macky and sister-in-law, Tamsin, some of Mylove's most cherished friends. Word was spreading somehow — those that couldn't make it were sending me email and texts — the world was pulling for her and cheering her on as she stepped across into the light.

I held it together until the last breath left her and then I fell apart.

****

It's now March of the following year. I'm trying to get this all down to finish this. It's part of the process of letting go. Even now almost six months after her passing, I get about three hours in a row before I fall apart for about ten minutes. Then I blow my nose, wipe my face, fix my make-up and get back to it.

"It" is the name for sorting through the myriad details of closing out her life. Banks. Insurance. House deed and title. Stuff. It's a full-time job.

We had two memorials for Mylove. One was 13 days after her passing. The same day that

Robyn and Tim were married in Italy. I had my dear friend Indira record a video of me breaking a coconut in their honor five minutes before 6:00 am on this day, which was five minutes before 2:00 pm in Italy — the beginning of their ceremony. Indira, her beau, KarlwithaKay and I, then met my dear friend Adam and we wrapped Mylove's body in her meditation shawls, annointed the body with some sacred ash and holy water and covered it with gardenia and rose petals. The four of us then sang one of Mylove's favorite sacred hymns as her body was cremated.

That night, while our house was filled with our Los Angeles-based friends, who had gathered to honor her passing, Granny and our friends in the Bay area gathered at Adam's mother's house to do the same.

I'm going to close out this chapter now. But I will include recipes for "perfect poached eggs, Mylove's "I need cocoa" cocoa & her new favorite, "Peach-Stuffed French Toaffles."

They are waiting for you on the next page.

PERFECT POACHED EGGS

There is nothing like a beautifully cooked egg. We all have our personal definition of that. Mine changed during my life with Mylove. I used to be an "over-medium" girl — mostly because I loved a nice runny yolk, but could never stand the uncooked white that un-caring cooks let pass for "sunny side-up" or "over easy." But Mylove was a sunny side-up girl — big surprise. One of our life-long jokes (mostly between Mylove and her bestie Weezie) was that she was an "Over-easy girl," which was a dig at me for forgetting (or not listening) how the love of my life wants things to be.) I guess it became a thing because I had insisted that I was right and she was wrong… about how she like her eggs…

Geezus Gawd — please tell me I've never been that stupid or arrogant. I won't compound my felony (or further cement my legacy) by also insisting it never happened… The point of this all is that… who knew eggs were such an integral part of marriage? Trust me honey — they are. So… in that spirit, I shall now, as an elder in the marriage tribe — (look when you've been married for more than 29 years, you can school me) bestow upon you the magic spell that will work every time. (I wish to now thank the many YouTubers who taught me this) Without further ado… behold! Perfection explained…

This is game of timing so get all of the above at hand so you're not fumbling around and fumbling past each person's perfection. The beauty of this system is that you can cook 1 or four pairs of eggs all at once — trust me people will think that you are a sorceress at brunch time — everyone eating their own perfection simultaneously. Ready?

Non-stick skillet (at least 2 inches deep)	**Slotted spoon**
A lid that will fit this skillet	**2 eggs per person**
Filtered water (enough to completely fill the skillet)	**Serving dishes for each person**
A small dish for each pair of eggs you will make (assuming 2 per person)	

Get the filtered water into your skillet to a rolling boil

Why filtered water? Cuz your eggs are going to swim in them — if your tap tastes good — then hats & horns, but if not, go filtered.

Crack each pair of eggs into individual small dishes.

This is how you can get the timing almost perfect — you will slide them in all at once (and since you have only two hands you can reload faster).

Watch the water return to a rolling boil (the more eggs you have the longer it will take as the volume of cold eggs has to be compensated by the boiling water — but it's only seconds).

When it hits the boiling point again — put the lid on — and shut off the heat!
When it's your idea of perfection...

Use the slotted spoon to lift out the first pair

> Now here's the scale —
> 2:00 minutes — super soft yolk — super soft white (Mylove's fav)
> 3:00 minutes — yolks soft — white cooked through
> 3:30 — yolks starting to solidfy — whites hard.
> 4:00 — why bother?

There will be uncooked white that falls away as you lift each egg from the pan.

This is good. Pull each pair at its preferred time and replace the lid when you can — but don't fret if you can't... after everything is plated you can pull the larger parts of the white from the water otherwise come back later to wash up — *eat that egg while it's hot!*

MYLOVE'S "I NEED COCOA"
(HOT CHOCOLATE)

There are days when this is the only cure. Mylove's lower lip pouts ever so slightly, and she has the wild look in her eye, and we both know it can all get better with a little bit of fire and whole lotta chocolate. My dad used to make this for us on the snowdays when he too was "too sick" to go into work.

I have also made this with pure (canned) coconut milk instead of evaporated milk — and it's amazing too. But in honor of my pops — here's his recipe.

1 cup milk for every one joining plus	**Dash of cinnamon**
1 can of evaporated milk for the pot	**Dash of ginger**
Your favorite unsweetened cocoa (I like Scharfenberger dark)	**¼ cup dark brown sugar**
1 exquisite dark (at least 67%) **chocolate bar**	**Dash of chipotle powder**

Whisk all the ingredients over a low flame until thoroughly mixed
adjust the taste accordingly — don't be shy with the chipotle — it really brings out the chocolate — the Aztecs might not have known how to treat women — but they did understand what makes us tick... chocolate and lots of it!

I use a hand mixer to froth before pouring into warmed mugs

I swear this recipe will cure just about anything especially a blue mood.

PEACH-STUFFED FRENCH "TOAFFLES"

Well, what would you call French toast made in a waffle iron? French Waffst?

Anyhoo... there's something about buying fresh ripe peaches... by the case. It inspires so much — so many possibilities. I put them in everything and when I thought of that eggy toastie buttery maple-y aroma filling the kitchen, there was only three things missing — Vanilla, Peach... and a fork!

We've burned out about three waffle irons during our marriage — this last one was an emergency gift rushed to us when my dear Auntieji Linda heard that ours had just broken. Now, that's a true friend!

2 eggs (for every 4 pieces of toast)

2 slices per person of good quality thick spongy bread (Brioche, Challah, Hawaiian egg)

½ fresh peach per person (sliced)

Spray vegetable oil (I have the kind you pump that doesn't use aerosol)

Pure vanilla extract

Dash of ground cardomom

Pure maple syrup

Butter

CLEANLINESS WARNING — THESE ARE VERY MESSY BUT WORTH IT!

Preheat your waffle iron

Whip the eggs in a shallow dish

Add two dashes of the vanilla and a generous sprinkle of cardamom, whip to mix thoroughly.

Soak the "bottom" slice of bread in the egg and put it on the iron

Lay the peaches on top of the bottom slice

Soak the "top" slice and lay that on top of the peaches

Close the lid. And push it down to squish the two slices together.

Cook until the edges crisp up

Plate, butter and pour the maple syrup and serve immediately.

"AFTER DINNER MINT"

It's been almost six months since our world ended...Since that time, we had several celebrations of the greatest love ever lived, I "un-did" thirty-two years of joint business relationships and "did up" a new solo act, and I ran away to Europe (if you're going to cry... and honey — you are going to CRY, so why not pick someplace pretty?) I stayed with the cousin of my dear friend, KarlwithaKay — Veronika was gracious, charming, generous — she held me when I needed a hug and left me to myself when I needed that. Because of the severe time change, we would share dinner and conversation, then go to bed like normal Viennans, and I would fall asleep at about ten pm... wake-up feeling refreshed and surprised that I had slept so soundedly... only to discover it was just shy of midnight.

Wide-awake, I'd move to Veronika's "Wintergarten" which was a cozy little glass-enclosed porch that looked down from the hills to the lights of downtown Vienna, snow-covered forest and winter stars... snuggled in a down comforter, stretched out in an easy chair, I would sob for hours, write some really bad grief poetry, and take solace in Austria's embrace.

You would be proud — I made apple chowder for Veronika for Christmas breakfast (she provided the fine Austria sausages) and we had spinach strudel and champagne for Christmas dinner.

For New Years, I was in my sister KJ's & her Fiancé, Jan's British embrace. Those who read GBTM will be happy to know that all is healed and well with Jan & I. She always was a fierce and wonderful lover of my sister (as I've always said) and now I can call her sister, too. KJ and I were able to resolve some of her bigger questions regarding my transition — which were oddly not so much about my gender, but the transformation of my "countenance." Things that were familiar from a lifetime of regard and comfort, like how I spoke, what I was interested in, and how I interacted with her, were just new — that's all. But so much of that had been in her imagination and supposition — and a week just "being together" smoothed that all out. We quickly got back to being the "buds" (I still define that as rose "buds" — whereas she may be seeing that as "Buddies" — and that's okay!) that we always were. As we both walk our own property on Avenue Q, we share something special that Lib & Shane will support but never need to truly understand — which is also okay.

Grief can be debilitating one moment — a gut wrenching. drive you to your knees, assault. I woke up one morning to discover myself on my hands and knees in the kitchen, cold air and pale light from the open refrigerator door, hand bruised from pounding my fists on the floor... clutching a jar of mayonnaise — the trigger. The only reason I was where I was, was because Mylove was gone. And she liked mayonnaise. Other times, grief comes as a sob that gets stuck in your throat and grows slowly, threatening to choke the life from you… and you don't care.

But grief is also a bittersweet breeze of her — a reminder that you did have it, you had achieved it — true love — it's horrifying pain is directly proportional to the love we found. We vowed to each other on April 29, 1989 to follow this thing we had as far and as deep as it goes… and we got there. So, I am, I know, in for a ride.

So, this is the last "apology" — I think, I've now broken all of the rules regarding the subjects that are traditionally not supposed to be covered in a cookbook. I do know that cooking for others has always been my savior — first to help me get through gender dysphoria, then the decline and losing of Mylove and now the grief. I hope you can forgive me if I pushed any of the wrong buttons on this journey together.

I set out to document a year in our kitchen — demonstrating that, as I said, the most important ingredient in any dish is love — and the particular place in your heart that your guests occupy gives love its special unique flavor that will make the dish you cook for them perfectly special. But, I had no idea that I would be documenting the last year of our marriage…

I am the woman I am today because of Mylove and her love of me. She taught me many things, and with full confidence and yes, some authority… I know what I'm talking about when it comes to love.

I hope I've made the case that tho' there are countless self-help books that would argue against me, confusing good intentions with bad discipline (or is it vice reverse as Mardie would say) declaring that food isn't supposed to be love…

… technically it is. Metaphysically, Quantum Physically and yes, Physically, Physically.

I know with every fiber of my being what it is to be loved. I am not speaking platitudes or abstractions or theories. She may have wavered in "how" to love me through our harder and more trying times, but she never ever faltered or hesitated in her love "for" me. Mylove gave me everything. And I, her. And together we lived in that love — it was the air we breathed, the light we bathed in, the "food" that sustained us for 32 years.

This is what I know.

We are best and brightest when we love one another — and so, when we cook for others with this in mind, it turns our humble kitchen into the holiest of temples. I don't just believe this — I have experienced this time and again. Being transgender has shown me many things (some I hope to never see again) but also, as I have shared my most "obvious" innermost self with people, it has been a divine vehicle for others to share their innermost selves with me.

And in that divine depth of the human heart, we have had a chance to revel in each's love for one another. You could see why it is absolutely mind-boggling that anyone could have anything but respect, reverence and love for transgender people — we both inspire with the example of how we lead our lives and give cisgender people license to be their own authentic selves, to be their own highest potential, to be their own noble selves — that any of the negative emotions or thoughts that could even be entertained by someone about the subject, is itself a reminder that there are some who are actively a part of their own evolvement and others who are simply incapable of being a true anything, most sadly, human. But... it is a new day in our world, and as the Rabbi who married us, (hi Shelly!) said many times and as Mylove reminds me after every rant or tirade I throw at those people...

... The brighter the light, the darker the shadow.

Which is actually a hopeful statement — acknowledging that a bright light, is in fact, already shining.

And there can be no brighter light than the gleam in the eyes of those you love, and the smile on their face when they taste a dish that you prepared for them in love, with love, for love.

It is the one irreplaceable ingredient.

I hope by now, I've illustrated this point that getting Recklass in the kitchen, with mindful abandon, wanton deconstruction and utterly delicious chaos will always be alchemically woven back together into something wonderful by your love.

And nothing else.

In every breath, in every moment of your life, in cooking and most certainly in love, may you always, always, always get Recklass!

All my love to you always.

Scottie Jeanette, March 2019

ABOUT THE AUTHOR

Mrs. Madden lives in La La Land with Aria & Bella in the house she and Marcy worked their asses off to get and hold onto. You know she loves cooking, and serving love on plates, glasses and trays. When she's not in the kitchen, she's following her Love's second to last request that she *"keep Zuzubean going"* — working to make the world a safer, more inclusive place for everyone — by opening one heart at a time with everthing's she got.

INDEX

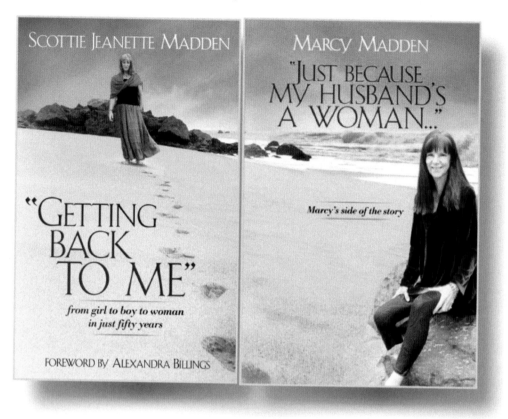

"Getting Back To Me"
from girl to boy to woman in just fifty years
by Scottie Jeanette Madden
Available at <u>amazon,</u>
<u>audible</u>

"Just Because My Husband's a Woman..."
Marcy's side of the story
by Marcy M. Madden
Available at <u>amazon</u>

Theirs was the storybook marriage that inspired others. For over twenty years, and after three failed marriages, Marcy had everything she had ever dreamed of in her husband, he was passionate, romantic, spiritual, generous, funny, loving, and... he cooked. She finally had someone who would love her as much as she could love. There was just one problem... a secret that could to shatter this storybook marriage.

An emotional journey where the only handrail is that gold standard love that they had forged over decades, they emerge to create a stronger, deeper and more loving marriage than either ever thought possible.

Praise for "Getting Back to Me" - from girl to boy to woman in just fifty years

In our lifetime we are rarely privy to the inner workings of a spiritual and emotional journey towards true newness. That is rare when it happens with such wit and beauty and pure courage under fire. Scottie's life is filled with joyful chaos and the elegance in which she moves through it ignites the transition we all eventually go through. We grow up, we come apart and we move on. It is the human condition.

Scottie has written this in her love for her life partner, in her devotion to her artistic self and in her hilarious look at the world at large through a Transwomen's lens. And so she speaks to us all, and so we are with her. And this is the great gift of both her story and the telling of it. We find ourselves on every page and our freedom in every event. You don't have to search long to hear your own voice even when the situations feel foreign. For it is her speaking to us with a clarity of honest inner reflection and the hope of carrying that with her, that is the summation of our journey through this world as humans.

Scottie is heart-breakingly funny, and mysteriously beguiling. And so this book, in our lifetime, has given us a small window into the hardest thing any of us can possibly do: Live our story and then share it with as many as are willing. And hopefully, we do what the book allows us to do, see who we are becoming because of who we once were.

And that is the great gift of Scottie's story. Once in this lifetime.

Alexandra Billings - Actress, Activist, Professor, 2016, HRC Visibility Award Winner

5.0 out of 5 stars This is the story of true love and being yourself.

This book was a wild ride and left me breathless, wanting more. Scottie's voice befriends you, draws you in like a really really good TV show where you think, "oh no, I'm never going to get to the dishes tonight." She talks to you like your best girlfriend, not holding back, not leaving anything out, revealing a depth of emotion and telling this story that is immediate, compelling, and also the story of what it's like to have the courage to be yourself enough to reveal your deepest secret to the one person you love the most in life, risking everything, and triumphing because love is love. And through it all, there is Scottie's heart, deep as the ocean, connected to Mylove and her heart, big as the sky.

5.0 out of 5 stars Buckle Up!

Scottie's book is a revelation, and a love story. Her exuberance about life jumps off the page and the reader is taken on a wild, headlong ride to clarity and the power of love, with a side of extreme survival show maneuvers both in front of and behind the camera.

5.0 out of 5 stars Inspirational

Scottie Madden's memoir, "Getting Back to Me" is not only eye-opening, it's heart-opening.

She reveals her life journey with such unparalleled openness and humor that you quickly feel intimately involved in her story, from her first experiences as a small child, through coming out in middle age to friends and family, to the legal hoops she has to jump through in order to establish what most of us take for granted. The strength and support of Scottie's wife is an inspiration. This isn't just a manual for 'trans' people (an imperfect term which the author explores) and others in their life. It should be required reading for anyone who wants a fulfilling marriage or who just wants to be a better human being.

5.0 out of 5 stars Ms. Madden Knows How to Tell a Story

Completely compelling — I could barely put it down — well-told, smart, funny book. Such a positive window into the story of a one person becoming more deeply herself. It is also a love story that is honest, rich, and beautiful. Please know you are going to love it, it's a book where the wisdom and love are given their day — and that's never easy. But it IS truly soul-deepening. Go ahead, and trust Scottie! I did, and I'm sure glad.

5.0 out of 5 stars superbly crafted

Thorough, thought provoking, and illuminating look into what it's like living this remarkable journey. Cleverly written, the book deftly puts you in her shoes from early life, through dealing with friends, family, career, and marriage! As entertaining as it is enlightening.

Praise for "Just Because My Husband's a Woman" - Marcy's side of the story

Engaging, fast-moving, poignant, fun and funny, I loved Just Because My Husband's a Woman … Marcy's Side of the Story from the moment I picked it up to its final page.

A true love story. Marcy shares her world, her life, and her voyage with lightness and intimacy. This true story is filled with exceptional individuals and amazing events. Marcy's commitment to her own authenticity and to her own True Love, no matter how exceptional the superficial changes, is awe-inspiring. This book is a sheer delight. I was left with a renewed belief in love, authenticity, courage and humor. Marcy invites you to join her, to visit her world, to travers her life with her. I felt as if I were Marcy, making all the same choices, moving through each age, each opening, crisis and opportunity with curiosity, vulnerability, strength, and, ultimately, with faith. I loved Just Because My Husband's a Woman … Marcy's Side of the Story and you will too!

Catherine A. Parrish President, NextLevel Leadership, Inc

5.0 out of 5 stars
Love trumps gender identity!

Ever since I read Scottie Jeanette Madden's book "Getting Back to Me", about her transgender coming out, I've been curious about the other side of the story, from the wife's point of view. This is that story. Both journeys are equally compelling. Marcy Madden has opened her heart and soul to anyone who is curious about how a woman, who married a man, can stay in a long term marriage after her "man" has transitioned to being a woman — all while dealing with her own health challenges. The answer is LOVE. Pure love. This beautifully written book chronicles how the power of love can transcend even the most extraordinary circumstances. It is a page turner and, although it stands well on its own, it is a perfect companion to Scottie's book.

5.0 out of 5 stars
Celebrating the transcendence of prejudice. Fearless andpowerful memoir.

Just Because My Husband is a Woman" is a memoir of a woman exploring the meaning of love and commitment amidst the shifting gender identity of her husband. Marcy Madden has written a memoir of profound honesty, vulnerability and courage. The author's exploration and ultimate triumph of love for her spouse transcends the rampant fear and discrimination the trans community faces, in a deeply mature and authentic way.

5.0 out of 5 stars Wonderful. Absolutely wonderful.
This book is outstanding. Both Marcy's book and her Love's (Scottie Madden) book are a must read for anyone who may be "sorting out" their own true gender or that of a life partner. I have benefitted greatly reading this book and I know those I will gift it to — will as well. Wonderful. Make a Movie now you two!

5.0 out of 5 stars
LOVE RULES

Amazing love story! If you need inspiration to overcome a life challenge, read this book!

ALL FEATURE PHOTOGRAPHY
BY MENA KERRY KEHOE

kerrykehoe.com

"STILL GIRL" MENA LENSING THE COVER SHOT

**MITCH MERBACK & KAREN FRANKLIN SHOW MY
SISTER KIMM EMERSON & I THE STUDIO...**

ADDITIONAL PHOTO CREDITS:
SPECIAL THANKS TO THE GENEROUS PHOTOGRAPHERS WHO "CAPTURED" MYLOVE & ME

pg. 34:   Mimi Fuenzalida - mimiimages.com
pg. 110:   Lara Tomov
pg. 139:   Lara Tomov
pg. 143:   Shivani Hawkins - sacrednatural.photography
pg. 145:   Shivani Hawkins - sacrednatural.photography
pg. 193:   Shivani Hawkins - sacrednatural.photography
pg. 211:   TJ Devadatta Best - LightinspiredArt.com
pg. 226:   Lara Tomov
pg. 273:   Lara Tomov
pg. 283:   Mimi Fuenzalida - mimiimages.com
pg. 288:   Mimi Fuenzalida - mimiimages.com
pg 290:   Mimi Fuenzalida - mimiimages.com
pg 292:   MitchMerback - merlinproductions.com
Back: M. Sharkey - msharkey.com

LARA TOMOV

SHIVANI HAWKINS

M.SHARKEY

MIMI FUENZALIDA

TJ DEVADATTA BEST

Made in the USA
Columbia, SC
03 January 2020

86190076R00164